D0442539

# So That Others May Live

Caroline
Hebard & Her
Search-and-Rescue
Dogs

# So That Others May Live

## Caroline Hebard & Her Search-and-Rescue Dogs

Hank Whittemore
and Caroline Hebard

BANTAM BOOKS
*New York   Toronto   London   Sydney   Auckland*

Grateful acknowledgment is made for permission to reprint two photos of Caroline Hebard and Pascha by Ed Pagliarini—The Courier-News, one photo of Sasquatch locating a "missing" person during training by Ray Jones, one photo of Caroline Hebard and Aly back from Mexico by Steve Kalaver—New Jersey Newsphotos, one photo of Caroline Hebard and Pascha by Reinhold Spiegler.

Book design by Caroline Cunningham

ISBN 0-553-09951-5

*Published simultaneously in the United States and Canada*

Bantam Books are published by Bantam Books, a division of Bantam Doubleday Dell Publishing Group, Inc. Its trademark, consisting of the words "Bantam Books" and the portrayal of a rooster, is Registered in U.S. Patent and Trademark Office and in other countries. Marca Registrada. Bantam Books, 1540 Broadway, New York, New York 10036.

PRINTED IN THE UNITED STATES OF AMERICA

# Contents

This book is dedicated to the victims, survivors, and their families, and to the wonderful men and women from all over the world who have cared enough as search-and-rescue volunteers to make a difference.

# Night on the Trail

THE PHONE RANG IN THE DIM LIGHT OF THE kitchen, where Aly lay half sleeping on the floor, and he heard the voice of his human partner answer it upstairs. He remained still for several minutes, but then a different noise reached his sensitive German shepherd ears, causing them to twitch and move forward. Now Aly listened intently to what, for him, was the most thrilling sound in the world: Caroline, up on the second floor, had swung open the door of her search-and-rescue closet, where all the gear was stowed.

Aly's huge, intelligent brown eyes snapped open as he lifted his oversized black head. He shifted the ninety-five pounds of his bulk, yawned, rose on his hind legs, and stretched, shaking the black and tan double coat that gleamed with robust health. Low, deep rumbles rose in his throat as he began to pace impatiently, waiting for Caroline to come down. When he heard her footsteps on the stairs and realized she was wearing hiking boots, his movements quickened with excitement; seeing her familiar orange coverall, Aly produced a joyful bark to let her know he was ready.

It was time to get to work.

On this Sunday night the call had come in at about nine o'clock, from park rangers in a wilderness area of the Delaware Water Gap in

Pennsylvania. Twelve children had disappeared. The oldest was four-teen, the youngest nine. They had gone out in the afternoon for a brief hike on the Appalachian Trail and had failed to return.

It had taken about four hours for anyone to believe the children were really lost. Then a few dozen rangers spread out to comb the trail for several miles. Even with reinforcements from local police, by the time it began to grow dark they had turned up only a set of footprints. The situation had escalated to an emergency.

The autumn weather in daytime had been pleasantly breezy and cool, but by evening the temperature had plummeted to ten degrees. Up on the trail, in the shadowy darkness of a moonlit night, it was bitterly cold, with a wind-chill factor of twenty below. If the children were forced to spend all night up there, they might not survive. Wearing only their light fall jackets, they would already be suffering from exposure.

And so the rangers called Caroline Hebard. From her home in Bernardsville, New Jersey, Caroline coordinated the U.S. Disaster Team Canine Unit, whose volunteers responded to catastrophes in foreign countries. She was also coleader of Northeast Search and Rescue, a group of handlers and dogs ready to search for missing persons or disaster victims anywhere within the United States.

Local officials in Pennsylvania had come to know Caroline as a pioneer in the field of volunteer canine search-and-rescue work. From working with her, some of them knew that a specially trained search dog could cover the same amount of terrain as a twelve-man grid team in less time and with a higher probability of success. The rangers also knew that Caroline and Aly, along with other handler-dog teams in her unit, would be at the scene as soon as they could get there.

She was mobilizing quickly, first by calling a member of her unit to start the phone chain by which other volunteers would be summoned with their dogs. "I've got a search," she told her husband, Art, offering just a few details as she kept in motion according to a practiced routine.

He and their four children were accustomed to these sudden missions, which occurred as often as once a week. Alastair, twelve, and

Heather, ten, were already asleep in their rooms. Joanne, eighteen, and Andrew, seventeen, watched as she pulled on some sweaters followed by the coverall and her red search jacket. The two older children received her last-minute instructions for the next day, in case she was not back by morning, and wished her luck. They understood, from long experience, that Mom was trying to get out the door as fast as she could.

When she heard Aly pacing impatiently down in the kitchen, Caroline thought how uncanny it was that he always knew when she was at the door of her storage place. It wasn't just his sense of hearing, acute as that was. Even when he was outside in the cold weather, with all the doors and storm windows of the house closed, he seemed to know when she was pulling out her gear for a mission.

With blond hair and gray-green eyes, Caroline at forty-four was a slight, athletic woman who had been leading this kind of double existence for sixteen years. Yet, as usual, her heart pounded with excitement as she bounded down the stairs with her duffel bag and backpack.

*Well, I'm an adrenaline junkie, too—always was, always will be.*

Caroline was used to Aly becoming hyper over the prospect of an imminent search mission. She suspected that he reacted to her heightened respiration and could pick up the scent of sweat secretions stirred by her adrenal glands, indicating to him that she was charged up. She also knew that the sight of her rescue gear and search jacket, which confirmed the initial information from his ears and nose, was all he needed to start barking, wagging his tail, and racing back and forth between her and the door.

To help calm him down, Caroline spoke as little as possible, except to tell him in German, "Aly, *hier*," and then, softly but firmly as he came to her, "*Sitz.*" Knowing the ritual, he sat still while she dressed him in his own orange vest, which had a white cross with the word *RESCUE* printed in tall black capital letters.

It was nine-thirty when Caroline and Aly climbed into her dark blue rescue truck, a no-frills Chevy Suburban with four-wheel drive, heading toward the Delaware Water Gap. She activated the blue emergency light on top and stepped on the gas. They could make it in about an hour. Sipping coffee from a mug as she sped through the darkness, she reviewed some of the facts and possibilities.

Twelve children, lost in the wilderness, were groping through bone-chilling wind in hopes of being found. They must have wandered across miles of unfamiliar terrain, becoming increasingly desperate as they sought to make their way out. With neither map nor compass nor flashlights, and lacking food, water, and proper clothing to protect themselves, they could survive only so long. By now, after about seven hours, they had to be exhausted and terribly afraid. And the drop in their body temperature could lead to hypothermia, resulting in light-headedness, confusion, disorientation, and panic. To rescue them alive, searchers would have to work within a rapidly diminishing window of time.

Four other members of Northeast Search and Rescue, three of them women, joined Caroline at the scene shortly after ten-thirty that night. While anxious parents had been waiting at park headquarters, the rangers had set up their command post inside a small fire station, where they spread out a topographical map of the surrounding wilderness. In this area, the Appalachian Trail narrowed to a rough track as it zigzagged in a north-south direction across high mountain ridges. Whether the youngsters had gone north or south was unknown. Tarmac-covered roads intersected the trail at various points, so it was possible the children had turned onto one of them. Earlier, rangers and police officers using searchlights had walked the trail and driven all along those roads, without success.

Park service officials briefed Caroline and her teammates as they studied the map. Then she quickly divided the trail into five sectors, one for each handler and dog. "You cover from this point to this point," she said, giving out assignments.

The missing children, some of whom had come to the park with their parents, were part of a large church group whose leaders had brought them to one of the campgrounds here. They had enjoyed a weekend of outdoor activity and Bible study. That afternoon, before their scheduled departure on buses, the adults had decided to hold a last-minute meeting at park headquarters. Meanwhile, the dozen youngsters had gone out for a quick hike by themselves, intending to be back by the time the meeting was over.

They had started up a steep side path leading to the Appalachian Trail on the high ridges. On the way they had passed a hiker coming down who told them they could make a loop on the trail by following a series of distinct tree blazes; but in fact there was no such loop, and no such blazes existed. Having continued upward, they apparently had not been seen again by anyone else. When the hiker reported his encounter with the children, he learned that he had misinformed them.

If they had gotten up to the trail and started following it, Caroline thought, they must have kept looking for the tree blazes while heading farther and farther away from help. On the other hand, they could have turned left or right on one of the paved roads.

The five handlers and their dogs climbed into official vehicles, and the rangers brought them to where the children had entered the side path. They made their way up to the location where the hiker had seen them on his way down.

Caroline had trained Aly to use his extremely sensitive nose to follow the airborne scent of human beings, alive or dead, across miles of wilderness. As night had fallen, the children's warm bodies would have given off a greater amount of scent in the cooler environment than in a hot environment, and the colder air descending from high ridges would have carried the scent downhill. That would be helpful, but by now the children's bodies had to be too cold to keep producing very much scent. Also the heavy, erratic winds and steep, varied terrain could pose all sorts of difficult challenges for an air-scenting search dog.

In his training, Aly had learned to distinguish human scent from all other odors. The complex structure of his nose, and the large olfactory lobe in his brain, gave him a smelling sensitivity up to a hundred times greater than that of any man or woman. He could track the scent with his nose to the ground like a vacuum cleaner, and he could trail by holding his nose a bit higher while casting around for the near-ground scent, weaving from side to side to catch its drift.

Most important of all was the air-scenting mode, by which Aly could find people without either a known starting place or a clear trail. He could do so by lifting his nose straight up, then ranging far and wide until he caught the invisible, floating scent. When that happened, he would wag his tail with excitement and suddenly move out with intense purpose.

The scent of the children was being dispersed downwind in a cone-shaped pattern, the smaller end of which was centered around their bodies. As the distance from them grew, to perhaps half a mile, the cone widened over a vast area. In air-scenting, it was the search dog's task to find this large end of the cone, then to work back and forth as it narrowed, leading him to the target.

The pivotal question now was whether the children were continuing to wander. Because their cold bodies were no longer producing as much scent as before, the ability of the dogs to find them would be much greater if the lost children remained in one spot. But if the youngsters were still moving, Aly's nose might lose the original scent cone. In that case he would have to start ranging all over again, trying to pick up a new—and probably weaker—scent.

On some missions, Caroline was able to "pre-scent" Aly—that is, to let him sniff some articles of clothing belonging to the missing persons—but in this case that was not possible. Instead the rangers offered detailed descriptions of some of the children's shoes, including the fact that one boy was wearing a pair of boots that had heels with distinctive markings. So it might be possible to pick up their tracks from time to time with flashlights; and here, at the point where the children had been seen last on the trail, the rangers showed the dog handlers a set of footprints. Among them was the boy's boot-heel design, impressed into the now frozen ground.

Because he was wearing his orange rescue vest, Aly understood from past experience that he would be air-scenting tonight. Without the vest on, he would have been either tracking or trailing; and, according to the different leads and collars Caroline used with him, he could tell whether it was to be one mode of searching or the other.

As they stood on the steep side path, Caroline removed the vest for several minutes and put Aly on a special lead for tracking. She steadied the beam of her flashlight on the children's footprints, letting him sniff them. Then she strapped on his vest again to signal a return to the air-scent mode. Now, although Aly would follow whatever human scent he encountered (other than that of the searchers, whose odors he understood he should disregard), he also would recognize the specific smell of those footprints. If he picked up that odor again, he would home in all the more excitedly.

All it would take now was a familiar command, in German, to *"such und hilf"*: he was to search for and help any human beings who might be wandering in that vast, dark wilderness.

Up on the Appalachian Trail, the handlers and dogs set off north and south to cover their five separate sectors. Each team was accompanied by three rangers. As they walked they radioed their positions to the ranger command post and to each other. Caroline had chosen arbitrarily to start at the northern end of the southernmost sector and to keep heading south, away from the others.

Bolting ahead of her, Aly seemed to be inventing his own combination of tracking, trailing, and air-scenting. At times his nose fell to the ground, but then he would raise it high in the air, trying to catch the human scent on the wind. If he lost it, this information from his nose was transmitted back to his brain, and he might return briefly to tracking or trailing. If a fox or a bear had crossed the trail and left its scent, he would recognize the animal smell but disregard it. In his methodical way, Aly could maintain this intense focus longer than any dog Caroline had ever known.

As she and the rangers followed him south on the trail, Caroline had no idea whether the children were somewhere farther ahead or miles away in another direction. Often there were steep cliffs on either side; at other times, the trail curved through black woods strewn with boulders. With his superb night vision, Aly could travel as fast in the darkness as he could by day, and he kept well ahead of Caroline's powerful flashlight beam. Two hours and nearly four miles later, Caro-

line learned via her radio that the other handlers had finished searching their sectors and returned to the command post. It was past one
o'clock in the morning.

Although Caroline was warmly dressed in layers of clothing, the
cold had gone through her entire body. She was exhausted, frozen,
and hungry. Aly was doing better. He had a thick double coat to
protect him and serve as insulation from all weather extremes; too, his
efficient body structure enabled him to keep working for many hours
without becoming overtired.

Suddenly Aly bolted toward a spot where he started sniffing
around with gusto. Caroline knew he had picked up human scent. His
animated body language told her he also had found the specific scent
associated with the children's footprints. Undoubtedly he had been
picking up drifts of scent all along as it blew and eddied on the wind.
He had been finding and losing it with his nose until, now, he had
come to an area where it was concentrated.

Caroline could see no signs of human passage on the trail, but she
had complete trust in Aly's judgment that the children had been here.
Maybe they had stopped to rest and relieve themselves, in which case
much of their scent would have settled to the ground. Now she aimed
her flashlight around the area that Aly had marked. A few minutes
later she saw footprints—and then the boy's unmistakable boot-heel
mark.

"We've got tracks and it's them," she radioed the command post
as Aly kept up his enthusiastic sniffing and pacing, with periodic
glances at her to make sure she understood him. "They're going in this
direction," Caroline added over the radio, "but how much farther
south they are is hard to say."

"Okay," the search leader replied, "just keep heading south until
you come to the next road. We'll bring a vehicle and catch up to you at
that point."

Caroline and Aly continued on, followed by the rangers, checking
every little side path or deer trail along the way. Most of these paths
petered out quickly in the forest, but you could never tell what people
suffering from hypothermia might do. In the darkness, the confused

and fearful children could not be expected to behave logically. And when the core temperature of their bodies cooled to below normal, their ability to think rationally would decline rapidly.

It was after 1:30 A.M. when Caroline and Aly reached an abandoned camp, where the rangers soon caught up with them. They checked through all the cabins, finding them empty. Caroline returned to the Appalachian Trail, now following Aly across the top of another wind-blown ridge, and after about a mile they came to another paved road that crossed the trail. At this point Aly seemed to lose the scent, and he stopped. The children could have continued straight on the trail, but they also could have turned east or west on the road. Alone with her dog, catching her breath, Caroline stopped to wait for the rangers.

"Now what?" she whispered to herself in the darkness.

Aly stood beside her, panting. He braced himself against the wind, frustrated but keeping still. The next move was up to him.


Caroline rested, giving Aly water from the canteen in her backpack, as the rangers caught up to her again and others from the command post arrived by car with hot coffee. While the park officials milled around and talked, she watched her canine partner as he maintained his solitary concentration, oblivious to the human commotion.

"Let's pack it in," the men were saying. "These kids must have turned onto the road, so the only question is whether they went left or right."

"How can you be sure they took the road?" Caroline asked.

"Well, it's obvious. They would have seen the pavement and said, 'Hey, we can get off the trail here. If we turn either right or left, eventually we're going to find civilization of some kind.' That's how anybody would react, even those kids."

"But they must be disoriented," she said. "Their reasoning is probably impaired."

"Hey, Caroline, we can't stay out here forever! It's nearly two o'clock in the morning!"

"We'll call the cops," another ranger said, "and we'll have them start on this road from each end of the park. They'll come in by cars from both directions and find 'em. They'll round 'em up for us. There's no sense going any farther on the trail."

Caroline herself was almost ready to give up, but she knew Aly was not a quitter. He was still alert and hard at work. He had come out here to win the game of life or death. And so had she. No other human being could take her place as his partner on this night, and by the same token, Caroline could not be successful with any dog but him. The unique bond between them had been forged during nearly two hundred missions together in the past four years, over the course of which they had learned to read and trust each other's silent body language.

What her dog's concentrated behavior told her right now was that she should let him alone, give him some time, and keep her faith in him.

She was about to disagree with the rangers again when Aly walked straight across the road to where the trail continued. Now he was operating on his profound animal instinct alone. Nothing in his training or experience could have told him what to do. Having lost the children's scent, he was not relying on the kind of logic that human searchers might employ. He ignored the road, preferring instead to continue in the lost youngsters' general direction of travel. In effect, his actions said, *This is the way they were going, and this is the quickest way to get to these people, in this straight line.*

Now he barked loudly, turning to look straight at her. Then he charged ahead a short distance, only to turn toward her again. *Come on,* he was saying to Caroline. *I've picked up their scent again! Follow me!* His nose was waving in the night air, working hard, and Caroline knew from his whole attitude that he was pleading, *I've got it, so please, let's get going!*

She ran across the road to the trail.

Aiming her flashlight at the ground, she saw no footprints. She looked over at Aly's face. For her it now came down to a choice between the dog and the rangers.

The dog won.

"Hey, guys," she yelled, "those kids did *not* go down the road. They're still heading south!"

"How do you know?"

"I'm telling you what my dog is saying," she insisted, "and he says they're still on this trail!"

Without arguing or waiting anymore, she gave her full attention to Aly, who broke into a dead run ahead. Caroline ran behind, scrambling in the dark over rocks and branches. She was unable to keep up with him, so he kept interrupting his progress to wait impatiently for her. The rangers followed reluctantly. Despite their skepticism, they radioed for a separate crew to come by car along another road that crossed the trail several miles up ahead.

About thirty minutes later and nearly a mile farther on, Caroline was wearing down and hoping against hope that she wasn't leading the rangers on some wild-goose chase. She had chosen to put all her trust in Aly, whether the outcome was successful or not. They were a team. As much as she depended on him, he needed her to read him correctly and then not let him down. So she had opted to believe in her dog, to follow through for him, and that was that.

Aly stopped to wag his tail with enthusiasm, then bolted around a bend and disappeared. Caroline held her breath.

A long minute later he returned with a large stick in his mouth. It was the signal that meant he had found them.

Caroline broke into a run again as Aly jumped with joy beside her. Up ahead, in the beam of her flashlight, she saw the entire group of twelve children. They were off at the side of the trail, shivering and whimpering as they huddled together for warmth. Caroline saw that they had been frightened when they heard the large animal running towards them in the darkness, but as she approached with her light, the children began to realize they had been found. Some appeared dazed; others began to cry with relief.

"It's all right," Caroline told them. "You're going to be okay now. Good boy, Aly, good boy . . ."

The smallest and most fragile child, a nine-year-old girl, was being embraced by two of the others. She was probably suffering from frostbite, Caroline thought. The tiny blood vessels in her ears, nose, hands, and feet would be constricted, and her general circulation would have slowed. Eventually her extremities could have frozen. Caroline whipped off her jacket and coverall, removed an Icelandic sweater she had knitted, and wrapped the girl inside it. She continued to bathe Aly in hugs and praise, then coaxed him to sit in the midst of the children so they could snuggle against his massive body for heat.

By the time the rangers behind her had caught up, Caroline was using her portable stove to heat some water with bouillon cubes. The rangers built a fire while she served the warm soup to the kids in two metal Sierra cups, handing them from child to child. They held the warm cups in their hands and took little sips, heating their bodies gradually from within.

Some of them kept hugging Aly, who sat there with the stick between his paws in front of him.

She learned that the children had indeed kept going along the trail, not turning onto the paved roads, plodding onward in the darkness until the little girl had begun to cry and complain. At that point they had given up, stopping so they could huddle together against the wind. They had tried without success to make a fire. They were inadequately dressed and totally unprepared to spend a night in the wilderness. What their fate might have been had they not been found was anybody's guess.

By now the park rangers had communicated back to their headquarters, calling for medical help while alerting the anxious parents. When the other trail crew came in from the south, the rangers and paramedics began the process of bringing the children out of the woods. Ambulances were waiting on the nearest road, a few miles farther south. None of the children was able to walk alone; most were carried out, one by one, on stretchers.

All the children would be taken to a hospital to be checked, but only the little girl would have to be held for further observation. She did, in fact, have early frostbite. If the others had been forced to stay out much longer, their condition would have deteriorated rapidly as well.

Caroline rejoined the other members of her team at the firehouse, where the rangers were dismantling their temporary command post.

By now, the leaders of the church group and the children's parents had left park headquarters. There would be no chance to see them, but the volunteer dog handlers were elated nevertheless. The rangers expressed their gratitude all around and turned finally to give special thanks to Caroline and her canine partner. If any park officials had been skeptical about the power and accuracy of trained search dogs, their doubts had been dispelled by Aly.

Dawn was breaking when Caroline arrived back home in New Jersey. No one was awake yet. She fed Aly and washed out the truck, then showered and dressed in some clean clothes. While the other family members slept, she and her dog had saved twelve young lives, but this was Monday morning and the Appalachian Trail now seemed a million miles away.

Soon there was breakfast with Art and the children around the kitchen table, while Aly slept on the floor. Caroline, still high from the mission's success, bubbled over as she gave a sketchy account of it and answered their questions.

"Way to go, Mom!" exclaimed Alastair, the twelve-year-old, who already had told her that he too wanted to be part of search-and-rescue work when he grew up. "Way to go, Aly!"

They went over plans and schedules for that day, and then Art was on his way to work in a science lab and the children went off to school. Caroline did some laundry and other household chores until, late that morning, her body began begging for sleep. Before climbing upstairs for a nap, she knelt down next to Aly, who opened his eyes and glanced up at her.

"*Feiner Hund,*" she whispered into his ear. "Good dog."

# Chapter 1

# Jaeger:
# A Taste for Freedom

"I DON'T WANT MY DOG TO BE A ROBOT," SHE told the instructor. "I want him to be able to express his own character. I feel that anyone who handles a dog needs to respect that animal's individuality."

It was 1969 and Caroline, a Stanford University graduate student, was taking her three-month-old German shepherd, Jaeger, to obedience class at the local shopping center.

She found it ironic to be setting up rules of behavior, even for her dog. Recently married, and in love, too, with the outdoor freedom of the Bay Area, Caroline finally had escaped a life that from childhood had been filled with matters of "obedience." Every detail of how to dress, speak, and act had been subject to the dictates of her father's role in the British Foreign Service, in which diplomatic protocol—defined by Webster as "a rigid code prescribing complete deference to superior rank and strict adherence to precisely correct procedure"—was of paramount importance.

So Caroline knew what it was like to be dominated by inflexible thinking and by punishments for breaking the rules. And that, she thought, must be how too many dogs were made to feel while being trained. Jaeger was barely out of the puppy stage, a playful, curious shepherd who had been a black and tan fluff ball only a month earlier. What he wanted most, she knew from her own experience, was to be himself and have fun.

Caroline Anne Ruthven Gale was a lonely child whose home base kept shifting from country to country as she grew up. As far back as she could remember, she had wanted a dog of her own. A dog meant comfort, stability, companionship, affection, love. Any kind would do.

Her father, Malcolm Gale, had met and married her mother, Ilse Strauss, a beautiful German woman, in England just before World War II. The Gales were stationed at the British Embassy in Santiago, Chile, when Caroline was born on June 20, 1944. Her brother, Ian, who had just turned five, had also been born in Chile, where her father had done undercover work during the early years of the war.

When Caroline was four, her father was transferred to Caracas, Venezuela, and her real memories began.

They arrived in the midst of a revolution, so no one from the British Embassy could meet their boat. Caroline's father found a man with a pickup truck and paid him to drive them while they sat in the open back, the dust from the dirt road blowing all around them as they headed up over the hills.

The embassy did not provide housing, either. Caroline's parents found an ancient, Spanish-style house without screens on the doors or windows. At night enormous spiders dropped onto Caroline's bed and crawled into her sheets, until she felt their presence and screamed in terror.

But the house also had a sprawling garden, filled with mango and avocado trees as well as an assortment of colorful, noisy parrots that became her pets and playmates. Another friend was the family gardener, who taught her how to catch the lively, wiggling snakes with a pronged stick, a diversion she practiced without the knowledge of her mother, who hated reptiles. She loved all animals—except those intrusive spiders, of course—and her mother would always remark that she had a way with them. But most of all she loved Mike, who lived out in the garden in his own dog house.

Mike was a pure-bred Airedale, a rare dog in Venezuela, and four-year-old Caroline had instantly claimed him as her own. In the tropical heat, his wiry black and tan coat tended to smell so bad—even within hours of a good washing—that he was never allowed inside the house. But outdoors was where Caroline preferred to be.

Airedales are the largest of the terrier group, and Mike was no exception, standing nearly two feet high at the shoulder and weighing over forty pounds—more than she did at age four. He delighted Caroline with some of his jumping feats. One involved the wall that ran along the edge of the garden. As people walked by on the street side, Mike would race next to the wall and then leap up, much to the surprise of the passers-by, and steal the hats right off their heads.

Mike was also a source of comfort. When Caroline did something to get herself in trouble, which happened quite frequently, she went out to the dog house and crawled in there with him to hide. Her father, having inherited the English tradition of strictness toward children, used a leather belt or slipper as his chief means of enforcing discipline. Caroline came in for her share of licks, unless she could lay the blame on her older brother for whatever she had done, in which case he got the punishment instead.

Caroline was by nature a tomboy and a free spirit, but as a diplomat's daughter, she was shoved into frilly dresses and white gloves and forced to take ballet lessons from a Russian teacher whom she hated. At home she was pressured to conform to rules and manners more suitable for Queen Victoria's time. She and Ian had to learn to eat even bananas with a knife and fork. When their parents went out, the children compensated by attacking their mashed potatoes with their hands and tossing clumps of potato at each other.

Social events were a large part of life in the British foreign service, which Caroline's father loved, and her mother, the perfect diplomat's wife, played her supporting role with style. She was a gracious hostess, dressing beautifully and immaculately, and at social functions Caroline was expected to be the same. Her parents held tremendous cocktail parties out on the lawn, where one of the parrots, a mammoth macaw with blue and yellow markings, lived in a mango tree. Caroline adored the macaw, who shared her rebellious attitude and sly sense of humor. The feathers on one of his wings were clipped, so he couldn't fly away, and he would walk far out on a branch above the crowd, maintaining a precarious balance on his toes. When guests at the party wandered into range, Caroline would watch, holding in her laughter, until the bird let loose an expertly timed *plop* on those beneath him. As his victims reacted, the macaw raced back up the trunk to a much higher position. Then he broke into wild, human-sounding laughter, and Caroline split her sides laughing with him.

Three years later, the Gales were transferred again, this time to Turkey. Ian, now twelve, would be leaving for boarding school in England, and Caroline would be alone with her parents. No dogs were allowed where they would be living. She could bring a bird named Lorrito ("little parrot"), a gift from her Spanish tutor, but Mike would have to stay in Venezuela. The thought of leaving Mike behind, of never being able to see him again, was unbearable. Yes, the Gales had found him another family, a good home, they told Caroline, where he would be happy. But she was inconsolable.

The morning he left, Caroline crawled into the dog house one last time, hugged his smelly body, and cried her eyes out. Someday, she vowed, she would get another dog, one that would go with her wherever she went, a dog that only death could take away.

Caroline's father was stationed in Ankara, the Turkish capital, an inland city crawling with diplomats and spies. Her family lived in an apartment building with other foreigners, and with her brother away at school, she was very much on her own.

In the morning she walked up Atatürk Boulevard with the Russian ambassador, who took her by the hand as he trudged to the Soviet embassy. A large man, he encouraged her to get a good education. Caroline had heard talk about Russians being bad, so it seemed strange that he was so kind and concerned.

The ambassador dropped her off at the Swiss legation, where she was the only girl among older boys studying with a French tutor. She also had to go out and play soccer with the boys, who often beat her up, but she quickly learned to fight back. Later she walked back down the hill for math, Latin, history, and German with Madame Kudret, a brilliant but fanatical Czech woman with a slight beard and mustache who threw her slippers at the pupils for emphasis. But she was a rigorous teacher, and Caroline was beginning to stand out as a student, particularly of languages. By the time she was ten, in addition to English, she could speak fluent Spanish, French, and German, and even communicate in Turkish.

When her parents threw parties, Caroline now displayed all the right manners; but offstage she dropped the pose and hung out with Ellie, the German housekeeper, who talked to herself, and with Bayram, the male cook, who played music on the radio and taught her Turkish dances. In the kitchen, while Ellie chattered and Bayram cooked, Caroline practiced belly dancing.

Her father also took her to see remains of the ancient Hittite civilization and to visit hills covered with fossils. She was happiest wearing old clothes on these adventures, and often went with Lorrito perched on her shoulder.

She learned that dogs in Turkey were treated as working animals, used as shepherds in the fields or else ignored. Few Turks, who were mostly Muslims, kept them as playmates or household pets. This was because the Koran regarded dogs as a low form of life and labeled them unclean. Caroline made friends with many strays, and one frigid winter day, on her way home from school, she found a puppy shivering with cold near a garbage bin. She put him inside her wool coat and carried him home.

He was an Anatolian sheepdog, pale tan, very young and still very small. Aware that residents of her building were not allowed to have dogs, she smuggled him up the stairs to the attic storeroom, making a comfortable place for him to sleep. It was her secret, and she told no one. In the mornings and evenings that followed, she sneaked up to feed him, give him water, and cuddle him. She named him Aeneas, because she had started to read Virgil with Madame Kudret, and this puppy seemed like a wanderer, too.

It worked well for about a week. Then Ellie or Bayram must have noticed that food from the kitchen was disappearing, because one of them discovered the secret and told her parents. The puppy was brought down from the attic and taken away while she was at school. When Caroline came home and learned from her mother what had happened, she fell silent for two days. No matter what her parents said, she knew he was no longer alive. That little fluff ball could not survive on the street, so the "humane" choice had been to put him down. She knew.

Soon afterward Caroline's parents were transferred to the island sheikhdom of Bahrain in the Persian Gulf, but because that country had no schools for her to attend, she did not go with them. Instead, at age eleven, she was deposited at an all-girls boarding school in England—no dogs allowed.

Caroline didn't live at home again until 1961, when her father was transferred to Washington, D.C. Kennedy was in the White House then, and she entered American University as a junior at age sixteen in a climate of excitement, liberation, and idealism.

Living at home, she was still sheltered. She was driven to and from the university by day, and she observed a nightly curfew of eleven-thirty. Yet in other ways Caroline was more advanced than her twenty-year-old classmates, having lived in a variety of different cultures in South America, Europe, and the Middle East.

Caroline joined a sorority, but soon decided that such an atmosphere was not for her. She was slim and pretty in a wholesome way, and could look like the perfect sorority girl if she wanted to, but she was really an outdoor person who preferred a sweatshirt and jeans. It was more fun hiking up in the Blue Ridge Mountains, climbing the Washington Monument at night with a bunch of guys, or going out spelunking in Virginia.

Although she was accepted for graduate studies at Oxford University, her memories of being stifled at boarding school in England were so strong that she elected to remain in the States. She continued at American University, earning a master's degree in French and applied linguistics while teaching languages to the wives of State Department officials.

In the summer of 1964, her parents were transferred to Portugal.

Caroline made her final decision to stay. Stanford University offered her a graduate fellowship along with a job teaching English to foreign students. Her father's farewell gift was a tiny car called a Sunbeam Imp, which he had gotten from Great Britain. Looking like a sewing machine and about as sturdy, it was the first Imp imported to the United States—a dubious honor, since the car took several minutes to get up to sixty miles an hour. If it broke down, no American mechanic would be able to fix it.

But her father, who had come to admire his daughter's independent and adventurous spirit, had given her more than just a car. The Imp was also part of her education; if she was going to drive cross-country on her own, she might as well learn how the car worked. Before she left, Malcolm Gale had her take apart the rear-mounted engine and put it back together again.

She made it to the foothills of the Rockies before the motor died. Caroline was beneath the car, investigating the problem, when she saw the boots of a state trooper coming toward her. The officer could see her sneakers and jeans, but that was all. "Hey, fella," he called, "you need some help?" When she emerged, her face covered with grease, he stared at her and said, "My God, it's a girl!"

When she arrived in San Francisco she found an apartment and lived on a shoestring, waiting tables until her scholarship money from Stanford kicked in. During her first year of graduate school, Caroline also worked as a model for Saks and JC Penney, saving her money for ski trips during vacations; she cooked twice a week for law students who lived together in a big house, earning free meals for herself in exchange.

The Stanford social scene was intense, and Caroline was soon juggling marriage proposals. At one point the pressure became too much for her. She wasn't sure what to do, short of deciding not to go out at all, but that was no answer. When her father came for a visit, she found herself confiding in him in a way she had never done before.

"I don't know if I'm coming or going," she told him. One of the proposals had come from an older man who put her on a pedestal. It was flattering, but it also made her feel too coddled and protected. "I don't think I'd have enough independence," she said.

"You don't have to marry anyone."

"I hate feeling stifled."

Her father smiled. "I know," he said.

She turned down all the marriage offers.

The little female dog was part Australian shepherd and part border collie, with a fluffy coat that was black and brown and white; she had eyes of different colors, one brown and one blue, and there were freckles all around her nose. As soon as Caroline spotted her at the pound, there was no question of looking further. Caroline named her Pickles. They shared an instant rapport that seemed totally basic and natural, and from that first moment, Pickles became Caroline's constant companion. They went everywhere together, especially all around campus, and Pickles waited outside the classrooms for her.

Having Pickles felt, to Caroline, like the fulfillment of a dream she had harbored since early childhood. The devotion offered by Pickles was unconditional; her canine friendship was, unlike human relationships, without reservation or complication.

When Caroline looked back at how she had been uprooted so often, moving from home to home in country after country, she realized that her world, along with the people and things to which she had become attached, had always felt temporary and subject to change without notice. A dog of her own was the opposite—constant, faithful, loyal. When Caroline felt miserable, Pickles was right there with boundless affection and love. Even if she just wanted to take a walk, Pickles was always ready to go with her.

She got rid of her "sewing machine car" in favor of an imported Triumph—again, a gift from her father. Through his connections, the green TR-4A convertible was specially put together and delivered to the docks at San Francisco. Caroline drove it down to Los Angeles, where she worked with mechanics who remodeled the motor into a racing engine. With Pickles seated beside her, she now had the sense of freedom and power that came from being behind the wheel of a race car on the open road.

The final touch came when she found a soft leather World War I flyer's helmet at a flea market. The devoted Pickles allowed herself to be dressed in the helmet and a long white aviator's scarf, and Caroline got to tool around Palo Alto with "Snoopy" at her side.

Soon there was a new passenger in the Triumph: Arthur Hebard, who was working at Stanford on his PhD in physics.

Caroline and Art dated for nearly three years, occasionally breaking off and seeing other people. The big difference was that with him she never felt any threat to her individuality or personal freedom. They enjoyed some of the same things, such as skiing and hiking and exploring the outdoors, but otherwise they valued their separate identities and interests. If they were to get married and have a family, Caroline felt, that essential distinction between them would be maintained.

She had developed a longing for stability and a sense of permanence, a foundation upon which to build her life, but she also needed to be herself. Part of her wanted peace and security, while the other part needed excitement and even risk. One side required structure; the other, freedom. As opposite as those aspects of herself might have been, they were both necessary. The challenge was to acknowledge those different sides at the same time.

Caroline and Art were married on May 4, 1968.

Her parents, who were stationed in Argentina at the time, flew up to be at the ceremony and reception, which Caroline herself catered with money she had made teaching. Of course, Pickles played a prominent role at the wedding and joined in formal poses for the photographer.


Art and Caroline moved into a small rental house while continuing their graduate studies. Whenever they could get away, they went off backpacking to enjoy the wilderness. Friends took care of Pickles when they were gone, and Caroline did the same for them. At one point she was caring for six canine boarders at once—a situation that did not always sit well with the neighbors or, for that matter, with Pickles, who was used to being the center of attention. What Pickles didn't know was that her place in the family was soon to change forever.

Caroline was thinking about getting another dog, a larger, more trainable one, the kind she had wanted since she was twelve—a German shepherd. Friends of her parents had had shepherds, and there was something about the look and personality of most German shepherds—their size and regal bearing, their intelligence and affection, a certain look in their eyes—that seemed to connect with her.

One evening she asked Art to go out with her for a ride in the Triumph. Caroline sped up the winding roads of the Santa Cruz hills above Monterey Bay.

"What's up here?" Art asked.

"We're going to see some puppies."

Amid the redwoods was the home of an elderly German breeder. On the phone, he had told her he had a litter of German shepherds only eight weeks old.

Sure enough, the black and tan puppies were scurrying around and rolling over each other. They were hardly over ten pounds apiece, and were just being weaned from the mother. Caroline gazed at them awhile and noticed one particular pup who was very black with just a little tan on him. She knew next to nothing about how to pick out a dog, but this little guy looked up at her with special eagerness. When Caroline moved, he seemed to want to follow her; when she lifted him and held him in her arms, he snuggled into her as if he belonged there.

"This is the one," she said.

It was dawning upon Art that a German shepherd was about to join their household. "Are you trying to pull a fast one?"

Caroline smiled. "You bet," she said.

On the way back down the Santa Cruz hills, with Art behind the wheel, Caroline held the puppy on her lap and cuddled him. She really did have a way with animals, especially dogs, and with this one she was already establishing a close bond. She decided to speak to him in the language of the country in which his breed had originated. She named him Jaeger, the German word for "hunter."

Although Jaeger was still a puppy, Caroline could soon tell he was a good, solid dog, with a wonderful temperament. He was energetic and high-spirited, and although he was independent, he was smart and highly trainable. His only flaw, so to speak, was an innate dislike of cats and an incurable urge to chase them. He was going to be big, too.

When fully grown he would stand about twenty-five inches high at the shoulder and weigh up to eighty-five pounds.

German shepherds had been developed, over hundreds of years, from sheep-herding and farm-dog stock. At the beginning of the twentieth century they had been perfected as large, muscular working dogs. Jaeger's parents and grandparents had been trained in a variety of specialties other than herding—as police dogs, message carriers, patrol dogs in war, and guide dogs for the blind. They also had been bred as family pets, which was how Caroline thought of Jaeger when they first went to obedience class.

One night a week she took him to the shopping center for classes, which were held by the local German shepherd dog club. She also worked with him daily by herself, for five or ten minutes at a time. After a short session of obedience work, she rewarded Jaeger by throwing balls and playing with him, to give him a sense of release.

It didn't take any longer than those few minutes a day to practice the basics, which she conveyed to him in crisp German—*"platz"* ("down"); *"bleib"* ("stay"); *"sitz"* ("sit"); *"steh"* ("stand"); *"fuss"* ("heel"); *"hier"* ("come"); and so on. At first the words were simply names attached to things the puppy did on his own quite naturally or even accidentally. Whenever Jaeger lay down, for whatever reason, she spoke the word *"platz"* right away, so that he would begin to link it in his mind with the act. As she said the word she also pointed downward. Before long he learned that *"platz"* meant he should lie down, and he happily did so. In that same gentle, easy manner, accompanied by happy voice tones, the various German words became his specific commands, along with the arm movements that Caroline incorporated along the way.

*"Feiner Hund!"* she would say, telling Jaeger that he was a good dog, and then played with him for maybe another ten minutes. The important part of obedience training was to make it fun for the dog, whose zest for performing would continue to grow if it was based on what trainers called "positive reinforcement."

One of the subtlest points of training, she discovered, was when and how to reward Jaeger. At first, if he sat down on command, she often gave him a treat; but once that particular behavior was established, the food was phased out and only verbal praise was given.

Some dogs—such as beagles, she noticed—were real "chow hounds" and did much better with treats as a reward; but most German shepherds became trained quickly with energetic praise or play as their reward.

Caroline also learned that obedience sessions were most effective when short, because of the puppy's limited attention span. Training was best done in stages, and it worked only if the dog's owner was in good spirits. If Caroline felt grouchy or tired, she skipped a session rather than subject Jaeger to such moods. Above all they were teaching each other, and learning how to learn, without rigidity. Just as she herself, as a child, had rebelled against attempts to make her do everything correctly, so would a dog react badly to harsh, inflexible treatment.

As Caroline saw it, Jaeger was developing self-esteem. Without fear of reprimand, he felt free to use his own initiative. Before long he would stay or sit or heel upon receiving the slightest cue from Caroline, who felt less and less need to repeat herself or raise her voice.

Caroline's instinctive love of freedom had gained a sharp edge during her four years at the St. James School in West Malvern, Worcestershire, where she had arrived when she was eleven. The place was a stuffy prison, requiring the girls to wear hideous uniforms with "bullet-proof" stockings, and its rules seemed specially designed to break young spirits.

Caroline's father received money from the Foreign Service for her to fly round-trip once a year to the Persian Gulf, where the Gales were stationed at the time, but during Christmas, Easter, and other holidays she was farmed out to family friends in England, Scotland, or Germany. At the boarding school, which was loaded with snobby girls from the horsy set, there were certain routes to popularity, such as parents who took you out on weekends, so you could invite a friend along, or receiving lots of care packages, so you could share the goodies. Caroline had neither of these advantages, but in other ways she deliberately set herself apart, becoming an outcast by choice. Although her father represented Great Britain around the world, she proudly identified herself as Latin American.

Trapped at school on weekends, she developed an ingenious system of breaking out by creeping up and down fire escapes, from building to building, and to the edge of the campus, where she had stashed some work clothes. After quickly changing into this disguise, she went downtown to buy the sexiest, trashiest paperbacks she could find; back in her dormitory room, she cut up each novel into sections that she "rented" to the other girls. She kept the racy pages stashed under the floorboards, along with candy bars and other snacks to be sold at premium prices. At a school where the hormones of puberty were raging, the market for sex and sweets was bullish, and the profits became her pocket money.

One of the few bright spots was the presence of Señor Peres, who taught an advanced Spanish class consisting of Caroline and three other girls. An exiled communist from Spain, he brought wine and invited the girls to drink with him while discussing Spanish literature. He also took them on "field trips" to London, where he went off to see his girlfriend, leaving Caroline and her classmates free to roam for the rest of the day.

These tastes of freedom were too few, however, so Caroline began to break as many rules as it might take to get herself thrown out. That victory finally came in the spring of 1959, when she was nearly fifteen.

It started with the rule that all girls had to attend church twice on Sundays—more than she could tolerate. During the services she and other girls rolled Ping-Pong balls back and forth down the pews, and one morning Caroline got caught. She was ordered by the vicar, whom she hated, to go pick gooseberries in his garden. The next Sunday morning, in retaliation, she skipped church altogether. It was a beautiful day, so Caroline and another girl climbed up to the dormitory attic and onto the roof. They took off their clothes and lay down on towels to sunbathe.

A military helicopter was practicing maneuvers nearby, and the pilot, catching sight of them, flew closer and hovered. Caroline and her friend stood and waved to him just as school officials, leaving church, saw the helicopter and spotted the two naked girls. Caroline, because of her past record, was told to find another school.

During the next two years she went to a boarding school in Lausanne, Switzerland, and by contrast with the English school, this one—the Pensionnat Brillantmont—was heaven. She could wear her own clothes. She could go into town on certain days, so long as her grades were good. The school even had a mountain chalet where the students spent a month during the winter combining skiing and academics. Here was a civilized environment, with students treated not as look-alike prisoners in uniform but as individuals respected as young adults. As a result, Caroline did well in her studies and graduated early, with advanced-level certificates, endorsed by the universities of Cambridge and Oxford, in numerous subjects.

And so, training Jaeger several years later, she recalled how quickly and easily her behavior had changed at the Swiss school. At the British school, where harsh criticism and constant punishment had been the only means of affecting her behavior, she had been unhappy and unmotivated and rebellious; but at the Swiss school, which had rewarded good behavior with more freedom and fun, she had flourished. Such was also the case, Caroline realized, for any dog that valued its pride and independence.

Caroline and Art both wanted children, and they had agreed to try starting a family while they were still young. Thirty months after the wedding, however, the pair of healthy twenty-six-year-olds had not yet succeeded in conceiving a child. Caroline started a long series of painful medical tests. After months of uncertainty, she and Art were called to the doctor's office for the final verdict. She could never conceive, they were told, because both fallopian tubes were blocked. Having a child of their own was out of the question.

It was a devastating disappointment, but it drew the young couple even closer together in their desire to be parents. After long discussions with both of their families, they decided to apply for adoption. Their names went into a file, and they were told it could be years before a baby was available. There was nothing to do but wait.

Jaeger had grown into a marvelous one-year-old German shepherd whose potential to learn seemed limitless. Caroline now began to explore the possibility of taking him beyond obedience into the Ger-

man sport of Schutzhund. Just being introduced into German shepherd circles in the United States, Schutzhund, or protection training,
included demanding tests of tracking, agility, and retrieving. Caroline
loved a challenge, and it sounded as if Schutzhund would demand the
best of Jaeger—and of her.

It was someone in the obedience class who spotted the difficulty.
"Look at his rear end," he remarked as Jaeger walked by. "Is it wobbly?"

Caroline watched closely with a sinking feeling; by now she knew
enough about the breed to be aware that this wobbly gait might be a
symptom of hip dysplasia, a disabling condition prevalent among German shepherds. Jaeger was a beautiful dog and she had thought about
breeding him, but for that he needed to be structurally sound. In
addition, the requirements of Schutzhund involved jumping, which
meant that his hips had to be healthy and strong. When the signs of
slight discomfort and lameness did not go away, she took him for an X
ray and waited anxiously for the results.

The radiographs revealed that in fact Jaeger had dysplasia in both
hips. In dogs, this congenital malformation occurs mostly in the larger
breeds, and it is found in nearly all species of big animals. It causes
joint instability and leads to partial or complete dislocation, not to
mention considerable pain and secondary osteoarthritis. Jaeger could
remain a lovable family pet, Caroline realized, but she could never
breed him, and he would never become a working dog.

Jaeger could be treated with pain relievers alone or also with sur-
gery. Caroline chose the latter. At that time the operation involved
cutting a small ligament as well as removing the heads of the femurs,
which, after being reset, would no longer rub in the same spot. The
veterinarian recommended moderate exercise and weight control, to
maintain muscle tone and slow the onset of arthritis. From that point
on, Caroline kept Jaeger obedience-trained while giving him daily
swims and brisk jaunts alongside her bicycle.

Her only goal for Jaeger now was to offer him the happiest, longest
life possible, with the least amount of pain.

# Chapter 2

# Zibo:
# Dogs in the Family

CAROLINE KNEW WHAT SHE WANTED. OBEDIENCE training with Jaeger had sparked her desire to work a dog to its fullest potential, so she asked other handlers how to go about finding the best German shepherd. She wanted a young dog, but one that was older than a puppy so they both could enter more advanced training right away.

Through members of the German shepherd dog club in the Palo Alto area, she initiated contact with an elderly German importer of dogs who lived near Atlanta, Georgia. This man had contacts with major breeders in his native country and reportedly was bringing over very strong, healthy shepherds. Caroline kept up lively contact with him, speaking by phone with him and writing to him in German. It was a risk to deal with someone she had never met and to buy a dog sight unseen, but they kept talking back and forth until at last he called and said, "I think I've found the right dog for you. His name is Zibo. I'm sending you a copy of his pedigree along with his photograph, and I want you to look at them."

When the package arrived, she stared at the snapshot of Zibo's dark body and black face, noticing that his eyes seemed set like those of a wolf. He was fourteen months old, the perfect age, and Caroline notified the importer that she agreed. Soon her new dog was on his way from Germany, through John F. Kennedy International Airport in New York, to San Francisco.

By the late 1960s, canine handlers in the United States had begun to feel the need to import more working dogs from Europe. Because the rules governing breeding in Germany were stricter, German shepherds bred in that country displayed very different temperaments than their American-bred counterparts did. They had inborn positive personalities, their inherited drive or need to work was stronger, and their genetic heritage made them tougher. Even as puppies they were seldom intimidated. Sudden noises or strange sights did not faze them; instead, they tended to be curious. If you started up a vacuum cleaner, for example, the shepherd puppies did not pee on the spot or shy away, as most dogs did; rather, the whole litter would descend upon the alien machine to find out what it was doing.

In her research, Caroline had also learned that most of the shepherds bred in Germany as working dogs had some ancestors in common. These pedigrees had been arrived at under careful breeding laws applied over many years. In Germany, unlike in the United States, a given dog could be bred into certain family lines but not into others; there were also regulations against breeding dogs that were too closely related (the probable reason for Jaeger's inherited hip dysplasia). Dogs in Germany had to earn a working title before they could even undergo the first of the two "breed surveys" required. Their hips had to be X-rayed; standards for weight, height, gait, and temperament had to be met. Only then were they allowed to breed. The dogs that passed such tests became, over generations, the producers of excellent working stock.

And that was Zibo's background.

When Caroline arrived at the San Francisco airport to meet the plane, she watched a customs official reach toward the open door of a dog crate with a hamburger. The entire piece of meat promptly disappeared. Then a big black bullet of an animal bounded out, full of energy. When he stared up at her with that wolflike face, which she recalled from the photograph of him, Caroline fell in love with Zibo on the spot.

Right there in the airport she deliberately began the bonding process, calling his name and speaking to him in German so he wouldn't be confused. She petted him and set down some paper so he could relieve himself, then gave him a large T-bone steak she had brought with her. Then she took him to a grassy spot outside the customs area and walked him around on a leash for half an hour. She praised him and hugged him, transmitting her own energy to him, until she felt that he was going to be her dog and hers alone.

Later she would look back and describe Zibo as "a very loving, quiet dog, good around children and family, very much an all-around dog." At that time, however, the only members of the Hebard family in California were Art and Caroline, along with Pickles and Jaeger; and when Zibo arrived, he was hardly a "family" dog who wanted to curl up next to his owner's feet. He had been bred and trained for action. In terms of sheer presence and zest for life, he could not be ignored. He was clearly a serious working dog, and as Caroline told her husband, "I have to put time into this guy. I owe it to him to find out just how intelligent he is, to see what he's really capable of learning and what he can do."

Jaeger had been king of the household up till then, so he had a hard time making room for the new German shepherd. He and Zibo walked around each other on tense, stiff legs, like two hostile fighters awkwardly circling. They kept their distance when Caroline was around, getting on together reasonably well, but a clash seemed inevitable.

It was also clear that Pickles, the original family pet, was becoming more and more withdrawn. This sensitive female dog had been accustomed, at least in the beginning, to having Caroline all to herself. By now she had learned to accommodate Jaeger's presence, but with Zibo's arrival she was pushed to the point of depression. "I'm not being fair to her," Caroline said, and soon afterward she reluctantly found her a new home with a couple and two children who obviously adored her. Now, as before, Pickles could be the queen. About six months later, when Caroline went to visit her, this lovable Australian shepherd–border collie mix was her old self again. Now she was "their" dog, and Caroline, with relief and sadness, knew that giving Pickles away had been the right decision.


She made contact with a group of several California police officers who, along with a few civilians, were starting Schutzhund training with their German shepherds. The group, called the Peninsula Police Canine Corps, gathered on Saturday mornings and Wednesday evenings to practice skills in obedience, tracking, agility, and retrieving as well as basic protection work. Because most members were in law enforcement, their goal was primarily to develop patrol dogs.

Until Caroline arrived, the group had consisted of only men, who seemed wary when she and Zibo arrived one Saturday at the training field in the hills behind Stanford University. "I just want to work my dog to his full potential," she explained.

"Nice animal," one of the men said as Zibo went through his exercises in obedience.

"Well, they're letting me join," Caroline told Art that night, adding with a laugh, "but I think it's only because they like my dog!"

Just as she and Zibo were getting started, however, there was a call from the attorney that Caroline and Art had hired to help with their adoption proceedings. "I hope you people are ready," the lawyer said, "because your baby is about to be born."

Joanne was three days old when Art and Caroline drove to the hospital to pick her up. Caroline would never forget the incredible mix of excitement, fear, and longing she felt that day. As she and Art stopped to gaze through the nursery window, they saw a row of sleeping newborns with one little pink bundle screaming its head off. "That's her for sure," Art said. "That's our little girl." He was right.

Joanne turned out to be a wonderfully easy baby, adorable and sunny-natured from the start. Even so, Caroline had her hands full. Ten days after the baby arrived, they moved to a new rental house and Art left to attend a scientific conference in Japan. Caroline had never known she could be so tired and so happy at the same time.

A month later, just as things had settled down a bit and Caroline was getting used to motherhood and diaper pins, she came down with what she thought was the flu. When the symptoms didn't go away, she went to the doctor for tests. A few days later she got a call from the doctor's office.

"Congratulations," the doctor's assistant said.

"For what? Having the flu?"

"No, ma'am, you're pregnant."

"I don't *get* pregnant," Caroline said.

"Well, you are."

"That's physically impossible. You must have made a mistake or switched the charts."

"No," the woman said, "there is no mistake."

Caroline clutched the receiver and glanced over at Joanne, who was sound asleep in her bassinet.

"Mrs. Hebard? Are you okay?"

"I—I think so."

She hung up and called the university physics lab.

"Hi, Art. Guess what?"

Ever since Joanne's arrival, Caroline had faced the need to make sure the baby was protected from Zibo and Jaeger. Neither dog was a fear biter (one that might snap at someone who made a sudden or unexpected move), but raising children around two huge German shepherds was potentially dangerous nonetheless.

Her philosophy from the start was that neither dog should be given any reason to be jealous of the infant. They must not view Joanne as a threat to their own status as family members, nor should they feel abandoned or left out. So she introduced them to Joanne as soon as the baby was brought into "their" world, letting the dogs sniff the delicious new-baby smell and including them in the baby's routines. Both dogs sat beside Caroline while she fed Joanne; when she took the baby out for walks, Zibo and Jaeger went along; and when Caroline put Joanne in the front carrier and went for a bike ride, they happily kept pace.

Their new rental had a backyard and a pool, so Caroline also spent hours outside on the grass, watching the dogs and the baby together. If she needed to go into the house for a moment, she placed Joanne inside a circular fence while the dogs lay outside right next to it. That way she never worried, and moreover the shepherds acted as the child's guardians.

By this point, if Joanne started to cry, Zibo and Jaeger clearly felt responsible. In exasperation, they would go to Caroline and shove their noses at her as if to say, "Hey, Mom, pay attention!"

Zibo was extremely protective, especially of Caroline, and one night Art made the mistake of testing to see how the dogs might react if a "stranger" entered the house. Art frequently worked late at the lab, because it was the only time he could run his scientific experiments. On this night he parked his car in the driveway and, instead of using the front door, walked around and slipped through a gate into the yard. So far so good; now he came to the rear door and quietly sneaked into the house. In that split second, Zibo hurtled toward him. The big, black German shepherd was totally airborne, mouth wide open as if about to slice Art in half.

"Zibo, *nein!*" he whispered.

Somehow Zibo stopped himself in that instant, within an inch from mauling the "stranger" in the house, and his feet landed on the floor. The huge dog stared, mouth open, hackles still raised, and Art swore on the spot that he would never, ever sneak up on him again.

Taking care to see that Zibo and Jaeger got along with each other, Caroline brought both dogs when she went out jogging, and she took them swimming as well. The exercise was to keep fit during her pregnancy, but it also served to keep the dogs themselves in shape. Too many so-called working dogs were overweight, Caroline had decided, simply because they were overfed and underexercised.

Physical activity with Zibo and Jaeger was just one form of quality time, which she had learned to value. It meant taking the dogs on walks, doing a little obedience work with them, having some playtime with a ball, and even just hanging out together. Such activities helped to ensure that they were happy, calm, and well behaved, especially in public. (Whenever she visited a dog owner who felt it necessary to keep the animal away from the guests because it was not properly socialized, Caroline silently understood that the pet was not experiencing this kind of quality time in the first place.) Just as a parent's relationship with a child was based on much more than teaching and enforcing rules, so was a handler's relationship with a dog based on more than formal training. In each case the bond was strengthened by simply sharing one's life.

To keep Jaeger happy she sometimes brought him out for training sessions with Zibo. There was a thin line, she discovered, between competition and jealousy. The dogs were motivated to learn through healthy competition; to that end, Caroline always brought treats for each of them. She made sure to reward them equally and, if possible, simultaneously, but if one became jealous of the other, there could be trouble.

One afternoon when Caroline and Art went out with the baby, they left Zibo and Jaeger unsupervised in the fenced yard behind the house, and the two dogs got into an unholy fight. Neighbors heard wild barking, snarling, growling, roaring. They peered cautiously over the fence to see the two large German shepherds trying to destroy each other. The spectators, unable to reach Caroline, were not about to climb into the yard and interfere with this ferocious scrap. It finally stopped when the canine warriors, joined in a tornadolike ball of whirling fur, spun over the edge of the swimming pool and splashed together into the water.

Caroline and Art never again left Zibo and Jaeger alone together in the yard. Oddly enough, the two dogs always got along fine in the kitchen, where they spent the night with each other, and in all other ways as well they were buddies.

As soon as Joanne had settled in, Caroline lined up some reliable babysitters, and she and Zibo continued to train with the police group twice a week. Saturdays were spent outside in the field, Wednesday nights at an indoor horse corral. She listened to the German instructor and the handlers, absorbing their different attitudes, and reading as much as possible to clarify her own ideas. She finally learned mostly by instinct and observation, taking into account the dog's personality as well as her own. Zibo's reactions were not quite the same as those of any other dog, so it was up to Caroline to tailor her training methods accordingly. As they continued to work on obedience, she learned to trust her gut feeling that Zibo wanted to be with her, that he listened to her, that he was motivated to obey and please her, that he would not quit on her. She used a more gentle approach than most other handlers did, without yelling at the dog or jerking him around, and the personal rapport between them helped their skills to grow and develop.

Zibo had completed his Schutzhund I training in Germany, so he already possessed a working title, but Caroline wanted to take him through the same initial trial so she herself could learn. In his native country he had received exemplary scores at the first level, so Caroline felt the burden of catching up to him in terms of experience; too, she needed to keep refining their ability to work as a team.

The sport of Schutzhund, which developed rapidly in Germany after World War II, remained virtually unknown outside Europe until the early 1970s. In the United States, it was still very much a male domain, so Caroline became a pioneer as both a handler and a woman. There were three levels, consisting of increasingly longer ground-scent tracks as well as progressively more difficult tests for climbing, jumping, and retrieving. At the third and highest level, one of the dogs' tasks was to carry fourteen-pound weights over a series of walls up to five feet high.

Training never went well if Caroline used a flat tone of voice; it was important to use a light, happy tone with Zibo, and in many cases the German words seemed to work better than the English ones. The command "come" felt dull and heavy, for example, while its German counterpart, *"hier"* ("hee-ah"), sounded much lighter, gentler, and more inviting to the dog. Voice tone was also a means of conveying various kinds of other messages. The word *"sitz,"* for example, rang with much greater emphasis than "sit."

It was not necessary to use many commands or to talk much to the dog; it was the *way* she spoke that produced results. (While some owners talk nonstop to their dogs and swear the animals comprehend everything they say, the dogs really are responding to the *tone of voice*; the animals understand that their owners are communicating with them, but don't know what is being said.) As Caroline found, one word was usually enough. When she used the command *"nein"* it was clear to Zibo that he should stop what he was doing. If he heard the more emphatic *"pfui"* ("phooey"), he understood that he should "get away from there!" It was a matter of expressiveness.

The timing of reward or correction was a delicate but essential element. It was useless to praise Zibo or give him a treat or play with him five minutes after his task had been accomplished; the response had to be immediate. And it was counterproductive to say "no" once the undesired behavior had already taken place; anticipating the bad move, and giving a forewarning, was much more effective. If Zibo ran away, for example, it didn't do any good to scold him upon his return; by that time, he had done the right thing by coming back! Instead, it was important to stop him the moment he made the slightest move to run off. And the correction was not a painful punishment but a firm statement of what was expected of him, as if to say, "This is what I want you to do, right now."

Fairness, patience, persistence, and consistency had become Caroline's watchwords. If she wanted Zibo to climb a ladder and he was physically capable but refused, she did *not* shrug and say, "Well, he isn't in the mood, so I guess we'll try it tomorrow." Instead she persisted, gently and patiently but firmly, until he climbed that ladder. She would not let him get away with *not* performing the task, but once he did perform it, she was right there with rewards of effusive praise and enthusiasm and affectionate voice tones, petting him or playing with him.

She carried Zibo's tug-toy and some food in her pockets, the better to give him those rewards on the spot. If she had reached for them even a few minutes later, he would not have linked them with his successful ladder climb. Through consistency, he learned that his reward would arrive quickly—after, never before, he completed the task.

If Zibo was supposed to climb the ladder, walk across a plank, and then climb down the opposite side, and if he started up but slipped off at the very beginning, the unpleasant experience might well cool his desire to try again. To maintain the dog's confidence, it was important to ensure his success every time in any endeavor. To let him get away with stubbornly refusing, however, would damage him as well. If he won any such contest with Caroline, he would win again in the future. So she insisted that he start back up and finally go across the plank and down the other side.

After rewarding him, she made sure to guide him through the agility test once more. Any more repetitions that day might make Zibo hate the whole thing, but to accept less from him would weaken her authority. Then, during any future session, Zibo would be eager to go through it again as if there never had been a problem.

In Schutzhund tracking work, a dog was given the whiff of a specific human being's scent and then required to follow it close to the ground without the handler's guidance. Although Caroline might have known where the physical track was located, she was not allowed to assist her dog. Zibo had to depend entirely upon his powerful nose to follow the path of someone who might or might not have left footprints.

The earliest sessions with a young dog involved tracks only five or ten feet long, to get him accustomed to going "deep nose" like a vacuum cleaner and following the scent step by step, without zigzagging from side to side. A stranger (never the dog's handler) walked over the ground to create a scent track, "baiting" this invisible trail with food as he went. By deliberately not having fed Zibo that morning, Caroline made sure he would be eager to eat breakfast out on the track. Then she took Zibo to the starting point, where she scented him on the "scent pad"—an area the track layer had scuffed. Since the goal was for the dog to keep his nose to the ground along the way, having him discover pieces of hot dog from one end to the other guaranteed his success in covering it.

"*Such*," she told him, using the German command for "track" but saying it slowly and elongating it: "*Z-u-u-ch!*"

During these practice sessions, the amount of food distributed would vary—sometimes more, sometimes less. Through this intermittent-reward system, the dog became accustomed to tracking human scent while hoping to find some treats. Then came the morning when Zibo, hungry as usual, was given the same tracking command only to find no food at all. By now, however, he had learned to associate tracking with the pleasant experience of getting food, and he followed the human scent as he had done before.

Then, and only then, did Caroline reward him with treats or praise or playtime. Eventually the transfer from baited to unbaited tracks was complete.

The California police officers were eager for their dogs to do well on clear or unbaited tracks. Obviously, felons would not drop hot dogs or Cheerios to help the dogs along. And in the actual Schutzhund trials, there was never any food. Instead, the track layer hid two or three "scent articles" along the track, often leather gloves or a wallet, because leather is one of the best scent retainers. The dog had to follow in the track layer's footsteps exactly, and points were taken off if it failed to find one of the scent articles. The response to a find was also very precise: the dog was supposed to go into a down (*platz*) position until the handler approached, picked up the scent article, and gave the command to begin tracking again. Handlers hoped there would be no crosswinds, because if the scent was blown sideways and the dog followed it through the air even as little as two or three feet off the track, a demerit resulted.

At the first level the track was only ten minutes old. At Level II, the age of the scent grew to thirty minutes, and finally, at Level III, the dog was taken to the track up to two hours after it had been laid. Also, the distances were gradually lengthened—from about 150 yards for the first level, to 500 yards at Level III—and the number of turns and cross-tracks was increased dramatically. Beyond Level III of Schutzhund, the dog and handler could go on to an advanced test that included tracking only. For this, several people in addition to the track layer crossed the track; the dog had to sniff its way past a number of confusing cross-tracks in order to follow the correct one. This track, many hours old, was close to a quarter mile long and went over various kinds of surfaces, from concrete to grass to sand.

In each of these trials, the dog was completely unassisted by its handler.

A Schutzhund-trained dog was also taught to do zigzag searching across a wide field, while the handler employed voice commands and arm signals to guide him. In an exercise called "searching the blinds," Zibo had to find a hidden person, usually a man (known as the "agitator") wearing a large padded burlap sleeve on his arm. Whether he was supposed to represent a "bad guy" or a "victim" was of no concern to the dog, who viewed the entire exercise as a game. The man with the burlap-covered sleeve, hiding in a V-shaped blind, was someone to be played with after being found; that by itself motivated the dog.

The trials Zibo went through also tested the dog's courage. A man would jump unexpectedly from the bushes to yell and wave his arms at the handler. Would Zibo charge him? Or back off? Caroline held Zibo while he gazed across the field at the menacing agitator, who brandished a soft leather stick and snapped it loudly against his leather pants. As the man taunted her and Zibo in a threatening manner, she told the dog in a zesty, playful tone of voice, "Watch that guy! Watch that guy!" Then she'd give the final command: *"Fass!"*—"Go get him!"

In the next breath Zibo was racing down the field to "attack" the man's thick, protective sleeve, while someone else shot a gun in the air to test the dog's reaction. No matter what sights or sounds confronted him, Zibo ignored the gunshot and cheerfully went for the man's sleeve in a tug-of-war game. When the agitator stood still, however, the dog had to release the sleeve immediately. At that point, he was supposed to simply sit in front of the agitator and bark.

There were various methods of training the dog to release, some of them quite harsh. Caroline preferred teaching Zibo with a correction technique called "double handling." That is, a second handler held on to a long leash while she herself had a short one. If the agitator stood still and Zibo failed to release the sleeve, she would yell *"aus"* to tell him to let go; simultaneously the handler with the long line gave him a tough jerk from far behind. *"Sitz!"* Caroline would then call out, commanding Zibo to sit. *"Gib laut!"* she would add, ordering him to "give noise" or bark. With repetition, Zibo learned to perform the routine with no leashes at all.

As a reward, the agitator would move his arm again and allow Zibo another "hit" on the sleeve—again, stimulating and encouraging the dog's play drive. When the protection exercise was over, the man would let his sleeve drop so Zibo could grab it and parade around the field as if carrying a trophy, much like a bird dog proudly retrieving its prey.

In training for police work, this exercise was a little different. A patrol dog was trained on a hidden sleeve worn by a man wearing a completely padded outfit. If the "bad guy" ran toward the handler or away from him, the dog could "hit" him anywhere on his body and bring him down. Then the handler, a police officer, would be able to get the person under control and handcuffed.

Schutzhund trials were contests that utilized judges and scoring, with control of the dog as the primary goal. To prepare for these, Zibo did both on-lead and off-lead obedience; he tracked over long distances; he went through tests for noise shyness; he climbed back and forth over walls to retrieve dumbbells; he searched the blinds in wide-ranging tracking exercises; and although he viewed the "bad guy" as a friend and only "attacked" the burlap sleeve as a form of play, he happily and unwittingly learned protection work.

One of the Schutzhund trainers was Gernot Riedel, a German breeder who had done a great deal for the sport. During his Wednesday-night sessions inside the horse corral, he seemed to single out Caroline (still the only female handler) and pounced on every mistake as if she were committing a crime: *"Du dumme Frau,"* he would yell. "You stupid woman! What are you doing? You have a good dog—how can you be so stupid!"

When she returned home in tears and Art suggested that she quit, Caroline shook her head.

"No," she said, "I really feel that Zibo and I are learning something important."

"So where's it all leading?"

"I don't know," she replied, "but wherever it is, we're going there."


Caroline continued to train twice a week with the police group until the very last stage of pregnancy. By then the officers, convinced she would go into labor right there on the training field, had begun carrying obstetric kits in their cars. They were actually disappointed when they learned that she had delivered in the hospital.

Joanne was ten months old when Andrew arrived, as demanding a baby as she had been easy. Now more than ever it was a juggling act, as Caroline rushed back from Schutzhund practice to nurse her hungry son.

Andrew was six months old and not yet weaned when Caroline put Zibo through the first official Schutzhund trial ever held in the United States. His scores were not quite as high as they had been in Germany, but once again he passed. Because Caroline had become a United States citizen after Joanne was born, she was also the first American woman to pass a Schutzhund trial. They started preparing for the second level right away.

By the summer of 1972, however, Art was due to receive his PhD in physics and had been shopping for work. When a research job at the world-famous Bell Labs in New Jersey came through, there was little question that they should move. The only thing Caroline knew about New Jersey was that it had a turnpike running through miles of oil refineries and polluted air, and she burst into tears at the thought of having to live there. On the other hand, the offer was exciting for Art, especially at a time when getting any kind of research job was difficult. Art's specialty, low-temperature physics, could be pursued in relatively few places, and many other talented scientists were teaching or staying afloat by doing work totally unrelated to their field.

They filled their new van with babies, dogs, and camping gear and set out for the East.

# Chapter 3

# Search and Rescue

THE RENTAL HOUSE OFF KING GEORGE ROAD IN Warren Township, New Jersey, was a dump of a place. The walls were covered with mildew. The water heater didn't work, so Caroline bathed the kids with water she warmed on the stove. There was no furniture, so she and Art slept on rollaway beds. In the mornings Art went off to Bell Labs in Murray Hill, thrilled to be putting his training into practice, while Caroline was left to figure out how not to go stir-crazy. But she did have a name and phone number.

"You should look up Margo Roebling in Bernardsville," a California friend had said. "She's always had German shepherds."

So Caroline impulsively called her.

"Come over tomorrow for tea," Margo said.

"Well, I have two dogs and two kids, but no baby-sitter, and even if I did, I wouldn't want to leave them in this hole-in-the-wall we're renting. What if I pile them all into the van and bring them with me? Would that bother you?"

"Not at all."

The next day she took the kids and dogs to see Margo.

"I've got to do something," Caroline said, "because I'm going nuts. We're still looking for a house, but I've got to get out and do something for myself and the dogs."

"You know," Margo said, "there's a new thing with German shepherds called search and rescue. They've just started a unit of the American Rescue Dog Association with people from New York and New Jersey. Maybe they'd have something you could do."

That night Caroline made contact with the group, speaking by phone to a woman who told her that a training session would be held the following Saturday morning near Bear Mountain in New York.

"Why don't you meet us there?" the woman said.

Caroline wrote down the directions.

"Do you have any survival gear?"

"Most of it is still coming across the country, with our furniture and other belongings, but I'll bring what I have."

Art stayed with the kids that cold, rainy Saturday morning in September 1972 while she hit the road in the van with Zibo and Jaeger, heading through the scenic Hudson River Valley near the Ramapo Mountains. When she arrived at a large field surrounded by woods off Seven Lakes Drive in Bear Mountain State Park, four women and three men were standing amid the drizzle with their German shepherds. Caroline was startled to find that more than half the handlers were female; it was certainly a change from the police group in California (although a few women had joined by the time she left). She was even more surprised that the two leaders of the search-and-rescue unit were women.

"I'm not going to work with Jaeger because he's dysplastic," she said, "but I brought him along because he needs to get out."

"What kind of training has Zibo had?"

"He's a Schutzhund I dog. He's ready to take his Schutzhund II, but we left California before that trial was held."

"Well, we don't take Schutzhund dogs."

"Why not?"

"They're killers!"

Caroline was shocked. "Do you understand Schutzhund?" she asked.

"It's a way of creating vicious attack dogs."

"No, no, no. It's a sport! There's not a nasty bone in Zibo's whole body! Does he seem vicious to you?"

"No, but—"

"He's a working dog, but he's also a loving family pet!"

"Well . . ."

She would have to prove it to them.

The rain began to come down harder, but Caroline threw on a waterproof poncho and started through the mud with Zibo and Jaeger. As the downpour continued, she worked with the dogs on basic obedience and tracking routines. The others, meanwhile, were taking turns hiding in the woods so their shepherds could practice finding them. The dogs, she was told, had learned to follow human scent not on the ground but strictly through the air. That was not something she had heard of while working with the police group, but then Caroline knew nothing about search-and-rescue work. By the same token, these handlers obviously had been misinformed about Schutzhund training.

When the session ended, they were all soaked and chilled to the bone. The others seemed convinced that Caroline would never show up again, but when they mentioned the date for the next workout she made a mental note. Clearly something new and different in the world of dog training was taking place there, and no matter what they thought, she would be back.

Modern search-and-rescue work in the United States was just getting underway when Caroline moved to New Jersey and joined the American Rescue Dog Association (ARDA), which had been founded the year before, in 1971, by Bill and Jean Syrotuck of Washington State. The Syrotucks had begun their pioneering work a decade earlier, in 1961, when they were members of a German shepherd dog club in Seattle. At that time, by chance, they happened to read about a little girl who had gotten lost in the woods with her two family dogs. When she sat down and cried, one of them had stayed by her side while the other returned home.

"Where is she?" her parents had asked the lone dog that had come back to the house. "Let's go find her! Show us!" they had begged, so the dog—spurred by their encouragement, and eager to please them—led the girl's father and mother into the forest and then all the way to the spot where she was waiting.

But how had the dog accomplished this feat? Had it memorized the route with its eyes? Had it followed footprints or smells along the ground? Or had it used some other method to find the child?

The Syrotucks, fascinated, wondered whether members of the German shepherd dog club could train their dogs, deliberately and methodically, to search for lost or missing persons. They formed a search dog committee to explore the question, starting with tracking lessons. In the early 1960s, tracking was the only known method of locating missing persons. The dogs were acquainted with scent articles, and were trained to keep their noses to the ground to follow the scent.

The notion that dogs could follow human scent strictly in the air—searching across miles of mountains and valleys, without depending totally on tracks and odors clinging to the ground—would have seemed preposterous to most civilians.

But the practice did, in fact, exist. In the Swiss and Austrian Alps, there was a long tradition of dogs using their noses to find buried avalanche victims. During World War I, dogs had been sent into the German and British trenches to search for the injured. During World War II, they had been used extensively by the British to check for people trapped in the rubble of damaged buildings immediately after the London bombing raids. And the U.S. military had trained dogs to follow the airborne scent of fuel in order to search for downed aircraft. Yet there had been no such application domestically in the United States.

After months of tracking practice, the Syrotucks and their small group finally went out to a designated field to conduct their first trial. When they arrived, they discovered that the ground had been fertilized from one end to the other with cow manure. It was a hot, humid day, and after taking in a few nostril-stinging whiffs of manure, the dogs kept their noses as far from the ground as possible. They wandered around, forgetting all about the tracks, and the test wound up as a fiasco. Clearly the tracking method had severe limitations.

The Syrotucks began to suspect that, in addition to following an actual scent track, a dog could "trail" by following particles of human scent that were scattered in loose, wavy patterns along the ground, or even just above it. In the latter case, the animal was working with its nose in the air. And therefore that same dog, the Syrotucks theorized, must be able to pick up the floating pattern of human odor (which might be a half-mile or more in length) and pursue it across the wind to its source—in other words, all the way to the person who was lost. They also conjectured that their dogs could trace airborne human smells originating from below the surface of the ground.

If air-scenting could be proven valid, it would be by far the superior method. Dogs could search regardless of weather, wind, terrain, elapsed time, ground contamination, and other factors that made ground-tracking extremely complicated. Yet many handlers remained skeptical, and their dogs, at least those already trained for tracking, were utterly confused about what they were supposed to do. In response, Bill and Jean Syrotuck gradually developed a scientifically based "scent theory" to support their new kind of human-dog training.

As the Syrotucks discovered, air-scenting is possible because of the microscopic dead skin cells, shaped like cereal flakes and known as rafts, which a human being sheds at the astounding rate of about forty thousand per minute. Each tiny raft carries its own bacteria and gives off its own vapor, and these rafts represent the unique combination of odors from any individual. This invisible bacterial, cellular debris enshrouds a sitting, standing, or moving person in his or her own personal "cloud" of scent. Portions of this cloud are constantly drifting away, most rising or falling with air currents or blowing with the wind, becoming an ever-expanding scent cone. It is this scent cone that the dogs would be trained to follow.

After building up evidence of the method's effectiveness through trial and error, the Syrotucks formed an initial search-and-rescue unit in the Seattle area. They began extensive training, delivered lectures, and gave demonstrations for county authorities, including the local sheriff's department. In July 1965 they got their first official call and reported to the site of a freight-train derailment to look for possible bodies. (The dogs confirmed that no one remained trapped.) After that the official calls steadily increased, and in 1969 the Syrotucks incorporated their unit as the Search and Rescue Dog Association (SARDA), a nonprofit corporation of unpaid volunteers. That year, a German shepherd handled by Jean Syrotuck made the first "avalanche find" by an American-trained dog, on a victim buried under seven feet of snow on Mt. Rainier in Washington.

Bill Syrotuck left his teaching job at the University of Washington to devote himself full-time to search and rescue. After compiling his data on victim behavior and air-scenting dogs for publication, he went to Europe and consulted on disaster techniques with canine search-and-rescue teams in Austria, Germany, Switzerland, and Scotland.

Word of the Seattle unit's work, accomplished by a number of pioneering dog handlers, spread across the country. Additional units were formed in New York, New Jersey, New Mexico, and Texas. In 1971 these combined units were given a new name, the American Rescue Dog Association (ARDA), signifying their attempt to cover the entire country, with Bill Syrotuck as cofounder and first president. At this point, the growth and development of a nationwide search-and-rescue movement began to coincide with the personal history of Caroline Hebard, twenty-eight, who had no idea that she herself would become one of its foremost innovators and leaders.

During the next training sessions, members of the Ramapo Rescue Dog Association quickly satisfied themselves that Zibo was anything but vicious. He was extremely affectionate and playful, and his bond with Caroline was so strong that they were already a well-functioning team. She had built up his self-confidence and motivation, training him to range and work independently, and had helped to increase his play drive, stamina, agility, and discipline without ever skipping steps by taking shortcuts. Caroline's main goal had been to gain control of Zibo while doing so in the most humane and patient way, in order to avoid diminishing his spirit.

It also became clear that what Zibo had learned in Schutzhund had given him a strong head start as a wilderness search dog.

In his ground-tracking work, for example, Zibo had already learned to use his powerful nose to discriminate between the scent he was supposed to follow and those of other human beings. And so, while it normally took two years for a German shepherd puppy to reach the level of scent-discrimination skill required, Zibo was ready for air-scent practice right away.

It began with simple games of hide-and-seek, first by having him sniff a glove or shoe or some other object to get its distinct scent, then hiding it nearby and having him go find it. (There was no ground track to follow, only the airborne scent.) Motivation was built by first having Zibo seek Caroline herself. She, after all, was the most important individual in his life, and her own scent was powerfully familiar to him. After she lay down behind some bushes, he was set loose; out of instinct, he dashed around with his nose lifted until he hit on her scent. Then he worked intensely to follow the airborne particles as they grew more concentrated and led him right to where she was hiding. In this way, he got accustomed to the air-scent mode while learning the joys of finding someone and being rewarded with praise and play.

Then others on the team replaced her as mock victims while Caroline herself reverted to the role of handler, and finally she directed Zibo to search for complete strangers who volunteered to act as "victims" lost in the woods. Gradually the distances were increased, up to half a mile and then much farther, while the time periods for searching grew accordingly. Working off-lead and staying out in front of Caroline, his nose raised in the wind, Zibo would initially follow a zigzag pattern to get a fix on the stranger's scent. And then—zoom!—he would race ahead, starting at the wide end of the invisible scent cone (which could be several hundred meters across and up to a half mile in length), narrowing his range as the skin cells grew more thickly concentrated. At last he would hurtle toward the smaller end of the cone, where the "lost" individual lay hidden.

By now Caroline knew that among the billions of persons on earth, each emits his or her uniquely individual scent. (A possible exception is identical twins, who may have identical scents.) And a specially trained search dog could distinguish the scent of any one human being on the planet from that of any other.

If, therefore, Caroline could produce a scent article from the missing victim, such as a piece of clothing, she could pre-scent Zibo by having him first sniff the object. When she also commanded him to search, the dog learned to understand his task—*Oh, I see, this is the scent of the person I'm supposed to find*—and soon he was charging into the wilderness ahead of Caroline. If, while trying to pick up that specific scent, he happened to meet up with someone else in the woods, he would take a whiff of the person and—with a wave of his tail—he would be off again, ranging with his nose in the air until he picked up the desired scent.

But the task for Zibo became somewhat different if no scent article could be produced. In that situation, which was more likely to be the case than not, Caroline learned to give him a chance to familiarize himself with the scents of the other searchers and dog handlers, by having him roam around and greet them all before they spread out. That done, he would behave as if he knew that these were *not* the people he was supposed to find.

Then, out in the woods, Zibo tried to pick up any new human scent that was drifting through the air. If his nose discovered the scent of a person who turned out to be a hunter or camper or someone else who was not the lost "victim," Caroline would praise her dog (by his reckoning, after all, he had succeeded) and then simply tell him to begin searching anew. The scent cone of the actual "victim" might be nearby or far away, but only the dog could detect it.

In practice sessions, they might cover miles of wilderness in two or three hours; and his reward, if he found the "victim" who was hiding, would be a stick, which Caroline often brought with her. Or, if she took too long to catch up with him, Zibo might get impatient and simply grab his own stick—at times, an entire branch or even a small log, if he could hold it between his jaws—and bring it to her as a means of communicating that he had made his find. This jackpot, along with heaps of praise and play, was Zibo's final source of pleasure during what had been, to him, simply an exciting adventure.

During the training, Caroline began teaching him to stay quiet when he found a "victim" in the wilderness. It might be frightening, for a small child or an elderly person or anyone, to hear the excited barking of a large dog. So, instead, she aimed to get him into the habit of coming right back to her (on a "recall") and barking directly at her for his stick reward.

But he was funny about it. Caroline was still very new at this, so after Zibo made a find and returned to her, she sometimes failed to "read" him as quickly as he demanded. In frustration, he would tear at the bottom of her jeans in order to yank her in the victim's direction.

"Zibo, stop it, I get the message!" She had to be quick about giving him the stick, in order to save her pants from being ripped to shreds.

After her first few local searches, Caroline realized that the group's biggest problem was to establish rapport with the authorities in charge of rescue operations. Too often the dog handlers were being summoned too late, past the time when they could be of any help.

Then Zibo made his first live find.


It was a morning in August 1973 when Caroline joined five other handlers with their dogs at Newark Airport for a flight down to a naval base near Washington, D.C. From there they were herded into a giant double-rotor helicopter bound for the Chesapeake Tidal Basin in Virginia.

"Yesterday," the copter pilot casually announced as they were taking off, "an aircraft just like this one crashed."

The passengers looked at one another. Someone joked about feeling "so much safer" with that information, and from then on, the gallows humor kept them laughing until they were deposited in an open hayfield surrounded by woods. It was just past noon and the temperature was in the nineties as they disembarked with their dogs. Within seconds it felt as though they had landed inside a steambath, filled with various crawling and flying insects, in the middle of nowhere.

An elderly black man known only as Amos had wandered off and was missing in the forest. He was suffering from the early stages of Alzheimer's disease and undoubtedly had become disoriented. One of the first questions Caroline had learned to ask when looking for someone with this condition was whether he was right-handed or left-handed, because that determined to an extent the way he would circle. The dog's air-scenting task would be more difficult if the victim kept moving; by the same token, it would be much easier for the dog to pick up the scent if the person was staying put on the ground. In their confusion, however, Alzheimer's patients had been known to actually go into hiding, deliberately evading the very people who were searching for them. All in all, Zibo and the other dogs were faced with a difficult task.

Amos was well known in the nearby community, having lived in the same area all his life, and many of the residents, most of whom happened to be white, had rallied to launch a massive effort to find him. After hundreds of them combed the area unsuccessfully for a few days, however, local officials called for outside help.

The handlers asked to be taken to the little shack where Amos lived, about a quarter mile through sloping woods from the open field, so they could let the dogs walk around and sniff the place. As Zibo became familiar with the particular scent he was supposed to find and then follow, Caroline gave him his search-and-help command. "*Such und hilf,*" she told him, with her usual emphasis on the first word when she wanted him to be air-scenting rather than ground-tracking. The six teams of handlers and dogs then returned to the field, where they split up and started away in different directions, according to their assignments.

His nose in the air, Zibo kept leading Caroline away from her designated area as he headed for one particular section of woods. The dog was insistent, so she followed him into that area and let him take charge. She could tell by his body language, and by her own gut feeling based on past experience with Zibo, that he was on to something. Just then, however, the sky darkened, and Caroline got word on her radio that with severe thunderstorms on the way, the teams were being ordered out. It was before six in the evening, but the elderly man—wherever he might be, and if in fact he was still alive—would have to spend another night in the open.

When they got to the motel where they were staying, the handlers discovered that their bodies were covered with ticks and mites. For hours they carefully picked the tiny parasites off themselves and their dogs. Later, as Caroline tried to sleep, she thought of Zibo's eager interest in that one section of field and woods. He had been excited, intensely focused, and determined, and had even become annoyed when she tried to redirect his searching. The man had to be in there, she was sure of it.

·  ·  ·

To avoid the daytime heat, they began searching the following morning at five o'clock. They went back out to the field, where the handler in charge began giving out assignments. As a relatively new member of the unit, Caroline was not accustomed to disagreeing with its leaders, but this time she found herself speaking up.

"I really want to go back into that same area I was in. I have a definite feeling about it."

"Why so?"

"My dog was very interested."

"Well," the woman said, "that's my area."

Caroline shrugged and set off to cover her assigned section with Zibo. This time she was with a local official, an amiable young man named Bart, who remarked, "I guess she wanted that area for herself."

"Seems so," Caroline agreed as Zibo wandered around without showing any specific interest. "This *is* the wrong direction," she said. "It is definitely not a high-probability area. Let's give it a hasty search and move back to the other one."

"Are you going to tell her on the radio?"

"Sure," Caroline said. She smiled and added, "But I'll tell her when I'm already *in* the area."

It was still only 6:00 A.M. when they trudged across a field and came closer to the section of woods in which Zibo had been so keenly interested the day before. All of a sudden the dog's nose picked up the scent, and his whole body reacted as if a jolt of electricity had rushed through it. Caroline and Bart could hear a whooshing noise as Zibo bolted through bushes and under branches, far ahead and out of sight. They followed as quickly as they could, but soon Zibo came racing back to Caroline with a stick in his mouth, his tail madly wagging. Then he turned and went ahead once more, until she caught up to him in a small clearing.

"Here?" she asked him. "Where?"

Zibo put the stick down and began to poke his nose at a cluster of vines and small trees. It was a kind of man-made shelter, Caroline saw. The vines had been twisted and braided, using uprooted saplings as supports, to form walls and a roof. When she tried to move closer to this unusual structure, however, the dog blocked her path.

"What's going on?" Bart said.

"Zibo's warning me."

"Is Amos alive?"

"I think so," Caroline said, "because otherwise Zibo would not have been so happy to find him. But now it seems that he's picking up that the man is mentally disturbed. The scent of such people is slightly different, I believe, and the dog picks up on that. He's trying to protect me."

Bart, who knew the man, moved closer. Then he called to him, "Hi, Amos! We're glad to see you! Whatcha been doing out here in the woods?"

"Just restin'," the man finally answered from inside his fortress.

"Well, we were hoping to find you."

"Why?"

"There are folks here that are worried 'bout you."

"What folks?"

"You feel like coming out of there?" Bart asked him.

At last Amos sat up. Caroline could see through the vines that he was a physically powerful man. He had stripped down to his underwear, probably because of the daytime heat, but during the night he must have suffered from the chill. There were scratches all over his massive body. It occurred to Caroline that he had uprooted the trees, and then had twisted and braided the vines, with his bare hands.

"What's *that*?" Amos said abruptly in a deep but frightened voice as he stared through the vines of his shelter and finally focused on Zibo's huge dark face. "A *wolf*?"

"No, no, that's a dog."

"What kind of dog?"

"Oh, that's a nice, *friendly* dog! We were just out walkin' with him."

Amos suddenly pointed through the braided vines at Caroline. "Who's *that*?"

"Oh, this is just a girlfriend of mine. I've just been out walking with my girlfriend and her dog. Amos, what were you doing out here?"

"I've been doin' the Lord's work! Clearing the forest!"

Bart kept up the dialogue while Caroline radioed the search headquarters for transport. She praised Zibo and threw another stick for him to fetch as his reward.

Rescue workers arrived and finally lifted Amos out of his shelter. They found that his whole body was covered by mosquito bites and ticks; he obviously had not eaten for days and was suffering from dehydration as well as exposure. With an ambulance waiting about a half mile away, someone drove a pickup truck down a nearby logging road to within fifty yards of the spot. From there the rescue people brought a stretcher.

Amos was too weak to walk, but he stubbornly refused to let them lift him onto it.

"You've been doing the Lord's work," Bart cajoled him, "so now we've got a chariot for you."

The rescue workers draped a sheet over Amos as if it were a toga, and at last he agreed to sit on the stretcher. Then they carried him out of the woods to the pickup truck and hoisted him onto the back. Finally an odd procession began along the logging road, as the toga-clad Amos sat on his stretcher aboard the truck, with the rescue people holding him steady, and sang at the top of his lungs: "I'm goin' on a chariot to see the Lord!"

Caroline walked alongside with Zibo, smiling and shaking her head at the bizarre scene. She was thrilled at the dog's success. Zibo pranced beside her, proudly carrying a small log in his mouth all the way back to the base camp.

*My God*, Caroline thought, *this dog really knows that he did a good job. I've just seen the proof.*

Everything had come together to enable her and Zibo to save a human life. They had found Amos in time because she had been so insistent on going back to that area, because she had put so much faith and trust in her dog. She felt a deep, wonderful sense of accomplishment. Now there was no turning back from life in search and rescue.

She was hooked.

## Chapter 4

# "Have Dog, Will Travel"

THERE WAS NO END, CAROLINE REALIZED, TO THE variety and depth of training for search-and-rescue work. As Zibo progressed, she herself became increasingly skilled in related areas such as heavy backpacking over difficult terrain, wilderness survival, and cross-country skiing. She learned to rappel down the steep cliffs of the Palisades while carrying the ninety-pound dog in a harness. Another priority was map and compass reading, the better to avoid becoming a missing person herself; in the eastern United States, with few mountain peaks for landmarks, it was extremely important to get a fix on your location and direction of travel, especially in valleys filled with seemingly endless swampland or snow.

Members of the Ramapo unit pledged "to be always ready, so that others may live." Because she could be called out on a mission at any time, Caroline kept ready a thirty-pound backpack filled with emergency gear and supplies for five days. The load included her hard hat with headlamp, a bright orange parka, topographical maps, a compass, a radio, first-aid supplies, food, sugar, bouillon cubes, a portable stove and cans of Sterno, water, a flashlight, flares, and signal mirrors. The citizen band radio of those days was particularly bulky and cumbersome, with a big heavy battery and a long whip antenna that often got snagged on branches, but carrying it was essential.

With her credentials in linguistics, Caroline knew she could have pursued any one of a number of careers in that field. Instead she had chosen child-rearing as her primary occupation, and volunteered for search-and-rescue operations. She knew she would not have been satisfied with most of the volunteer opportunities available in suburban communities. Unless she could face mental, physical, and emotional challenges such as those offered by search and rescue, she felt unfulfilled.

One of her goals was to keep setting herself new, and higher, professional standards. She wanted to be able to treat live victims at the scene, so that the rescue phase of her missions with Zibo would not end in tragedy. After the family moved to a house in Basking Ridge, Caroline went to work as a volunteer in the emergency rooms of two New Jersey hospitals. In related courses, she learned to perform the fireman's carry so that she could lift victims her own size or heavier, was shown how to transport people on stretchers by herself, and became skilled at extricating injured people from cars.

Caroline passed state and national exams that qualified her as a registered emergency medical technician (EMT) and became an American Red Cross instructor in first aid and cardiopulmonary resuscitation (CPR), eventually becoming certified at advanced levels. She also learned basic veterinary care.

"Have Dog, Will Travel" was the Ramapo unit's informal motto, and Caroline and the group's other members responded to official calls for help from emergency-management agencies in the region. She was ready to drive her van to situations in New York, Connecticut, Pennsylvania, and other nearby states, as well as New Jersey, to search for lost hikers, skiers, hunters, children, elderly persons, and so on. As their reputation spread, the small East Coast group was also called for missions farther away. In that case they would race to Newark Airport, where a U.S. Air Force C-130 transport plane or helicopter, on special assignment from Scott Air Force Base in Illinois, flew them to searches in Maine, Virginia, Minnesota, Wisconsin, and elsewhere in the country.

They trained together at least every other Saturday, giving the dogs a variety of searching problems to solve in the woods. In addition, Caroline was often called away on two or three missions each month. Even if the missions were brief ones, the increasing activity was becoming tougher on the routine of her family life. Art worked long hours at the lab, so he could not always cover at home for her, and maintaining a network of instantly available baby-sitters was not easy.

The solution came in the person of Palmira Chavas, a Portuguese woman who had worked for Caroline's parents when they were stationed in that country. Palmira wanted to emigrate, so Caroline and Art sponsored her for a green card, and she moved into the Hebard household. She thrived on the controlled chaos of kids and dogs and emergency beepers, and Joanne and Andrew took to her right away. They were too young to understand that Mom had a different life away from home—which, in one way or another, had been true since her own childhood.

In the fall of 1975, the recently formed National Association for Search and Rescue (NASAR) held its first big conference. Caroline, who was pregnant with her third child, drove down to Nashville, Tennessee, with both Jaeger and Zibo in the van.

NASAR was an umbrella group for men and women in all aspects of search-and-rescue work, from mountain climbers to divers, and the "dog people" had yet to become a recognized entity among them. Members of the other rescue groups still had little understanding of the dogs and their purpose or abilities, but that changed a bit when Jaeger and Zibo, along with their canine companions (who also sported orange rescue vests), became highly visible at the conference. By the end, Caroline and the other handlers had gained ground in their quest for acceptance.

Bill Syrotuck died the following year. He had lived to see his pioneering vision of a nationwide network of canine search-and-rescue teams finally taking shape.

The Hebard family had moved by July 1977 to a larger house in nearby Bernardsville, where they had a big backyard that bordered on some woods. Caroline and Art had a new son, Alastair, who was already almost a year and a half old, and Caroline had just discovered she was pregnant with her fourth child. Joanne, six, and Andrew, five, were using Zibo and Jaeger as floor pillows, the better to watch *Sesame Street* on television, when a call came at dinnertime.

"We need you out at the floods."

"You'd better fill me in," Caroline said as she stirred a pot on the stove.

"You haven't seen the news?"

"Look, I have no idea what's going on. The kids are into their own show and I'm fixing dinner. What do we have?"

It was then that she learned about western Pennsylvania having been hit by one of the worst flash floods in a decade. Johnstown was getting the most attention, but many surrounding areas and towns had been hurt even worse by overflows of the Conemaugh River. Fifty thousand residents had been displaced; the death toll, currently at twenty-five, was climbing; and hundreds of people were still missing.

In the great Johnstown flood of 1889, about 2,300 persons had been killed after the crumbling of an earthen dam on the Conemaugh River. And following another disaster in 1936, the Army Corps of Engineers had spent millions on flood-control projects. Now, in the summer of 1977, another flood disaster had struck after a nightlong, torrential rainfall of nearly twelve inches. Johnstown was still knee-deep in water and its forty thousand inhabitants were cut off from normal communications with the rest of the world. Helicopters, serving as the city's lifeline, were also picking up bodies in addition to rescuing people stranded on housetops and bridges. National Guardsmen had been brought in to protect Johnstown from looting.

Caroline threw extra clothing, gear, and dog food into a duffel. She tossed it into the van with her rescue backpack and took off with Zibo, driving through the night until they came to the small community of Seward, on the outskirts of Johnstown. Three other handler-dog teams from Ramapo also had arrived, and they slept in their vehicles for a few hours until dawn, before heading off to find the command post.

As she and Zibo walked with the others, they saw mud-filled

vehicles and even railway cars that had been overturned. Parts of frame houses had been ripped off, while other houses were listing, and some, having been demolished, lay crumbled in piles of debris. Above, helicopters were ferrying medical supplies, drinking water, food, emergency generators, and personnel into Johnstown. Receding floodwaters had left shattered roads and mounds of muddy rubble scattered through more than two dozen small communities. Serious flooding had occurred along a seventy-mile stretch, which was declared a major disaster area by President Jimmy Carter. Damage was estimated at $100 million.

Thousands of residents were living temporarily in centers set up in schools, armories, and firehouses. Four hundred refugees from Johnstown were crowded into the gymnasium of one elementary school. Twelve bodies had been found in West Taylor, but about fifty people were still missing.

Caroline and Zibo were taken to a trailer park where nine residents had been swept away. The site, which included not only trailers but other buildings, presented a scene of total destruction. It was inside a U-bend where the river turned against a bluff. The Conemaugh Dam was above it, and when the dam had burst, a thirty-foot tidal wave of water had come down the river, smashing into the clifflike embankment of the bluff and washing right back over the trailers and other buildings, burying them under tons of mud.

Caroline had never seen such devastation. The nearest kind of experience she could recall was when, as a child, she had seen mud slides during rainy seasons in Venezuela. People living in shacks directly in the path of the slides had been buried or swept away. It was one of the cruelest kinds of disaster, because few victims could escape the mud's overwhelming force.

In some areas below the Conemaugh Dam, the wall of water had crashed down so suddenly that people had had no time to get away from it. Some had tried to drive faster than the water, but they had been caught. Their bodies had been found in their cars.

In the trailer park there had been sufficient warning for most, but not all, residents to flee before the dam had burst and the tidal wave had enveloped their fragile homes. Caroline and Zibo were assigned to do a "clearing job" to make sure no one was still buried under the mangled metal of what had been the trailers, many of which had been overturned.

Caroline struggled through the deep mud in her high rubber boots, past the strewn remnants of furniture, family photo albums, toys and dolls, kitchen utensils, shoes, pieces of clothing, and other artifacts. Hills of rubble were everywhere, and occasionally she came across the bloated, maggot-infested bodies of dead dogs. The stench of death and rotting food, combined with Caroline's morning sickness from early pregnancy, made her feel faint. She vomited in the bushes and kept going.

She and Zibo worked for several days, virtually round the clock. Mounds of debris thirty to fifty feet high towered over the scene where Caroline and the three other dog handlers from ARDA kept searching. They trudged through bushes, briars, and thorns, traversing deep mud holes and often crawling on their bellies behind the dogs. In one bog, Caroline lost a ten-foot pole as she poked the water-logged earth to see if she could walk across. Covered with mud, she and Zibo were barely recognizable as they continued farther toward Johnstown, "clearing" areas as they went.

They were followed by bulldozer teams, whose members wanted the dogs to check out areas before they disturbed any bodies that might have been overlooked. She had learned to trust the dog's body language completely, and when he failed to give an alert for a live or dead find, she was able to reassure the other workers.

"No one is here, it's okay," she told them with confidence before going on; but when Zibo did show interest, she left markers notifying rescue teams to look for buried corpses.

They came to a tavern from which patrons, upon hearing the wall of water roaring its way down, had run for their lives. However, it was possible a few had remained drunkenly on their stools and been buried, so Caroline approached with trepidation. Inside, half-empty beer bottles were lined up along the bar as if time had stopped. Zibo alerted, clearly picking up human scent. Another search dog alerted also, pawed at the silt, and dug down eight inches before coming up with a mud-covered wallet in his mouth. Here was tangible evidence of the accuracy of trained dogs.

Because Zibo had alerted in the tavern, members of the bulldozer team made sure to take it apart slowly and carefully. They found nothing, but later Caroline learned that a body had been taken out of there the day before. Her dog had been correct.

The final death toll was sixty-eight.

At home, Caroline washed Zibo over and over to get the smell out of him. She took a long shower, tossed away her stench-filled clothing, and made a mental note to tell people, in one of the talks she sometimes gave to community groups or at schools, that search-and-rescue work was often rewarding but seldom if ever glamorous. It was usually filthy and exhausting. It could expose a person to devastation and death and engrave images of suffering on the mind and soul.

Zibo, too, seemed tired, even depressed. She would make sure to give him extra attention and playtime in the next few days. He needed to rest, for sure, but after their companionship on the mission, he could easily feel abandoned if she left him alone.

She had been exposed, on this mission, to some of the best and worst sides of human nature. There had been looting, but also acts of courage and selflessness. Thousands of residents, often complete strangers, had banded together to spend days and nights helping each other.

In the darkness of her first night back home, Caroline was tired but exhilarated. Her first disaster experience had opened up a whole new field of search and rescue to her. Trying to fall asleep, she wondered at the conflicting extremes of her experience at the floods. On the one hand, she had seen so much personal tragedy; on the other, she had shared in a triumph of the human spirit.

As part of Caroline's quest to expand her competence, she had applied a few years earlier to the Basking Ridge Fire Company for membership as a volunteer first-aid technician. She had wanted to gain experience during actual fire emergencies in order to increase her ability to assist victims during search-and-rescue work and also to extend her service to the community.

The obstacle had been that all fifty-eight volunteers were male and no woman had ever been allowed to join. It had taken a while to get up the courage to apply, but one day, after dinner in town with Art, she decided to walk over to the old brick firehouse.

"They'll turn you down," Art said.

"That would be ridiculous. I mean, they know my search-and-rescue work. And I've put in several hundred hours in emergency rooms by now, so I'm fully qualified. I'm already *teaching* first aid to some of the firemen. Well, here goes."

"I'm behind you," Art said as they started toward the building.

Caroline went alone down to the basement, where a social room and bar had been created for the firefighters. Hanging about were several of the volunteers, who were startled to see a woman in their midst. When she inquired about joining, they were flabbergasted. One of the men, politely telling her to wait, made a quick call to the chief.

"That dog lady, Mrs. Hebard, is here," he said into the phone, "and she wants to join the fire company. What do I— Yeah, okay."

He hung up and turned to Caroline. "The chief says you should join the ladies' auxiliary," he said with a smile.

"I want to volunteer as a medical technician," Caroline said. "Could you call him back and tell him I want to fill out an application?"

The fireman used the phone again, then reported the chief's reply that no women were allowed. She could not have an application form.

But the Basking Ridge Fire Company did not reckon with the quiet determination of a woman who hated stupid rules, who had a long history of using her ingenuity to bend or break such rules, and who, because of her dog training, had been refining her skills in the art of gentle persistence in order to get her way. The macho firemen, who had excluded women from their ranks for generations, were about to get a lesson in obedience.

The key to obedience training was to keep praising the subject—a dog, a child, a fire chief—for doing the right thing. Shouting angrily or being abusive in any way was counterproductive; it was a matter simply of motivating and guiding the subject into the correct behavior. So Caroline called the fire chief and invited him to her home. When he arrived, she rewarded him with cheerful voice tones and praise, the way she would have given Zibo his positive reinforcement.

"Thanks for coming here, Chief. I appreciate it."

"Look," the chief said, hoping to preempt the discussion, "the fire company is very old, with a long tradition, and no woman has ever belonged. To let you join would disrupt that tradition. Besides, members of the company feel they couldn't rely on a female firefighter. It's my duty, Mrs. Hebard, to dissuade you."

Caroline spoke in an even voice. "I see. Well, fine. Then I'd like to become an associate member, so I could still help in a first-aid capacity."

She knew the chief, just like Zibo or any good working dog, wanted to please her. Here was his opportunity, but he failed to seize it. "No, you'd have to be a full member of the fire company to do first-aid work."

It was just as if Zibo had refused to climb the ladder for his agility test. So she took the next step, according to the fairness-consistency-persistence doctrine. "Well," she said with a warm smile, "in that case, I'll have to learn firefighting."

The chief looked at Caroline as if it had just dawned on him that he might be facing a formidable opponent. Her appearance was deceptive—blond hair, gray-green eyes, slim figure—and her gentle, polite, cheerful manner was disarming.

"I'm sorry," he said, "but you can't become a firefighter."

Caroline nodded. "Would you speak to your members?"

Now the chief, like a puppy finding bits of hot dog on the track, took the bait. "Sure," he said. "I'll put it to a vote."

"Fine," she said, praising her subject. "I'd appreciate that very much. And thanks again for coming."

If the fire chief left that night with a feeling of victory, it was only because Caroline wanted him to. In obedience training, the essential underlying ingredient was that the subject must always feel successful.

Caroline waited nearly a month. When she still hadn't heard from the chief, she called him herself. He reported that her request had been vetoed by the fire company, and therefore she could not have an application. Democracy had prevailed.

She had known beforehand, of course, what the outcome of the firemen's vote would be. "I appreciate your information," Caroline said, maintaining the same cheerful tone as she prepared her next move.

Accompanied by another local woman interested in first aid and firefighting, Caroline went to the Basking Ridge Township Committee and asked for help. Would members of this local governmental body take a position? Or would they at least mediate the matter?

That move was followed by endless phone calls, meetings, and discussions. The mayor voiced concern that if women were allowed to join the fire company, it would disband. The township committee, following up on an idea put forth by the fire chief, suggested that Caroline and other females form a separate first-aid squad.

"There's no *need* for two," she replied.

Sensing a fight shaping up, the fire company hired an attorney. Caroline went to the mayor and asked if he, personally, would get her an application. Then she waited patiently, for two months, until the mayor confessed he could not help. That same day, she also learned that the township committee would not mediate between her and the firemen.

Having attempted all possible routes to her goal and found them blocked, Caroline next went to the State Division of Civil Rights in Trenton, where an attorney was assigned to investigate. The key issue, she explained, was that no one had given her a chance to demonstrate her capability as a firefighter. She was willing to train, if necessary, but she believed she already could perform the duties required. And she could be available at any hour to respond.

"Are you willing to go to court?" the attorney asked.

"If necessary," she replied. "I'd like to see these guys take the stand and try to explain themselves."

The lawyer warned that it could take a long time.

"Patience and persistence," Caroline replied.

"If we win," the attorney said, "it would be a landmark case."

Victory came in September 1977, following state hearings on Caroline's formal complaint against the Basking Ridge Fire Company. That day, posing for a *New York Times* photographer, she stood smiling in front of the Hebard home with one arm around Andrew, six, while holding Alastair, nineteen months, in her other arm. Joanne, the oldest, was off somewhere; and Caroline was visibly pregnant.

Because of her persistence, the fire company was ordered to open its ranks to women. Found guilty of violating state antidiscrimination laws, the department was told to amend its policies and regulations forthwith. Caroline, at thirty-two, was granted probationary membership; but because in the interim she had moved to nearby Bernardsville, the fire company was excused from having to admit her.

In the future, Caroline's case would be used as a precedent by lawyers for women bringing similar suits against the New York City Fire Department as well as other organizations around the country. It would also be cited in law school textbooks. What would not be cited was the campaign of harassment against Caroline and her family, along with attempts to intimidate her, which had started after she filed her suit. She had received anonymous letters, nasty and threatening, and had had garbage dumped across her front yard, but these actions had only served to strengthen her resolve.

Soon after the Basking Ridge decision, the Bernardsville Fire Department announced it was expanding its membership, so Caroline called some of her female first-aid students. "They need some new volunteers," she told them, "and you're going with me." The women marched down, Caroline leading the way, and they became the first females to join that department.

It was all a matter of patience, persistence, consistency, and fairness, as the life lessons of obedience training continued.


During a terrible ice storm in January 1978, Caroline had to go pick up Andrew from a sports practice at the school gym. She was driving with Joanne and two-year-old Alastair in the van when the vehicle hit some ruts in the ice, skidded, and spun out of control, slamming up against a stone wall. Alastair was okay, but Joanne suffered cuts, bruises, and a mild concussion. Caroline, whose jaw was fractured, went into premature labor.

Heather was born two months early, weighing just over four pounds. The tiny infant remained in the neonatal ICU at Newark Beth

Israel Hospital for weeks while Caroline commuted back and forth, going to the hospital at least once a day to deliver breast milk and stay close to her. The baby girl went into cardiac arrest three times, and Caroline and Art could do nothing but hope and pray. At first she was too weak even to nurse, but slowly she got stronger and stronger.

During this entire time, Caroline's jaw was wired, and all she could have was liquid food; after her jaw healed, she swore she never wanted to see another milk shake again.

Heather came home to her parents and siblings after eight weeks.

By August, Heather was thriving, and Caroline was starting to ease slowly back into search and rescue. She had purchased a stick-shift, four-wheel drive Suburban truck, with plenty of room for dogs and gear, and the number of calls for help kept growing.

# Chapter 5

# Sasquatch: Puppy Personality

ZIBO WAS NOW EIGHT YEARS OLD, AND CAROLINE decided that her partner deserved some retirement years. She began to look for a new dog.

One day Margo Roebling called to say that a friend who ran a nearby kennel had a new litter of German shepherds whose father had been a champion U.S. show dog. So Caroline went to look at the puppies. The one that caught her attention was a cute little male with extremely large paws. When she brought him home, one of the kids said, "Let's call him Bigfoot." Art found that the Salish Indian name for Bigfoot was *Sasquatch*, and that, the family agreed, was perfect.

From the beginning, Sasquatch was a happy-go-lucky fellow with a winning personality. He loved Zibo, and as a youngster he often accompanied him up into the woods behind the house by playfully hanging on to the bigger dog's tail. The family members all chuckled at the sight of the puppy racing behind Zibo and jumping up to grab the big shepherd's tail by his teeth. As the two dogs disappeared in the woods, Sasquatch's rear paws kept flying off the ground as he bounced up and down through the air.

The night before Andrew's ninth birthday, in June 1980, Caroline took Zibo and Sasquatch out for a walk. It was extremely warm, so when they returned she decided to keep the dogs in their open pens behind the house, rather than in the kitchen. The following morning, a Saturday, her mind was filled with plans for her son's party as she went outside to walk them again before giving them their breakfast. Immediately she knew that something was wrong. Normally both dogs would be standing at the wire fence with their tails wagging, barking to greet her enthusiastically. Now there was a strange silence.

Sasquatch, quiet but extremely agitated, was trying to poke his nose through the wire into Zibo's adjacent pen. As Caroline drew closer, the younger shepherd turned and whimpered as if to say, *Listen, I'm really confused and upset, so you'd better come over here and help!*

Zibo was lying on the ground toward the rear of his outdoor pen. As she opened the wire gate, he tried to get up but was unable to raise his ninety pounds. *He can't get up*, she thought as he made an extra effort and attempted to drag himself toward her with his front legs. Caroline went in and sat beside him. "Hi, old buddy," she said.

Caroline had a sudden flash of the older dog's behavior the evening before, when Zibo had been his normally bouncy, energetic self, but all that had changed literally overnight. Now he was totally silent and could not use his hind legs or even wag his tail. *Oh, God, he's had a massive stroke*, Caroline found herself thinking as she petted him gently. He tried to bark, but no sound came out. Instead he could only gaze up at her with pathetic, pleading eyes that seemed to be saying simply, *Help me!*

"It's okay," Caroline said softly, her voice choking. "You're a good boy, Zibo. It's okay. . . ."

She petted him some more, but then could no longer bear the sight of him this way, and went back into the house. She and Art had planned to supervise Andrew's birthday celebration together, but Caroline found her husband and, holding back tears, said to him, "I think Zibo has had a massive stroke. I think . . . I think I have to put him down."

"Oh, no . . ."

"Art, listen, I've never missed a birthday party, but this one is yours. Take the kids out somewhere. You handle it, Art, because I *can't* do it. Please. And please just *keep* handling things when you get home with them, because I won't be capable of helping you. That's my partner out there. I have to say goodbye to him, and after that I can't see myself celebrating.''

She called the vet and said, ''I've got this dignified dog out there, and now his hind legs are paralyzed. I want him to maintain his dignity.'' And she added, trying to keep her voice from betraying her emotions, ''I can't . . . I won't . . . let him go on this way.''

''Can you bring him over here?''

''Yes, I'll . . . I'll get him there soon.''

Then she called Margo Roebling, knowing she would understand. ''I'm going to need your help doing this,'' Caroline told her. ''I can't do it alone.''

''No, of course you can't,'' Margo said. ''I'll come right over.''

Now it was time to tell Andrew and Joanne. It was her policy never to lie to the kids, but this moment of truth-telling was going to be difficult.

''Listen,'' she told Andrew, ''Dad is going to have to take over your party, because Zibo's had a stroke.''

''Are you taking him to the vet?'' Andrew asked.

''Yes. Margo's going to help me bring him there.''

''So the vet will take care of him. Why can't you come back and be at my party?''

''Because, Andrew,'' she said, hesitating, ''I have to put Zibo down.''

Joanne burst into tears, but Andrew stared back at her in silence. They both rushed outside to the pen, where they could see for themselves what had happened. When they returned, Joanne was still crying, but Andrew soon grew furious. He was annoyed at first that Caroline was abandoning his birthday party; then came his real anger.

''Why can't the vet help him?''

''The dog is paralyzed,'' she said in a quiet voice, ''and the vet is not a magician.''

''But why do you have to *kill* him?''

''It's the only humane alternative, Andrew, because—''

''You have no *right*, Mom! No right!''

''German shepherds are dignified, clean animals,'' she told her son, "and if they become helpless and incontinent, they lose all of that dignity. I would rather allow Zibo to die with whatever dignity he can still claim." Andrew was listening, but was clearly in no mood to agree with her.

Someday, when he was older, she would tell him the rest of her thoughts. *We human beings,* she continued inwardly, *unfortunately don't have that choice. When we get paralyzed, senile, and incontinent, the doctors just keep us going. So we wind up in nursing homes, wearing diapers and sitting in wheelchairs, sometimes needing machines to keep us alive. The dignity of life is taken from us. But dogs* do *have the choice, if their guardians make it for them.*

Andrew walked away, dark with resentment. *He's only nine,* Caroline thought, *and his anger right now is understandable.*

When Margo arrived, they got Art's help to lift up Zibo and carry him to the back of the truck. Then the two women drove the several miles to the veterinarian's office, where a man came out and helped them carry the heavy dog inside. They sat with Zibo on the floor of the treatment room. Caroline held his head in her lap as the vet, who agreed that nothing could reverse the dog's paralysis, prepared to inject him with a lethal dose of the anesthetic sodium pentobarbital.

The vet put a tourniquet around one of Zibo's front legs, then injected the solution into a vein. Caroline watched as her partner drifted into sleep. She waited while the overdose took effect, causing his heart to slow down and finally come to a halt. At last, when Zibo had stopped breathing altogether, she held his head a bit longer until it was time to let go.

Before long they were outside the vet's office again. Everything seemed to have happened in a blur. Caroline drove Margo back to the house to pick up her car, but then she decided to continue driving by herself. She took the back roads, winding through the most rural sections of Bernardsville and surrounding towns, and for the next few hours she drove aimlessly around while recalling scenes from Zibo's life. In her mind Caroline saw images of her past dogs—Mike in Caracas, Aeneas the puppy in Ankara, Pickles in California, and of course Jaeger, her first German shepherd—and said goodbye to them once more as well. Days later, Caroline scattered Zibo's ashes in the woods.

Sasquatch, in the last stages of his puppyhood, was devastated by Zibo's absence. He went into mourning, hardly touching his food. Caroline found an old push broom that had a black and brown handle the color of Zibo's tail and bristles resembling Zibo's wiry, coarse hair, and she gave it to Sasquatch for comfort. For more than a month, the lonely young dog slept with the broom as if it were Zibo himself, his mentor and friend.

As he grew, Sasquatch displayed the outgoing, friendly temperament of a collie or golden retriever. He loved everyone and everything—his food, the kids, the missions. He was tremendously affectionate, a wonderful family pet. Swarms of children could climb all over him and he wouldn't be bothered.

By this time, Caroline had begun to host wilderness-survival programs for local students and adults, teaching them how to avoid getting lost in the woods and what to do if they did. When she brought Sasquatch along for one of her "Hug-a-Tree" presentations, however, he proved to be a born show-off and a master clown. At one school auditorium, Sas stood next to her at the podium onstage as she spoke. So far, so good, but then he lay down and started making all sorts of grunting and groaning noises. Encouraged by giggles from the audience, Sasquatch proceeded to roll over onto his back. Belly up, his paws waving in the air, he gazed out at the audience with those big eyes of his, until the students roared with laughter. So much for Caroline's program, as Sasquatch thoroughly distracted her listeners and stole the show.

In the field, Sasquatch displayed a limited attention span and worked only when he felt like it. When he did happen to feel like working, he gave his all, but Caroline needed a dog whose drive would produce more predictable, consistent performances. He also loved chasing rabbits or squirrels or deer. One time, on a mountainous search in Pennsylvania, Sasquatch led Caroline half a mile through the woods until he stopped, eyes gleaming with pride over having treed a wild turkey. On another search, he raced into a farm and sent all the chickens into the trees. He was proud of that feat, too, and when he rewarded himself with a stick and circled around Caroline with his tail flapping, she could only shake her head, trying to hold in her laughter, and tell him, "Good boy, Sas, great going! You did it again!"

She decided not to bother doing Schutzhund work with Sasquatch in any concentrated manner. He was her "failure," Caroline told colleagues with an affectionate smile. And he was an example, she added, of how a dog's innate temperament was crucial. Even with the best training in the world, and no matter how skillful the handler, the personality of the dog could make all the difference, one way or the other.

The news bulletins in November 1980 from southern Italy were grim. Powerful earthquakes had struck the region, and the casualties would eventually total more than three thousand dead and several thousand injured. At one point fifteen hundred victims were still missing. As the death toll kept rising and rescue teams attempted to reach isolated towns in mountainous areas, their efforts were slowed by shattered roads and bridges as well as by severed phone lines and heavy fog. It was the worst quake disaster Europe had seen in sixty-five years.

When the U.S. government announced it was sending military helicopters, a thousand tents, and financial aid, Caroline wondered aloud why human beings and dogs could not be sent as well. Based on what they had learned about the capabilities of their dogs, Caroline and other Ramapo handlers knew they could help. The Swiss Disaster Dog Association had proved successful in finding live victims at the scene of several European earthquakes. The governments of other nations were supporting national canine teams. Why not the United States?

Caroline had lived in Italy with her parents one summer, so she had a feeling for the country and also spoke some Italian. She called OFDA, the Office of U.S. Foreign Disaster Assistance, run by the State Department, to offer the services of the Ramapo unit.

She was turned down coldly. There had been no request for such assistance, the official said.

Next she called the Italian Embassy in Washington, D.C. "Yes," she was told, "we do need your help. We can get you a flight on Alitalia, with the dogs, at no charge."

Excited, Caroline called OFDA again. "The Italians have a flight for us," she said. "If I can get the dog handlers to meet that plane, can we go as representatives of the United States? We're paying our own way."

"No," she was told, "and if you try it, you might have difficulty getting back into the country."

"Why so?"

"Well, your passport might be questioned."

Caroline knew that it was perfectly legal to take her dog overseas as a volunteer, but the implied threat was intimidating. Clearly the State Department people felt that if the U.S. government did not send an official canine unit, no one else should go, either. In fact, canine search and rescue was still so new that it was not even recognized as a resource. Caroline backed off. This was a battle that would take time.

In Italy, meanwhile, hundreds of victims were still missing, trapped under wreckage, and undoubtedly many were alive. Because the affected areas were spread across such a vast region, the rescue teams needed as many search dogs as possible.

"We need government sanction to be able to load some dogs into a plane and take off," Caroline told her colleagues. "We need our own government to realize that we're a resource for helping people in other countries. I am sure that some of the victims died because we didn't go there."

Sasquatch was unpredictable, so it was frustrating for Caroline to have him as her partner until she could get a new search dog. In November 1982, they were called to a search in northern Maine with three other female handler-dog teams from the Ramapo group. They were joined by four Wisconsin men with their dogs from a new ARDA unit, which Caroline and her colleagues had helped to train. Maine game wardens met them in Bangor and then drove north until they were not far from the Canadian border.

This wild, remote wilderness, primarily used for logging and hunting, was covered with nine inches of snow. There was a ski resort in the area, but otherwise they seemed to have left civilization far behind. The hilly countryside was filled with huge trees and networked by swamps, rivers, streams, and lakes. The daytime temperature was still above freezing, but the wind made it seem much colder, so Caroline was glad she had worn lots of wool layers and thick gloves. She had on hiking boots, which kept her feet warm, but it occurred to her that snowshoes might work best in the future.

On their way into the area, they were briefed on their mission. A hunter named George Wescott had gone out with a group of men but failed to return to the logging road where they had parked their cars and pickup trucks. Members of the hunting party had stayed at the same spot all night, waiting for him. They had blown their horns and fired rifle shots. They had even run a chainsaw for two hours in the hope that Wescott would hear the noise and find his way back.

The next day a massive search began. The wardens organized teams of hikers who formed loose grids as they tromped through the snow-covered woods, while a helicopter flew overhead to check ponds, streams, and other logging roads. After that effort failed, it was decided to bring in some dogs. By that time, of course, Wescott might have moved miles away in any direction. In that case, his fresh scent cone would have moved with him, while the less recent particles of airborne scent would have drifted to the ground and been covered by new snow.

After their dogs were pre-scented on Wescott's car, the handlers studied a topographical map and were given their various territories to cover. Caroline was assigned to one of the wardens, with whom she hiked through a wooded area until she saw Sasquatch stop and put his nose in the air. Because of his other adventures chasing after game, however, she had learned to be wary.

"He's alerting," she told the warden with a rueful smile, "but I'm pretty sure it's on game."

"There he goes," the warden said as Sasquatch took off.

Caroline and the warden charged through the woods after him. About a half mile later, huffing and puffing, they caught up to the dog and found him standing nose to nose with a huge moose.

"Oh, God," Caroline muttered.

The moose stared at the German shepherd in wonderment, then snorted, pawed the ground, turned, and bolted away. In a flash Sasquatch took off again in bold pursuit, leaving Caroline to burn with embarrassment as the game warden grinned at her.

"That's it for you, Sasquatch," she said under her breath as her dog disappeared into the snow-covered landscape. "Sasquatch, my boy, that's it!"

"Well, flatlandah, let's take a rest," the warden said. (Caroline had already learned that a flatlander was any "foreigner" from south of Maine's borders.) "We might as well just sit here and wait."

They brushed off a log, sat down, and waited.

Sasquatch finally returned with his tongue almost down to his knees and a clearly submissive look. He knew he had done something wrong. Caroline could only glare at him. True to her principles, there was no point in correcting him after he had done the right thing by coming back.

They went a bit farther until she noticed some fresh paw prints in the snow. Caroline had taken enough tracking courses to recognize various kinds of prints, but these were gigantic.

"Mmmm," she said. "The animal that's been leaving these prints is a big one. Is this the same moose? Or another one?"

"Nope," the warden said. "That's a bay-yah!"

"A what?"

"Bay-yah!"

"Oh, a *bear*," she said, taken aback. "Which way is he going?"

"Well, flatlandah," the warden replied, glancing at her, "*he* goin' thataway." He turned, now pointing in the opposite direction. "And, flatlandah," he said, his voice suddenly changing, "*we* goin' *thataway!*"

Searching went on until dusk and resumed at dawn each day. But a week later, the dogs had still turned up no trace of George Wescott, and the search was finally called off. Wescott was presumed dead.

The wardens drove the dog teams south to Portland, where Caroline and the other handlers picked up boxes of live lobsters to take home. Then they boarded a C-130 military transport, flying first to Wisconsin to drop off the fledgling team from that state. The Maine-to-Wisconsin-to-Newark route seemed weird, but such was the flight plan.

Cooking the lobsters after midnight, Caroline told Art how Sasquatch had frightened a moose nearly to death. "I love him dearly," she said, "but he needs to retire from search and rescue as soon as possible. I'm definitely ready for a new dog."

Three weeks later, in December, Caroline received a report of how George Wescott had come out alive.

After hunting that first day, he tried to use his compass to get back, but because it indicated he was heading northwest—farther into the vast, remote, rugged, unpopulated wilderness—he refused to believe it, thinking it was frozen. He had no topographical map to guide him, and he could not orient himself in relation to the sun, because either snow was falling or the sky was almost completely overcast.

During the first night he used up his matches, trying without success to get a fire going, and the next day he wandered in search of high ground, but the heavy tree cover prevented him from seeing much of value. Then his route was blocked by a large lake which, because the daytime temperature was slightly above thirty-two degrees, was only frozen around the sides.

Wherever he went, Wescott met up with icy cold ponds or rivers blocking his way. He spent most nights at empty logging camps. He found a Sunfish sailboat and put it into the lake, but fell overboard and nearly froze to death. A week later he sailed down the lake to a landing, then walked along the road until a telephone repairman picked him up and took him to Greenville Hospital.

It was quite a saga, Caroline thought, and it pointed up the fact that successful searches with dogs often depended upon getting them to the scene quickly. By the time Sasquatch and the other dogs arrived, Wescott had gone out of range and was nowhere near the search areas; also, fresh snow had covered his older scent particles, making them more difficult for the dogs to pick up. Wescott had come out alive, but it might well have been otherwise.

To find her third canine partner, Caroline consulted a friend named Ursula Kempe, a German woman who had been active in the Schutzhund world. Ursula lived in New Jersey, but every year or so she returned to her native country, where she had many contacts among the breeders.

They agreed that if Ursula saw a terrific dog in Germany that she thought would be right for Caroline, she would phone her right away.

In June 1983 Caroline and another dog handler, Millie Curtis, formed their own volunteer group. The original Ramapo outfit, whose members were invariably outspoken individuals, had previously been fragmented by the creation of an offshoot called Palisades Search and Rescue, which Caroline and Millie had joined. And now, starting off with five women and one man from *that* group, they called their new unit West Jersey Canine Search and Rescue.

Caroline and Millie, who lived about thirty minutes from each other and had worked together on many searches, decided to create the new unit for two reasons. On the practical level, they could not afford the time and expense of traveling long distances by car for the ongoing practice required by handlers and dogs. So, they felt, why not train by themselves, closer to home? It also made practical sense to concentrate more on local searches in New Jersey and nearby states; perhaps they had been neglecting the area in which they lived. The value of search-and-rescue dogs was being recognized by more and more regional officials, who were spreading the word among themselves, so emergency calls from these sources were on the increase.

Caroline was also feeling the need to be home for her children as much as possible. They were demanding more of her attention these days, not the least because they were older and needed to be driven here and there to their many friends and activities. Joanne and Andrew were thirteen and twelve, respectively; Alastair was seven and Heather was five. Palmira had become a true member of the family, and Art could often cover at night, but Caroline was determined not to be an absentee mother. It was sometimes an exhausting juggling act, racing back and forth between her two worlds. Although the new unit was still on call for special missions across the country, she hoped it would keep her closer to home.

On the philosophical level, Caroline and Millie objected to the Ramapo group's rule excluding dogs other than shepherds. When the Syrotucks had made the transition from tracking and trailing to air-scenting, they had believed that German shepherds, being natural air-scenters, were the only dogs that should be used in search and rescue. It was true that the breed had numerous advantages. Shepherds were large enough to work their way through a maze of forests, yet small enough to be transported by helicopter. They had the stamina to search night and day, and their thick, protective coats enabled them to endure extreme temperatures.

But Caroline and Millie believed that many other breeds were suitable. The six teams in their unit included three German shepherds, a Doberman pinscher, a Rottweiler, and one large mongrel whose family heritage was unknown. Theirs was an all-breed unit, allowing any kind of dog to train and undergo testing. If the dog passed, that was sufficient.

Whatever their breeding, the dogs were still carefully selected. They were judged for stamina, intelligence, adaptability, curiosity, trainability, motivation, temperament, agility, work drive, play drive, and persistence. At the same time, they had to be family dogs; all of those in the new unit were lovable, gentle pets at home.

"The last thing we want is a guard dog," Millie and Caroline told people. "We never train any aggression into the dogs. They work simply for the fun of it, and to please their owners. If we're threatened, they'll protect us, but they're never a threat to anyone who's lost or hurt."

Millie, whose partner was a ninety-pound German shepherd named Strider, had a deeply personal reason for her own involvement. Ten years before, her seventeen-year-old son had been hiking alone along the Appalachian Trail in Vermont when heavy storms broke. As they later reconstructed the accident, the stream he had wanted to cross was swollen, and a bridge had collapsed. He waded in anyway and was swept downstream. For five days and nights, rescue parties searched in vain. They finally found his body half a mile from the collapsed bridge, where the receding water had left it.

"It changes the way you think about life," Millie later said. "After that I left my office job and took up nursing, then got into this work as a volunteer. The loss of my son was the start of my commitment to search and rescue."

With the original Ramapo group, along with the Palisades and West Jersey units, now responding collectively to five emergencies per month—about sixty missions each year—Caroline got word from Ursula that a new dog had been found for her in Germany. He was descended from a top-of-the-line shepherd.

He was a king's son, a prince.

And his name was Aly.

# Chapter 6

# Aly:
# The Prince Arrives

*ALY VON DER HEISSENER HOHE SchHI, KKIA.*
That was his name on the ID papers from Germany. The abbreviations indicated he had passed the Schutzhund I trial and had been certified, after qualifying in terms of temperament and structure, to be allowed to breed. He was eighteen months old. Having been raised at a large kennel near Hamburg, Aly had spent lots of time around other dogs, but not children. He had never been part of a home and was not a family dog. He knew nothing of search and rescue.

*Father: Barry von Harberg SchHIII, AV*
*Mother: Gina von Haus Reolich SchHI, AV*

Aly came from royalty, no question about it. His owner had given Caroline an idea of his bloodlines and working background. She knew both his parents had Schutzhund titles; his father had passed all three of those trials. Because she belonged to a dog club in Germany, receiving its monthly magazine from abroad, she had kept up with information on lineage. She knew which owners in Germany were producing the top litters and which working lines were best. She also knew many

of the German judges and breeders, because of her Schutzhund training with Zibo, and had called them to check details of Aly's history.

Even so, he was arriving sight unseen.


Caroline felt nervous and excited as she drove with Andrew, now
thirteen, to Kennedy Airport to meet him. In Germany her friend
Ursula had checked Aly out personally before putting him inside a
crate for transport, and now she was escorting him overseas to the
United States.

Caroline had told Ursula she wanted a male. Although females
tended to be less aloof and to bond more easily, she had always
wanted male dogs, purely as a matter of personal preference. Caroline
knew that Aly had not been neutered; there was the possibility of
eventually breeding him, in which case his good bloodlines would help
produce some better working dogs in the United States. But her gender
preference mainly had to do with the need she felt to test her abilities
as a handler. If someone could not control an intact (unneutered) male
shepherd, Caroline felt, then that person needed to work with a different breed. Learning to handle such a dog was a challenge she relished.

Caroline knew that Aly's German owner had noticed he was growing too big for the breed-survey norms, in which the height limitation
was twenty-six centimeters. If the adult dog exceeded that height, the
breeder would not be able to show him or use him for breeding in
Germany. It seemed likely that Aly would grow beyond that, so his
owner was willing to let him go, despite his certification.

Regardless of the dog's size, a German shepherd of such quality
was very expensive. When Caroline had negotiated with the breeder
by phone, she had been sure to mention that she planned to use the
dog in search-and-rescue work. Breeders who knew that a dog would
be worked, not just shown or kept as a pet in the backyard, would be
more likely to name a fair price and send a good dog. Caroline wound
up paying just under $3,000 for Aly.

Sadly, though, it was becoming a real racket to sell poorly bred
dogs in the United States for large sums. By the early 1980s, some
European breeders had learned they could charge $8,000 to $12,000
for nonworking dogs, and some American buyers wouldn't know the

difference until too late. Caroline knew people who had paid $20,000 for dogs that came over and sat like marshmallows in their backyards. That happened a lot in Japan as well. After paying all that money, many new owners could do nothing with their dogs.

She knew Aly's coloring was black and tan, and that he had a big dark snout on a large face. His temperament had been described as "tough." She had been told that his fight drive was excellent; in his Schutzhund work, she had learned, he loved to go after the burlap sleeve and play tug-of-war.

But no matter how much information they had given her, she still had no real idea of what Aly was like. She understood that each dog in the world was unique. The biggest mistake a trainer could make was to compare one dog to another, or to expect that a given animal was going to be a clone of its parents or grandparents. Each dog would have its own stronger and weaker points. They were individuals, just like people. But what Caroline could not know was how she and the dog would relate to each other.

She stood waiting with Andrew in the international-arrivals building, and her heart was pounding. It was something like being an adoptive parent waiting to pick up her new child; she remembered the way she had felt when they had gone to get Joanne.

Then she saw Ursula, who had a German shepherd on-leash, and her heart sank. The animal looked like a good dog, but it was not Caroline's type at all. It was too low-slung, not what she had been led to imagine. She almost always had an immediate, gut reaction to a dog, as if she were picking up some invisible energy.

And the one with Ursula made her think, *Oh, no, not for me!*

"This is *my* new dog," Ursula said, as if reading her mind.

Caroline and Andrew followed her back into the customs area, where a plastic airline crate stood waiting. After the trauma of flying across the ocean in cargo, she knew, it was important that a working dog be greeted first by its new handler; the bonding should begin at that instant. So she approached the crate and opened its door, reaching her hand inside to grab his collar. The furry, muscular, eighty-five-pound German shepherd inside the crate was such an incredible ball of energy that Caroline could barely hold on to him so she could snap on the leash. Liberated at last, the dog almost pulled her over.

Then he turned and stared up at her with big brown eyes, as if seeing a vision.

This one, Caroline knew, was Aly.

They looked at each other. Then he came to her. She put her hands around his huge, dark head, and they formed an instant bond. For both it was love at first sight.

Then and there he made her his total focus. After his long and disorienting ride from Frankfurt, here was a woman who called him by name, who brought him water and snacks, who spoke to him in German. Having emerged from the lonely darkness of his crate, Aly fixed his attention on Caroline as if he had already decided: *This is the person I'm meant to trust, to follow, to give my devotion to.*

As they walked out of the airport, she was aware of how this big dog ignored crowds the way a king walked past his subjects. Yet he would not take his eyes off her. He watched Caroline's every move and gesture, each expression, and listened to whatever tone of voice she used.

She could see by his dark, sensitive face that Aly was capable of great devotion. He was strong, yes, and already he was being protective (no doubt he could scare someone when he needed to), but even such a short while after meeting him, Caroline knew he was not as tough as the owner had described him as being.

*This guy is anything but a wimp,* she thought, *but inside he's all heart and soul.*

Caroline and Andrew coaxed Aly into the van for the ride of under two hours to Bernardsville. His crate was in the rear, but she decided not to put him in it. She wanted him right there in the seat behind them.

Ursula had mentioned there was a gift beneath the pad in his crate, so Caroline checked and found some boxes of chocolates. She handed them to Andrew. It was dinnertime and he was hungry. Fighting traffic on the Belt Parkway, she turned to him and said, "Why don't you have a chocolate? Grab a box and open it up. I'll bet they're extremely good."

Andrew ate a piece, then another one, then another. He looked at her. "Mom, I don't think you should have any."

"Why not?"

"Because you're driving."

"What does that have to do with it?"

"Well, Mom, these are filled with liquor!"

Caroline burst out laughing.

"So how many have *you* eaten?"

In the backyard Caroline had built a second dog run in preparation for Aly, so he and Sasquatch could have separate spaces surrounded by high wire fences. Although a desire to fight each other might have been expected, they adjusted well enough—Sasquatch was an easygoing and sociable dog, to begin with—and at night they both came inside, sleeping in the kitchen together without tension. If dogs also could have good and bad chemistry between each other, theirs was good.

Aly established his dominance at the house simply by showing up. Caroline never saw her new shepherd do anything specific to let Sasquatch know his rank had been lowered. Instead Aly looked at the other animal as if to say, *I'm the top dog now, and if you don't mess with me, I won't mess with you.* The reason Sasquatch would not challenge him seemed related to Aly's regal attitude.

She could only describe it as presence.

She began life with Aly early the next morning. It was important to be the first person to handle him—to take him out, feed him, play with him, do obedience work with him, reward him—in order to continue their initial bonding process in his new environment.

Because he was still only a year and a half old, Caroline knew he would continue to grow and develop for the next six months. Some breeds matured more slowly than others (she had met black Labs who hadn't seemed fully mature until age four), but for shepherds and golden retrievers, among others, full physical and mental maturity was achieved around age two.

Aly's bones, muscle tone, and general strength would continue to develop over the next half year. Caroline planned to complete his obedience training and cement their working alliance during this time. She would also continue the socialization process. During the remainder of Aly's second year, she would expose him to many different environments to make sure he would not be confused by new places and scenes. And she would give him a real sense that he belonged—not only to her, but in his new home.

She continued his work in Schutzhund and started training him in search and rescue. He picked up on air-scenting fast, going off on his first mission in the late summer of 1984, just a few months after his arrival, when he helped find a lost hunter.

Aly was a methodical dog that loved to search with exactness and thoroughness. There were faster shepherds around, but none more conscientious. Motivated and, indeed, driven to please Caroline, he would not stop until either his body gave out or she told him to quit. She was building his stamina, jogging or cycling beside him as he trotted at a steady pace. In an endurance test, he would have to keep up this gait for twelve miles, with only two evenly spaced water breaks.

They took off in the Suburban to searches in New Jersey, New York, and Pennsylvania, where local police departments now often requested them by name. One evening in September 1984, en route to the Shenandoah Mountains with Aly in the seat behind her, Caroline stopped at a toll booth. Apparently what Aly saw was the collector reaching out to touch *his* vehicle—which, by now, had become his second home—to possibly harm *his* partner. In a split second he was in the front seat and on his way over her lap, heading out the window.

"Whoa, Aly! *Nein! Pfui!*"

She held him back from the terrified man in the booth, her own heart pounding. Caroline understood that Aly was not attacking, just warning a potential enemy, but how was the collector supposed to know that? Apologizing, she paid the toll and drove to the side of the highway. This was not the first time Aly had acted to protect her and the Suburban from a toll-taker: *Someday*, she thought, *some poor guy is going to lose his fingers.* The time had come to use the wire crate she had installed in the rear.

"Sorry, Aly," Caroline said, ushering him inside. "I know you were just trying to save me, but we can't take any more chances. That poor guy nearly had a stroke!"

Keeping him in the crate back there was also best for Aly's own safety; if she had to brake suddenly, the container would restrain him even better than a seat belt. Having him in the crate would also be cleaner. During that Shenandoah mission, they spent three days and nights scouring a vast section of muddy woods for a man suffering from Alzheimer's disease, and on their return, Aly's confinement in the crate served to prevent the entire inside of the truck from becoming a mud hole.

She took Aly up to Bear Mountain, New York, for his first wilderness test, administered by members of the American Rescue Dog Association. Cofounder Jean Syrotuck flew in from Washington State to help supervise it strictly and impartially. Each member of Caroline's local ARDA group was given both a daytime and a nighttime test; one by one, with their dogs, they had to cover a thirty-acre tract and find two persons hidden in separate locations. Depending on the terrain, temperature, and wind conditions, they could spend up to three hours completing their tasks.

The test, simulating an actual mission, was also part of Aly's continual training. Caroline brought a backpack with sufficient gear to survive for five days, including first-aid equipment for herself, Aly, and any victims. The dog's performance was important, but even more emphasis was placed on that of his human partner. Dogs tended to learn their routines faster than people did; failing the wilderness test usually meant the handler's skills were lacking.

She told Aly, as a way of telling herself, "Hey, partner, it doesn't matter if we pass the test or not. We're here to enjoy ourselves, and to learn about our weak points."

Neither Caroline nor Aly knew where the "victims" were located. The test involved air-scenting, so her first task was to plan their approach according to prevailing wind currents. These generally depended on the weather and time of day. In the morning, as the sun first warmed the highest ridges, that air would rise and cause updrafts from below; at midday, the human scent would stay trapped down in the valley; and toward sunset, the cooling air above would gradually start downward. Caroline wanted Aly to "work into the wind" so the scent would be coming toward them.

Having gone through the test with Zibo and Sasquatch, she did not feel anxious or nervous. She had learned how to assess a dog, to know whether he was ready, and there was no doubt in her mind about Aly. He trusted her completely; she, in turn, simply let him know what she expected. To work effectively as a team, each relied on the other to fulfill his or her part.

"*Such und hilf,*" she told him, indicating their general direction with an outstretched arm. Racing forward, Aly ranged much farther than she herself did; he zigzagged back and forth in a wider arc, eager to pick up the first new rafts of airborne human scent. If she wanted him to range here or there as they went, she gave a slight wave in that direction and he reacted.

He was almost an extension of herself.

As he could read her, she could read him. She knew by his expressive face, by the slightest change in his body language, whether he was "just working" or becoming interested or getting really excited.

She carried her full backpack and used a topographical map and compass. She was also accompanied by an evaluator along the way. Her task, while helping Aly to pick up the scent cone, was to cover the wilderness area properly and fully. She needed Aly to use his sensitive nose, but he depended on her to give him the best possible advantage. This meant staying alert to the shifting wind patterns and adjusting accordingly.

The wind could switch abruptly. Instead of coming toward Aly, it might turn into a crosswind or turn around completely. Some handlers carried little containers of talcum powder to test the wind periodically; they often threw it upward only to have the stuff blown back in their faces. Caroline preferred to set little smoke bombs on the ground. This also helped her avoid the mistake of testing the wind too high above the level of the dog's nose; down where Aly was, the pattern of air flow could be very different.

The wind could change yet again when they came to ravines or gullies. An air current might be flowing straight across, so Aly would lose the scent in a dead spot as soon as he descended. Or if a victim was down below, that person's scent might be floating right up to the sky, so Aly would miss it if he stood on either side. Caroline's answer was to bring him down into each of the small gorges to check for scent before proceeding farther.

Aly worked within the scent cone to its source and located the first hidden person, picking up a stick to reward himself. She praised him accordingly, then used her portable high-band radio to communicate their exact position back to base. The "victim" wore a tag indicating a set of injuries or health problems, so Caroline opened her pack and administered the relevant first aid. For hypothermia, a frequent symptom, she heated water on her portable stove and served it with bouillon cubes in an aluminum cup.

To begin searching for the next hidden person, whose location might be far from where they were, Caroline got Aly into the sit-heel position. It was the same procedure she used in obedience training to let him know a new exercise or game was about to begin. She calmed him down by putting a hand on top of his head and stroking him between the ears; then she focused him by moving her other hand along his muzzle toward the front, gently aiming him in the new direction until her arm was fully extended and she was pointing as if to say, "We're going to go *this* way now."

She gave the search command, and he bounded off again.

Back at base camp, after Aly had found the second "victim" in the woods, she drew lines on her topographical map to indicate the area of wilderness they had covered. The ARDA officials announced that she and Aly had passed.

Caroline was preparing Aly for the unknown.

She took him to playgrounds, presenting him with all sorts of fun-filled activities requiring agility and concentration. He loved to climb ladders, go down slides, balance on seesaws, and crawl through tunnels. He was lowered from the edges of cliffs and walls in a harness. She got him accustomed to the different surfaces presented by fire escapes and other types of metal grates. On construction sites, he negotiated even more difficult terrain—piles of wood or rocks or concrete rubble, along with broken glass—similar to what they could expect at the sites of building explosions, bridge collapses, tornadoes, and other disasters.

She worked him without a collar or leash. There was too much potential for a dog to become snagged and hurt, if not literally hung, and she herself could be injured when he pulled. The answer was to give Aly complete freedom to use his natural agility based on instinct. Only he knew how to avoid hurting himself and, amazingly, he never cut his feet. She watched in awe as Aly walked carefully and nimbly over strewn pieces of glass, his toes spreading or pulling together, in constant compensation, until he got through unscathed.

She took him to busy airports, subjecting him to the chaos, to the slippery tile floors, to the loud engines of the planes. They went to shopping malls, where Aly got more exposure to sudden noises and large crowds. He let people approach and touch him. It was crucial for him to take these pressures in stride, to stay calm in the midst of any distraction. They visited school grounds, where kids flocked around Aly and further tested his patience by climbing on his back and tugging on his fur. And Caroline subjected him to other extremes—bitter cold and intense heat, bright light and utter darkness—to get him accustomed to whatever they might face in the future.

Perhaps his toughest challenge was to remain on a down-stay outside Burger King and McDonald's and other fast-food places while being enticed by the powerful smells of the cooked meat and fries. He received praise and playtime just for lying there and drooling, not moving a muscle, much less begging.

When Caroline told people she was "working him to his full potential," she meant it.

Testing herself as well, she carried Aly in her arms for hundreds of yards in the woods, in case he ever became incapacitated and she needed to bring him out alone. By now she had also become an active member of the volunteer Bernardsville Fire Department, responding to local emergencies at all hours and gaining further experience. And in September 1985, when the annual conference of the National Association for Search and Rescue (NASAR) was being held in Nashville,

Tennessee, Caroline was determined to attend in order to learn more about new developments in the field. She drove down with Aly, unaware that Mexico City had just been struck by a devastating earthquake and that she was heading instead for her first international mission.

# Chapter 7

# Earthquake in Mexico

SHE DROVE THROUGH THE NIGHT. WITH HER WAS a man from a Pennsylvania search-and-rescue team who had asked for a ride. Aly slept inside his wire crate. She had brought a variety of gear, as usual, to be prepared for any unexpected search mission. Stopped for speeding on the Tennessee border, she talked her way out of a ticket. They arrived in Nashville on Friday morning, September 20, 1985, in time to register for the NASAR conference.

Caroline went out with Aly to buy tickets for the Grand Ole Opry. They wandered around town and returned to the hotel by early afternoon. Walking through the lobby, she noticed several other dog handlers waving to get her attention. Among them was Linda Wallace of Dogs-East, a search-and-rescue group in Maryland.

"Hey, Caroline, do you realize they've had an earthquake in Mexico City?" Linda said.

"Earthquake?"

She learned that current reports were still sketchy, because international telephone and telex lines had been knocked out. The eighteen million inhabitants of Mexico City were virtually cut off from the rest of the world. Amateur radio operators were doing their best to pass on vital information. Early estimates of the death toll ranged from hundreds to several thousand, with untold numbers of victims still missing beneath the rubble of at least four hundred buildings.

Thirty hours had passed since the quake had struck. Experienced rescue people felt that most people buried in the rubble could survive without water and food for seventy-two hours—perhaps longer, they said, depending on injuries, the traumatic effects of shock, and the physical circumstances they were enduring. But it was best to get there within that three-day window of opportunity.

"We're trying to get government clearance to send some dogs down there," Linda said. "You want to go?"

"Well, I've got Aly with me and I brought my gear along, so sure— I'm ready."

She learned that the quake had registered 7.8 on the Richter scale. (The figure would be revised later to 8.1, indicating a release of three times as much energy as in a 7.8 quake, making this earthquake one of the most powerful ever measured.) The first tremors had been felt the previous morning—at 7:18 A.M. on Thursday, September 19—just as the rush hour in Mexico's crowded capital was beginning. The city rumbled and shook for nearly two minutes. Buildings shattered every which way, and numerous fires broke out. Electric power was cut in large sections of the sprawling city. The subway system, normally transporting more than four million passengers per day, stopped working, and its riders, both adults and schoolchildren, were evacuated to the street. Traffic lights went dark and electric trolleys jolted to a halt. Normally hectic traffic came to a standstill in gridlock.

The Mexican government's TV network, still in operation, reported that hospitals in the capital were filled to capacity with casualties. Urgent pleas were being issued for donations of blood and plasma.

The dog handlers in Tennessee could not ignore the fact that they, along with leaders of many other kinds of volunteer rescue groups in the United States, were assembled under a single roof while a neighboring country was in trouble. The need for canine units seemed obvious, but apparently the U.S. government had been caught unprepared, in the same way it had been unable or unwilling to send dog teams to Italy five years earlier.

But the value of air-scenting dogs at disaster scenes had been confirmed again and again over the years. In April 1979 a Texas unit of ARDA had assisted authorities in searching for survivors of three tornadoes that had ripped through Wichita Falls. The Israeli army's medical corps used dogs in 1983 to locate American marines trapped in the U.S. Embassy in Beirut, Lebanon, when it was destroyed by terrorists. The same year, two dogs from the California unit had searched the town of Coalinga after an earthquake. Even so, as Linda Wallace made urgent calls, State Department officials in September 1985 were still reluctant to send volunteers with trained dogs to Mexico.

The handlers in Nashville learned that canine units in other countries had already been mobilized. Ahead of the pack was Switzerland, whose twelve dogs and handlers were accompanied by a large extrication crew as an integral rescue component. They were already aboard a chartered Hercules transport. France was sending a team of 280 rescue specialists, including 33 search dogs; and West Germany had dispatched 56 members of a disaster-relief unit, along with a dozen dogs. Even a Russian-trained Cuban dog team was reported to be on its way. But the United States had no such official international team with a canine unit, and continued attempts to rouse officials in Washington were met with silence.

"This is ridiculous," Caroline said. "We're *neighbors* to Mexico. How can the Swiss, French, and German teams come all the way from Europe, while we have qualified people and dogs right here and can't get in to help?"

By that evening, however, the Office of U.S. Foreign Disaster Assistance (OFDA) told the Nashville group to place four handlers and their dogs on standby. Members of the prospective U.S. advance dog team would include three women and one man, with their four dogs: Caroline and Aly; Linda Wallace and Bourbon, her yellow Labrador retriever; and the husband-and-wife team of Judy and Hatch Graham, from the California Rescue Dog Association, with Sardy and Pepper, their female German shepherds. Although selected because of their experience and proven capabilities, as well as current readiness, they had never been to a catastrophe such as this one.

Set to go also, but without dogs, were Bill Pierce, assistant chief ranger of Shenandoah National Park, and Marian Hardy of Dogs-East. As "overhead," they would coordinate with the U.S. Embassy in Mexico while deploying the teams in the field, using hand-held radios with high-band frequencies to communicate with them as they went from one disaster site to another.

Caroline and her colleagues were scrambling to get ready when they learned that a second major earthquake had struck Mexico City just a few hours before—at 7:37 P.M. on September 20, a day and a half following the first. This one, measuring 7.5 on the Richter scale, had been an aftershock; dozens of smaller aftershocks had occurred, but this was the largest so far, and others could be expected. The second quake had caused additional buildings to fall, trapping new victims.

Linda Wallace learned at 11:30 P.M. that day that the State Department's request was official: The advance unit of four dog teams would leave from Nashville in the morning. Last-minute activity at the hotel became even more hurried and, out of the chaos, this small group emerged as the first U.S. international-disaster dog team in history.

The handlers were up all night getting everything together, too excited to sleep. Some of the team needed gear, so they persuaded a local sporting goods store to open up at one in the morning. They collected donations of cash to buy freeze-dried food, hard hats and goggles, dust masks, a water-purifying kit, veterinary supplies, surveyor's tape, sturdy gloves, surgical masks, flashlight batteries, jugs of distilled water, and ten days' worth of dog food.

Caroline called Art at 2:00 A.M. to tell him the news. "Joanne has a school play on Wednesday," she said, realizing he was still not really awake enough for her news to sink in, "and Andrew has a dentist appointment on Thursday. And, let's see, there's some frozen pizza you might want to use. . . ."

She rang her parents in Europe. "Hi there. I'm going to be in Mexico. If you see someone who looks like me on the newscasts, you'll know it really is me, so please don't worry."

Then she found the keys to her Suburban and handed them to the Pennsylvania man, who promised to drive it back to New Jersey.

Shortly after nine o'clock on Saturday morning, a mammoth military cargo plane from Washington, D.C., landed at the Nashville airport to pick up the team. The C-141 Air Force StarLifter transport had stopped in Pittsburgh to pick up personnel from the U.S. Department of Labor's Mine Safety and Health Administration and the U.S. Department of Interior's Office of Surface Mines. Their truck carried specialized seismic and remote-TV equipment to help rescuers.

A crowd of participants from the NASAR conference was on hand to cheer on the advance team as its members boarded the cavernous transport plane. Inside it was like a flying warehouse. There were huge tanks of extra fuel; all the supplies and gear, including the truck, were strapped in piles on pallets in the midsection. Although Caroline had flown on C-130s in the States, this was her first experience aboard the C-141 aircraft, which was even larger. She and the others sat with their dogs on benches along the massive inner walls, as if they were waiting their turn to parachute out.

The cargo plane's entire rear end could open up for loading. Otherwise, there were only a few small windows, and it was hard to see out. Amid the deafening noise of the propeller engines, it was also impossible to understand what people said unless you could read their lips; all the human passengers were supposed to wear ear plugs to minimize hearing damage, but Caroline removed hers whenever someone yelled to say something.

The noise and vibrations were making her drowsy, so she lay down on the floor to sleep. Aly jumped down, too, and she used him as a cushion for her head. Dozing on and off, she thought how she had never expected to return this way to Latin America.

The State Department had told them that this would be the first U.S. military aircraft to land in Mexico for more than a decade. Diplomatic relations between the two countries had been shaky for years, partially because of Mexico's large debt to American and other foreign banks, and more generally because of Mexican resentment of U.S. political and economic power. Also, the Reagan White House was angry at Mexico's coziness with the leftist Sandinista regime in Nicaragua. How, Caroline wondered, would members of the American search-and-rescue team be received?

The pilot banked as he made a pass over Mexico City, and so the passengers could see out the few windows. The world's largest megalopolis, sitting on a 7,300-foot-high plateau atop a former lake basin, consisted of nearly nine hundred square miles of low, crowded buildings ringed by tall volcanic mountains. To Caroline's surprise, everything appeared normal—aside from a cloud of cement dust hanging in the air amid the industrial pollution—but then, toward the center of the city, she saw it: the terrible pattern of random destruction, as though a monster had stomped and crashed through, flattening some buildings while leaving others upright.

She had learned that the epicenter of the first quake had been about three hundred miles west of the sprawling city, about forty miles offshore and far below the surface of the Pacific Ocean. Movement of the earth's crust had caused a slab to break loose, and the shock had produced a series of long, intense seismic waves. They thundered through layers of sediment beneath the old lake bed upon which Mexico City rested. In effect, the sand and clay below the buildings had turned to vibrating jelly.

Caroline saw smoke billowing from fires. The most severe damage seemed concentrated within the city's central business district—about thirteen square miles, she later learned. Even there the devastation was selective, according to which structures had been more or less resistant. Some of the tall modern buildings of more than forty stories, designed to sway flexibly during an earthquake, remained intact; many with less than fifteen stories, whether old or new, apparently had been shaken to pieces.

An amazed Air Force pilot came back from the cockpit to where the cargo and passengers were. Shaking his head, he shouted above the noise to give his verdict: "Reminds me of Beirut!"

Lines of Mexican police held back crowds of reporters, photographers, and onlookers at Benito Juárez Airport. Watching from a door of the plane, Caroline and her colleagues put on their orange NASAR caps so they could keep track of each other amid the confusion. As they got set to disembark, however, U.S. Ambassador John Gavin and other American Embassy officials climbed aboard to greet them.

Ambassador Gavin, wearing a dark business suit, was accompanied by his wife, who wore a navy-blue dress and heels. When Gavin saw the handlers and dogs, he drew back. Mrs. Gavin managed to smile, but kept her distance. By the disdainful look on the ambassador's face, it seemed he did not realize that Caroline and the others were search-and-rescue volunteers. Apparently all he saw was a group of grubby people with their smelly dogs. He refused to shake their hands, as if they were not clean enough. The handlers glanced at one another. The handsome Gavin, a former Hollywood actor, might just as well have climbed by mistake into the animal pens behind a circus tent.

*Maybe*, Caroline thought, *no one had briefed him.*

Now she was confronting the stodgy diplomatic world that used to be hers, but this time she was an outsider looking in. She was playing a new role (with a new costume, consisting of a denim shirt and jeans with large pockets), and was accompanied by her German shepherd.

Her rebellious side could not help but feel a sense of triumph.

The embassy staffers, far more welcoming than their boss, ushered them into a van that headed into the downtown district. There was still time in the late afternoon to see some of the damaged sections and get an idea of what they were facing. They rode through some blocks where nothing seemed wrong, only to turn a corner and see a building that looked as if it had been hit by a powerful bomb. Caroline had been ready for Mexico City's poverty, but nothing in her past could have prepared her for this destruction. Several downtown hotels had tumbled into the streets. Many of the newer concrete structures, built cheaply without steel reinforcements, were squashed and leaning over.

"We need to start working as soon as possible," Caroline said as the van passed squads of masked and helmet-wearing rescue workers swarming over the rubble to find sparks of life.

Crowds of Mexican citizens were stranded on traffic islands with all the belongings they had been able to carry. Apparently, because of the continuing aftershocks, they were too terrified to go back home—or they had no homes to go back to. Hundreds of thousands of homeless people were using makeshift tents provided by the government and camping out with pieces of furniture, cooking utensils, clothing, and whatever else they could salvage.

When the quake first struck, an embassy official said, some people had jumped from high windows—not always to safety. Crowds of citizens had rushed into the *zócalo*, the square outside the National Palace, seeking solace and information. At first survivors were shocked, dazed, and confused. Then they frantically rushed to find their missing relatives. Children stood sobbing on street corners, looking in vain for parents and family members.

Inside one hospital, victims of the initial tremor were being treated when the second quake hit. The building began to shatter, so those patients had to be quickly evacuated. In the Roma district and other sections, the original damage was compounded. Offices of the National Medical Center, referred to as "the pride of Latin America," were destroyed; many other buildings, seriously impaired by the original quake, were reduced by the second to jumbled chunks of concrete and twisted steel.

Three or four thousand bodies had already been recovered. Temporary morgues had been set up at government offices, but most of the dead were being taken to Mexico City's baseball stadium and placed in rows on the grass for relatives to identify. Thousands of other victims remained buried—dead or alive—in tangled wreckage.

The strike team arrived at the Sheraton next to the U.S. Embassy. This hotel was still functioning, although walls and ceilings in the lobby had developed fissures. On hand were media people from around the world, hungry for news. Reporters rushed toward the dog handlers; photographers and TV crews focused on Aly, Bourbon, Sardy, and Pepper.

"What can the dogs do?"

"Can they perform?"

"Give us a demonstration!"

Caroline and the others fled to their rooms on the twelfth floor. In charge was a pleasant and efficient Mexican man, who promised to keep members of the media at bay. "It's off-limits to them up here," he said.

Alone in her room with Aly, she gazed around and noticed a crack in the wall above the bed. Then she saw a rather substantial hole in the ceiling. During one of the quakes a light fixture or a chandelier, along with a chunk of the ceiling, must have fallen to the floor. The opening, about three feet in diameter, was now covered by carpet from the room above.

Caroline was rummaging through her duffel bag when she noticed that Aly's ears had pricked up. The fur on his back rose as he glanced around, eyes widening. He circled quickly as if wanting to flee from the room. A couple of minutes later she heard a faint rumbling noise, like the sound of a subway train on its way through a tunnel. Soon the rumbling grew into a roar, as if indeed a train were barreling through the hotel. It was an aftershock.

The noise and shuddering plunged her back into one of her earliest childhood memories. Caroline was about two years old, asleep in her crib, when a horrendous shaking woke her. The crib, with her inside, careened across the bedroom and back again. Her parents rushed in to grab her and her brother. Then the family huddled in the doorway while the whole house seemed to be breaking apart. That, she learned later, was the safest place. After some quakes, the door frames were all that remained standing amid the piles of rubble that used to be houses. So now, there in Mexico City, she grabbed Aly and crouched with him by the door of their hotel room. The shaking lasted several more seconds. When it was all over, she marveled at her dog's ability to sense the seismic waves nearly three minutes before she herself had heard a sound.

Caroline went out to the hall and, with the other handlers, memorized the location of all fire escapes and stairways. No way would they take an elevator, not under these conditions. Getting it down to a science, they held "earthquake drills" by timing how long it took each of them to run down the stairs to the lobby.

The American team met that night with Mexican engineers and architects, each group briefing the other on what to expect. The handlers explained how their dogs worked and what their capabilities were; the structural experts would accompany them in the field, to advise which of the damaged buildings could be searched for possible live victims.

"There's no such thing as safety in those places," an engineer said. "There is *less* unsafe and *more* unsafe. It will be a question of which buildings are simply too dangerous for you to climb into."

# Chapter 8

# Crash Course

CAROLINE WAS UP AT FOUR THE NEXT MORNING TO join the handlers and go over their search plans. But first she gave Aly his breakfast—one of two daily meals which, combined, would amount to three cups of dry food, one cup of instant oatmeal, and a single can of moist food. She mixed it all together with water in a single bowl, adding yeast and garlic supplements as well as vitamins. In the field, she would give him plenty of water and occasional snacks loaded with protein.

The U.S. Embassy, which was using its own system of purifying water, had allotted each search dog two gallons to drink per day. Working in the heat, Aly and the others would need a good drink every twenty minutes, to keep from dehydrating and to maintain the sensitivity of their noses.

Caroline had lived in Latin America long enough to know that if a bus was scheduled to pick them up at six o'clock, that meant it would be there at seven. To expect otherwise and get angry wouldn't help. At her suggestion, therefore, the van had been requested for five. It arrived at the hotel—promptly, so to speak—at six, and the team members piled in.

Aly sat beside her. Nearby was Bourbon, the yellow Lab, with Sardy and Pepper, the shepherds. Caroline saw Aly glance at the other dogs now and then, but otherwise he focused his attention on her. Like her teammates, she was handling the tension by making wisecracks, but she knew that Aly could sense her high level of adrenaline, and he seemed, by the look of eagerness in his eyes, to understand they were going to work.

A police escort led them through the maze of streets amid swarms of traffic. Rescue vehicles frantically waved red flags and honked to get through. Fire trucks raced by. Ambulances with sirens wailing sped more survivors to hospitals. Lights at intersections were still out, causing some massive jams, and roads were blocked with firefighters working at smoldering ruins. The van was forced to circle through dozens of side streets to get to its destination.

Hatch Graham, six foot three and a thirty-five-year veteran of the Forest Service, jumped out whenever they got stuck in traffic. The sight of this huge *gringo* in his yellow helmet, towering over everyone else in the crowded street while directing traffic in Mexico City, made the other handlers roar with laughter—*probably because we're all so nervous that we need the release*, Caroline thought.

The van halted shortly after 6:30 A.M., near a collapsed office building. As their first briefing had led the handlers to expect, the site was represented by a sector chief in charge of the immediate neighborhood, or *barrio*. It would be up to this man to give the Americans permission before they could go in and search. Now he came forward, glared at them, and shook his head. Where did they think they were going? Why hadn't the U.S. government asked his personal permission? What were those animals, those dogs, doing there?

Caroline listened, thinking that the *barrio* chief, proud and territorial, was first of all a male. He was not accustomed to having any female—especially a blond *gringa* wearing a small U.S. flag on her lapel, with a big German shepherd panting at her side—inform him in his native language, with authority in her voice, what she intended to do in his domain. *Well*, Caroline thought, *I wasn't a diplomatic brat for nothing.*

"We're here to help," she said, holding in her impatience and softening her voice. "How can we help you?"

This was her way of reassuring him that they hadn't come there to take away his prerogatives. It was useless, she realized, to push him and lose her temper. If she had an idea about how things should go, it was best to hand him the plan, so to speak, so he could say it was his and save face. She could not dictate, especially because she was a woman. Instead she had to make him feel he was in charge, so he would help the handlers do what they had come there to do.

After much negotiation, it worked. Her father would have been proud.


Cleared for passage, Caroline and Aly entered a blur of bewildering activity and noise. There was the thunderous sound of bulldozers and other heavy moving equipment, along with the constant racket of jackhammers. The air was filled with thick dust and foul odors. Men breathed through masks as they worked with picks and shovels to break through piles of concrete and assorted wreckage. There were shouts and screams all around, blending with the noise of machines and sirens. When a body was brought out on a stretcher, there was a hush followed by shrieks of horror. Then came long, loud moaning and, finally, quiet sobbing.

Many of the volunteers, some removing concrete debris with their bare hands, were young men and even boys. Theirs was a remarkable effort. And, Caroline realized, she was seeing something that had never before happened in Mexico City: the unemployed man and the street cleaner working alongside the government official and the attorney. In the midst of this fierce struggle to save lives, long-standing class distinctions had been dissolved by a common humanity. Later, she knew, the traditional class system would return and life would go back to the way it had operated before the earthquake. Meanwhile, though, all the volunteers and other survivors were freed from the restrictions of social status, and to Caroline it was beautiful to watch.

The handlers decided to rotate their dogs among work, standby, and rest periods. They agreed to let the dogs search for twenty or thirty minutes, no longer, to maintain the animals' energy and motivation. According to this plan, one handler would send her dog off-leash into the wreckage and follow behind, while another handler would go without a dog to observe. If the working dog started digging and barking, giving a "live alert," this result would have to be confirmed by at least one more dog. Only then would they ask rescuers to attack the wreckage by digging, cutting, pulling slabs away, and shoring up rubble to create a treacherous debris tunnel to reach the buried person. If the handlers deemed it necessary, they would even use a third dog to triangulate the scent source and give the extrication crew a more accurate location in which to dig.

Caroline had put Aly's orange rescue vest on him, so he knew from experience that he was going to be air-scenting. The semitropical heat was unfamiliar to him and made his breathing slightly more difficult, but Caroline felt he was becoming accustomed to it. Whether Mexico City's high altitude would affect his scenting ability remained to be seen.

When it was their turn, Caroline saw that Aly was watching her face and listening to the tone of her voice to learn what she wanted. She used the words *"such und hilf,"* commanding him to search, watching as he started into the rubble where she was pointing. He made his way ahead of her over the heavy chunks of debris, working with his nose and focusing his attention to pick up new human scent while ignoring the odors of rescue people.

Climbing behind Aly as Hatch followed to observe, Caroline wore her hard hat with its light (she also carried a flashlight in one pocket), goggles, gloves, and heavy-duty hiking boots. She also carried a mask to wear over her nose and mouth, so she wouldn't breathe the heavy cement dust directly. (The Americans had been warned to wear their dust masks only away from crowds, however, to avoid adding to the needless panic of citizens who had heard false rumors about disease epidemics caused by dead bodies.) As they moved into the collapsed office building, it was impossible to avoid the terrible stench in the air. She tried smearing oil of cloves and even Vicks Vaporub on the inside of her dust mask, but nothing worked.

They had climbed and crawled up into the shattered remains when, on a high floor, Aly came to a wall of rubble and suddenly turned away. *Whoa!* he seemed to say, as if expressing his utter revulsion. Here on this first rubble pile in Mexico City, where bodies beneath the debris had been decomposing rapidly in the heat, the blast of one particularly putrid odor had come into his nose and clearly disgusted him. He whined; his ears flattened slightly; and he tucked his tail between his hind legs. Now he turned away, his entire body curving into a V, as he pleaded with his face and eyes to be allowed to escape.

Caroline had seen him express avoidance in the presence of death before, but never so dramatically.

The handlers and dogs continued to search while Mexican rescue workers went up to the same floor. After pulling away debris, they located the body of the building's female janitor, who had been trapped and crushed. The woman's corpse had been partially excavated—only her face and upper torso were visible—when Caroline approached one of the men with a request.

"Excuse me. We do not mean to be disrespectful to the dead, but we need to bring each of these dogs up to this lady's body. We need to be able to read what the dogs are telling us, in terms of their body language, so we know exactly what to look for next time."

With permission granted, the four handlers took their dogs up to the woman's body and observed. Aly had the same reaction as before, but each of the others behaved in its own way: one dog's fur stood up, while another started to pee on the spot, and a third began backpedaling as fast as his legs could go. All, Aly included, refused to proceed any closer to the corpse. These responses had never been taught to the dogs by their handlers; instead, Caroline knew, their distinctly different behavior was innate to each individual dog.

What the handlers *could* do, she realized, was reinforce that instinctive behavior by praising their dogs. So, in effect, they let each dog know that finding a rotting corpse—and having such a natural reaction to it—was acceptable and even desirable. As a result, each handler could read his or her own dog's body language indicating death, as well as recognize the different signs given by the others. It would help them work together as a more efficient search unit.

Inventing as they went along, the handlers agreed among themselves to employ a simple code to mark their finds. They would take strips of orange surveyor's tape and tie them onto pieces of rebar (long metal rods, used as reinforcement in concrete structures) that protruded from the rubble. This way, whatever the dogs had found would be readily apparent; before leaving each site, the handlers would make sure that members of the follow-up rescue teams understood the code.

Three tapes meant someone was definitely trapped alive, and the rescue teams should hurry up and dig. Two tapes meant the unseen victim was possibly living. A single tape indicated the person was definitely dead.

After a few hours at this initial site, they left a number of single orange flags, but that was all.

They radioed their results back to Bill Pierce at the U.S. Embassy and then proceeded by van to the giant Colonia Tlatelolco complex of government-subsidized apartment buildings. All thirty-five of these huge gray blocks of concrete and glass had been evacuated. Most of the high-rise structures had survived the earthquake with only minor damage; but two thirteen-story vertical slabs of the Nuevo León apartment building had completely collapsed, crushing or otherwise trapping up to a thousand men, women, and children beneath the many tons of concrete.

Caroline stepped out of the van with Aly, but they could not see daylight. People had already descended on them, surrounding them as they waved their arms and pleaded: "Find my husband! Find my wife! My brother! My sister! My child! Please!"

Caroline saw that Aly was basically unfazed by the chaos, although he remained alert to any possible threat to her. With sideways glances he watched her carefully, reading her face to see if she was afraid or needed protection. He always knew her emotions and moods, often before she did. Standing there in her hard hat, blue jeans, and denim shirt, surrounded by this crowd of agitated, excited relatives of missing victims, she appeared to be calm and completely in control; but, she realized, her dog knew otherwise.

Neither of them had ever experienced anything like this.

As the only member of the team who spoke Spanish, Caroline explained who they were and what they were trying to do with the dogs. They approached Aly as if he represented their only hope, maybe a miracle. Children stroked his furry coat and hugged him. Women prayed over him with rosary beads. Some people gave both Aly and Caroline scraps of food and even offered their own precious water, which she politely refused.

Also at the scene was Spanish tenor Placido Domingo, looking utterly distraught. He had come to Mexico City to discover the whereabouts of relatives believed to be buried in the building's ruins. (It would be confirmed later that his uncle, aunt, and cousin, and the cousin's child, had been killed inside.) Caroline noticed that he had not shaved for two or three days. He had come all this way only to stand there, not knowing what else to do.

"Oh, shit," the handlers blurted out when they saw how the tall apartment building was damaged.

The activity here was frantic and confusing, as the Americans encountered international teams from France, Germany, Switzerland, and Italy. Caroline's ability to speak their languages, as well as English, Spanish, and Portuguese, put her in a unique position. Through her, all the teams could talk with each other and with the Mexicans as well. There was an urgent need for all the foreign units to coordinate their efforts and avoid overlapping personnel, so Caroline began serving as the communications link between the nationalities.

"Have your people had tetanus shots?" the Swiss asked her.

Caroline, Linda, Judy, and Hatch knew that the biggest health hazards at disaster scenes involved diseases such as cholera and typhoid, caused by bacteria in contaminated water. They could see, too, that the cement dust was causing an array of upper respiratory problems. But they also knew that exposure to the tetanus bacterium—which produced one of the most potent toxins known, one that attacked the central nervous system—could follow almost any type of injury, especially puncture wounds.

"It might be wise," Caroline said, "for us to get new tetanus shots." Looking around, she saw several Mexican doctors from a nearby clinic who were working at the site. She walked over to one of them and said, "Excuse me, but would it be possible for us to get tetanus shots? We had to leave the States in a big hurry."

"Sure," the doctor said, reaching for his needles and gauze pads drenched in alcohol.

"Hey, Caroline," Hatch whispered, "they're using those needles over and over! Ask him if they sterilize those things!"

"Okay, Hatch," she whispered back, "but let me do it diplomatically."

She turned back to the doctor. "Could I see your facilities? I'm an emergency medical technician, and I'm interested to see where you work."

"Of course."

He led her to the clinic, where needles were being sterilized. It was being done in an old-fashioned way, but she could see the procedure was safe.

Caroline returned with the doctor. "It's okay, Hatch," she whispered. "They'll use clean needles on us."

They let their dogs continue to rest in a grassy area near the Swiss team and went to the clinic, taking turns to get their tetanus shots. They joked and laughed, meanwhile, about all the different ways it was possible to die while helping other people to live.

The Americans used their dogs at the Nuevo León site to confirm two strong alerts by Swiss dogs, indicating that people were alive. The victims were somewhere beyond the far end of a debris tunnel created with jackhammers and pickaxes by Mexican workers, who had shored up the tunnel as they went.

Aly's scenting ability remained undiminished despite the altitude and the heat, but Caroline could see that the constant stench of death was taking its toll on him. She let him rest often, giving him water and some treats, and played with him to lift his spirits. She herself drank plenty of water and occasionally munched on one of the granola bars in her pockets, if she hadn't already given them to various children.

In the heat, dehydration was a constant threat to both the handlers and their dogs. The U.S. Embassy supplied them with bottled water that was available in the van, and Caroline carried a canteen for herself. But because Mexican citizens on the street were waiting hours in line for daily rations of water, she decided to avoid having Aly drink from a large bowl in front of them—especially if he drank only half that amount, forcing her to toss away the other half. To do so would only make people understandably angry. So instead she gave Aly water in small metal Sierra cups, about three quarters full, letting him drink two or three cupfuls at a time.

Leaving this collapsed building, the U.S. unit split up—Caroline and Linda forming one team, Hatch and Judy the other—to try to cover several more sites in other parts of the city before nightfall. They knew they would have to work quickly, since demolition teams wanted to blow up buildings deemed hazardous and beyond repair. The most precious commodity of all, which no one could offer, was time.

The handlers arrived at a new block, looked at a collapsed building and said, "Okay, this one looks safe. We can go on in." At another building they took one look and said, as before, "Oh, shit, we can't go inside this one! We'll do a peripheral."

They walked around the edges with team coordinator Marian Hardy, checking to see if any pieces of wreckage had fallen so as to create a void or hole. Perhaps they could send their dogs inside and follow behind. But having circled the building, they just shook their heads and muttered, "Nope. Too dangerous."

If there was a strong chance that survivors were inside, rescue teams could bring in cranes to pick up heavy slabs of debris and carefully remove them; then, with jackhammers and pickaxes and even shovels, workers could try to dig partway through. After a certain point, the handlers could return and follow their dogs inside.

But even before the structural engineers could give a professional assessment of a particular building, Caroline and her colleagues made their own rough classification. It was either an *okay* building or an *oh, shit* situation, based strictly on their gut reactions.

Caroline was proud of Aly, who seemed to approach each new search as if it were a game filled with unexpected obstacles. Nearly all the physical, mental, and emotional tests that a dog could face had been thrown together in a series of different mounds of debris, with teeter-totter slabs, steep climbs, sudden drops, narrow ledges, and dark holes. He went into buildings in which the floors, walls, and ceilings swayed and threatened to crash down as new aftershocks rocked the ground. In his methodical, painstaking manner, Aly moved amid the dust and heat over jagged concrete, broken glass, and twisted metal. He burrowed into openings too small for Caroline and allowed himself to be lowered into pits. He climbed onto ledges to check air spaces between floors and ceilings sandwiched together.

While doing all this, Aly tried to pick up and follow human scent that drifted through openings and cracks like curling wisps of invisible smoke. When his nose told him a person was definitely alive somewhere inside the rubble, he was ecstatic, and Caroline had no trouble reading him. She had trained him, when making a live find in the woods, by praising him only when he came back to her; so now he returned excitedly, tail standing high and wagging back and forth, to have her go back with him to the spot where he had alerted. If she failed to have his stick ready at this point, he found one himself or impatiently grabbed her portable radio or whatever else was in her hand. At the place where the scent was strongest, he barked and dug, frustrated because his path to the hidden victim was blocked.

There was no mistaking his joy in finding human life.

Inside the remains of a building, where the first two or three floors might have been crushed together under the weight of the upper floors, Aly would alert at a particular spot either downward or upward or sideways. But with so many paths for air to travel through the twisted chaos, from which direction was that human scent drifting? Where was its source? What was the effect of the temperature changes on the air currents? (In the daytime, when the outside air was hot, the cooler scent-laden air drifted downward, to the lower voids or elevator shafts or stairwells. Earlier in the morning or later in the evening, when the outside air was cooler, the victims' body heat would propel scent toward the higher floors.) Taking these and other conditions into account, Caroline could give the Mexican rescue workers a fairly accurate direction in which to excavate and even tell them how far they might have to dig.

When a victim had died and Aly came upon the smell of that buried, invisible body, his repugnance was triggered both by the odor and, Caroline was convinced, by his emotional reaction. Aly regarded people as his friends, and to be surrounded by so many dead friends was overwhelming. His aversion for human suffering and death was instinctive; each time he alerted on a dead body, it seemed that his spirits sank. It was, she felt, as though he became depressed the way humans do.

Other human smells drifted from victims who, while still hanging onto life, were critically hurt. Their floating body odors were different, generated by a combination of shock, terror, and approaching death. In such cases, Aly grew interested yet remained calm. He followed the scent around, over, and through the wreckage, going as far as he could, to wherever the odor reached his nose with the most power. There he stopped. If the smell was that of injury or fear, indicating the slightest possibility of life, he refused to leave. His body language expressed both sadness and curiosity, but did that mean the person was recently dead or still barely alive?

Aly fervently wanted his stick reward, and equally wanted to please Caroline, but as long as he was uncertain about whether he had found someone alive, he would not even reward himself. Here in this gray area, rules of logic no longer applied. Caroline was forced to make a critical choice based solely on Aly's behavior.

*Do I mark this spot for the rescuers to come in here right away and dig? If I do and the person is dead, these workers will have risked their lives and used up precious hours; but if I fail to mark a live alert when this victim still has a chance, then I've doomed that person to die in there. What if a second or third dog fails to confirm a live alert, but my gut feeling about Aly's response tells me otherwise?*

Now it all came down to knowing her dog and reading him correctly, to trusting her own instincts as well as his. She would tell the workers, in carefully phrased language, that she felt there was life "based on what my dog is showing me," and leave it at that.

This was the situation at the collapsed Juárez Hospital, formerly a twelve-story facility containing nearly 1,200 staff members and patients. At least 800 persons had died within a fifty-foot honeycomb of debris, but rescuers were still bringing out adults and infants from one side of the building. On the opposite side, where many doctors had been trapped, Aly and other dogs gave strong live alerts. If the excavators came and moved some of the large slabs, however, the part of the building where people were already being saved might well collapse. Could the handlers be absolutely certain that their dogs were correct?

"These dogs say there's life in there," Caroline said, hesitating only a second before adding, "and we believe them."

The handlers moved on. Unlike the members of the Swiss unit, they had yet to become formally integrated with a rescue component from their own country, so it was difficult to learn the results of their efforts. In this case, however, they were told that teams of workers, after carefully breaking through that section of the hospital and crawling way in, had found five doctors and brought them out alive.

It was evening when Caroline and Linda came to an underground parking area buried beneath a large office-apartment complex. When the first quake had hit in the morning, people would have been walking through the garage and getting into their cars to go to work.

Linda led the way down, but soon both dogs abruptly abandoned what they were doing. They turned around as if wanting to escape. Caroline had seen Aly behave this way in the hotel room, when he had sensed an imminent aftershock; now he and Bourbon were becoming skittish, which was unusual. Linda spoke first.

"Caroline—look at the dogs."

"I know."

In Chile at age three, Caroline recalled, she had gone with her family to a farm when a quake had struck. First came a distant rumbling, and then the earth began to move. Frightened and fascinated, she heard a tremendous noise and looked across the field. The ground opened, and an entire barn literally dropped from sight into a huge hole. Then the earth closed again. Caroline remembered how, beforehand, they had been having lunch on the patio when everything had become quiet. All the birds and insects had stopped making noise. There had been a ghostly hush.

Now there was that same eerie silence as the dogs glanced around and the fur on their backs went up. Caroline broke into a sweat.

"We can't go down there!" Linda cried. "We've got to get out!"

"Right," Caroline said.

They yelled to their dogs and ran for it. Caroline could feel a faint rumbling as they made their way back out. As they hit the street there was an enormous exploding sound and the earth shook. Both women, seeing their dogs were safe, dove for the pavement as parts of the building crashed down behind them.

# Chapter 9

# War Stories

CAROLINE STOPPED AT THE SHERATON'S NEWS-stand and bought several of the city's newspapers, hoping to find information about rescues. It was after 9:00 P.M., so the handlers had worked a fifteen-hour day. They had no way of knowing the full impact of what they and their dogs had done; this information would have to come piecemeal from various extrication teams, some of whose follow-up efforts would continue through the night.

She lingered at the newsstand to speak with the elderly woman and the young girl who ran it. The woman mentioned that half the girl's family, including her mother and brother, had been trapped in their apartment building. People were still digging at the site. If the girl was frightened or upset, however, she hid these emotions behind a solemn exterior. Caroline told her how she and Aly had come to Mexico City to help find survivors; in the case of her family members, it was now up to the rescue squads.

"I am saying many prayers," the girl said in a quiet voice.

As the girl shyly gazed at Aly, Caroline reached into her pocket and gave her a treat to feed him. The girl extended it tentatively toward his large face. Aly, perhaps sensing her trepidation, sniffed the treat and then gently took it from her. As he gobbled it up, the girl began to pet him. He looked up at her, as if to say thanks, and for the first time she began to smile.

·  ·  ·

Caroline gazed around her hotel room until she focused on the crack over the bed. It had definitely grown several inches longer. Then the carpet over the hole in the ceiling was rolled to one side. A man's face appeared.

She looked up at him. "Can I help you?"

The man introduced himself as one of two Scandinavian reporters occupying the room above. After a brief chat, he covered the hole again to give her some privacy.

She and Aly were exhausted and covered with dust and grime. One of the main water pipelines into the capital had been interrupted by the first earthquake, but the hotel facilities were working and she was able to take a long shower—although, even after long scrubbing, it was impossible to wash away the smells completely. She left the water running and, before toweling down, went to get Aly. His black and tan body was covered with cement dust, making him look like a gray dog instead. Caroline held him under the shower until his normal coloring reappeared.

In her duffel bag she found some saline solution, used for contact lenses, and rinsed Aly's eyes with it. She also took a cotton swab and cleaned the front of his nostrils—too much dust in there could diminish the powerful accuracy of his nose, as well as give him upper respiratory problems of his own—and then she checked his ears.


Word came from Bill Pierce that Mexico City's sector chiefs had agreed to have a meeting that night with the American team, to arrange better coordination the following day. Because she spoke fluent Spanish, Caroline was elected to help deal with these men—some of whom, she was warned, were self-appointed neighborhood leaders who had used less-than-honest methods to secure their turf.

She left Aly asleep on the bed and was driven over to a partially damaged government building, where the sector chiefs had gathered. As they studied a detailed map of the city, the men began arguing with each other over which of their sectors would get help first thing in the morning. Their rivalry, involving power and control over the various neighborhoods, was all too obvious.

Caroline told them she had been born in Chile, so they promptly decided she was South American. This information increased her credibility. Also, she wore eye makeup, earrings, and lipstick, as she often did in the field. These feminine touches tended to increase her effectiveness in a predominantly male world.

Getting down to business, she argued politely that it made sense to adopt a schedule based on the geographical layout of the sites. That way, the handlers and dogs would not waste time in the van as it zigzagged back and forth across town in heavy traffic. This suggestion also had the virtue of providing a reasonably objective standard, sparing her from having to make decisions based on status and other political priorities. They accepted the idea and made it their own.

Caroline then congratulated them for coming up with such a good plan, and told them what a wonderful job she thought they were doing in view of all the problems they faced because of the earthquake. This show of respect, laced with flattery, helped the warring sector chiefs to make peace. And they agreed to her plan, giving her what she needed.

Back on the twelfth floor, Caroline was drafted to translate for members of the American, Swiss, German, French, Italian, and other international dog teams. At once high on adrenaline and heavy with fatigue, they were all up talking into the wee hours. They needed to discuss their experiences and get some emotional release more than they needed to sleep. They hashed over their war stories from the day, often with gallows humor. Caroline was not one to readily reveal her vulnerabilities, but found herself laughing at each new story from the day's work. She had often enough heard EMS technicians jokingly refer to dead bodies in traffic accidents as "road pizza," or to charred bodies in burned buildings as "crispy critters." It was not meant disrespectfully, she knew; sometimes that kind of humor was necessary for the rescuers to get through the night.

When word came hours later that rescue workers had brought out several live victims from sites the dog teams had marked, their exhilaration was counterbalanced by a new sense of urgency to continue.

As Caroline entered her room, she saw Aly open an eye and then go right back to sleep. Then she saw the carpet being removed from over the hole in the ceiling. A pair of hands reached down. She went to the stocked in-room bar, grabbed some bottles of beer, and lifted them up. The hands took the bottles and disappeared. The carpet was flopped back over the hole.

Caroline's meeting with the sector chiefs was paying off. At each site during the second day, she made a point of immediately going up to the man in charge to get clearance. Consulting a list of their names, she greeted each one individually, and told him how honored and grateful the dog handlers were to be able to help him in his district. They were able to get to work quickly.

Four days, or ninety-six hours, had passed since the first earthquake. The search team was well beyond the seventy-two-hour period when victims had the best chance of being saved. Still, only sixty hours had passed since the second quake.

The advance unit had been joined by nine more U.S. handler-dog teams from California, whose members had arrived aboard another military plane at three in the morning. The new dogs included four more German shepherds as well as a giant schnauzer, a Doberman pinscher, two golden retrievers, and a little female Australian kelpie. The kelpie, originally a cattle dog, was nicknamed Tunnel Rat for her ability to scurry through rubble holes that were too narrow for the larger dogs. The U.S. group now had thirteen dogs ready to search, but the advance team remained a separate unit.

The panic of family members was now being replaced by mounting impatience and anger, and again and again the searchers were inundated by anxious crowds wherever they went. As they pulled up in the van at one site, something in Caroline snapped. She turned to Linda Wallace and said, "I can't go out there yet. You've got to get out first and get these people away from me. I need to be *untouched* for the next few hours! I just know I can't take it!" She was losing all composure as she spoke. "I have to stop being pulled at—my hair pulled, my clothes pulled. *I don't want to be touched!*"

Linda and the others got out, while Caroline stayed with Aly in the van. *He needs some space, too,* she thought. *He never objects to people pulling at him and pleading with him, but he has his limits as well.* When she realized that Aly was gazing up at her with a worried expression, she touched her face and felt the tears.


Caroline learned how closely the low-tech work of the dog teams was being complemented by the high-tech abilities of the U.S. government's seismic sound teams and remote-TV crews. The sounding devices, dropped by cable through layers of toppled concrete slabs, could detect the breathing and even heartbeats of trapped victims; but because of the noise during the first day, the seismic team had gone back to work from midnight until six in the morning. They confirmed live alerts made earlier by the dogs.

In the daytime a low-light, miniature TV camera was being snaked by fiber-optic cable through cracks and crevices, including holes bored deeply through the rubble. The probe could record human shapes and movement that were hidden from the rescuers by five hundred feet of wreckage. At one point the video monitor showed that the camera had come to an impasse; then, suddenly, the on-screen blob opened to reveal a woman's eye.

"The light of the camera must have made her blink," said Jesse Craft of the Office of Surface Mines, whose TV probes, following up on information provided by both the dogs and the seismic teams, were used primarily to help rescuers find the safest ways to pull away debris. In one case, the probe cable was even used to lower water to a couple trapped far below.

With the dog teams and the high-tech crews supporting and complementing each other in a common effort, Caroline came to the conclusion that all the different disciplines and capabilities that make up rescue work should be used at disasters. At the same time, she felt, her dog was a unique and irreplaceable resource. "They have yet to come up with any machine that's more efficient," she remarked to Hatch Graham, who agreed. "No invention is as effective as Aly's nose or as agile as his body, and a well-trained dog is certainly not as costly as some piece of equipment, especially one that breaks down and needs spare parts. If we treat them right, our dogs last longer. And they don't need gasoline, either, just food and water. And, of course, love.''

During that second day the dogs still made live alerts to suggest human life beneath the rubble. Several victims were saved as a result. But there were many more alerts on dead bodies. Among the most depressing places was the Conalep Technical School, where the dogs came upon room after room with bodies already in advanced stages of decomposition. On the third day, there were only five live alerts as the team investigated wrecked government offices, factories, apartment buildings, and other schools. Having confronted the smell of death over and over, Aly was gradually losing his eagerness and intensity. He never failed to do whatever Caroline asked of him, and invariably gave his all, but she gave him increasingly frequent rest periods and water breaks, along with praise to maintain his motivation. When she finally crawled into the sheets late that night, he jumped up on the bed by her feet.

She tried to sleep, but too many images of Mexico City flashed through her mind. And, too, she thought of her family and felt the frustration of having no way to communicate with home because international phone service was still knocked out. Domestic lines were now working, but the only way to get through to the States, they had been told, was from Ambassador Gavin's special ''red phone'' in his embassy office. The U.S. volunteers had been barred from using it.

Tossing around, Caroline glanced at the clock. It was a quarter to three in the morning; in just over an hour, the team would be meeting again to go over plans for that day. At the far end of the bed, Aly was fast asleep. Finally Caroline got up. Aly opened his eyes. As she pulled on her work clothes and boots, he climbed down and disappeared.

''Aly?''

She walked around the bed and saw he was trying to hide behind it. His big, brown eyes were mournful. *No, please, don't take me out there again! I don't want to do any more of this!*

She spoke to him gently. ''Aly? *Hier.*''

*Do I have to?*

"Aly . . ."

With extreme reluctance, he got to his feet.

They went down the dozen flights of stairs. *No one's going to hurt me if I go out for a walk*, she thought, *especially not with a big dog like him.*

Conspicuous in the otherwise empty lobby was a tall, muscular man wearing a ten-gallon hat, a colorful cowboy shirt, and denim trousers. He also wore fancy boots with high heels and a pair of spurs.

Caroline and Aly started for an exit, but the man waved and strode toward them. He grinned, pointing toward the U.S. flag on her shirt. "You're an American!" he boomed, acting as though he had come upon civilization after years of wandering in the desert.

"Yes, I am."

"I'm from Oklahoma! I don't speak this lingo. Maybe you can help me. I need to get a room here."

They went to the desk and she helped him fill out a registration card.

"Hey," he said, "you know anywhere we can get a cup of coffee?"

"Probably around the corner. There's a little place that stays open twenty-four hours."

"All right! My treat! On me!"

Caroline learned over coffee that Mr. Oklahoma was an undertaker. His specialty was "mass disasters," he said, adding that he'd ordered truckloads of body bags to be sent down to Mexico City. He was planning to set up shop.

"You're going to sell body bags?"

"Naw, I'm gonna *donate* 'em."

"I see," Caroline said, not believing him for a second.

The undertaker from Oklahoma discovered he needed Mexican change to pay for the coffee. "Sorry 'bout that," he said with a big grin, "but I guess it's *your* treat." Caroline smiled and left some of her coins on the table.

They walked back around to the lobby. "Well," Mr. Oklahoma said, "I'm gonna go telephone my secretary."

"Telephone? To the States?"

"Yeah. I got a way of gettin' through."

Caroline's mind raced. "You know, there's a bunch of Americans here whose families don't even know if they're still alive. If I give you their names and telephone numbers, could your secretary phone them and say that so-and-so is fine?"

"Oh, sure! No problem."

"Here's my room number. I'm going up—we'll be getting our morning briefing soon—but if you come up to that floor, I'll collect all the names and numbers."

"Sure," he said. "So, you really speak this lingo?"

"Yep," she dryly replied, "I speak this lingo."

"How'd you like to work for me? What would you need? I'll pay you. Are you being paid now?"

"Nope."

"I'll pay you big bucks. When is your team quitting?"

"Well, probably in about three days."

"You just stay on down here. I need somebody who understands these Mexicans, a go-between. I'll pay all your expenses and a salary. Name your price."

"I don't think so."

"You think it over. Now go on up there and get those names and numbers."

When she and Aly got to the team meeting on their floor, the others confronted her. "Jeez, Caroline, where were you? We knocked on your door. . . ."

"Well," she said, grinning, "I just met something I don't think is real!"

Hearing about the undertaker's offer, they were as skeptical as she was.

"You want to lay bets on his coming up here?"

Caroline shook her head and laughed. "I never heard such a fast talker before in my life!"

They were going over the map when Mr. Oklahoma showed up, spurs and all, to collect phone numbers. "My secretary back home is gonna call 'em," he said, "and I'll report back to ya."

Caroline was stunned. "We really appreciate this."

"Hey, no problem! Listen, have you thought about goin' to work for me?"

She felt her face redden as the others looked on. "No, I really—"

"Well, keep thinking about it."

Much later, when she learned that each team member's family had indeed been called by the man's secretary, Caroline realized she had never asked him how he could get through to Oklahoma.


Caroline set down Aly's breakfast in the room. She'd been feeding him once in the morning and once at night, never varying his basic diet. Stressful conditions and fundamental changes in a dog's food could combine to give him diarrhea. She knew it was okay if she *added* to Aly's meals, however, so she'd given him parts of the white-bread sandwiches provided in the van by the U.S. Embassy.

Aly had eaten each meal so far, but this morning he approached his bowl of food and stopped. He sniffed it a little and moved away. Had he lost his appetite? Did the smell of his canned moist food remind him of the odors outside in the wreckage piles? Was he suffering from too much stress? Or contact with injury and death?

"I think my dog has had it," she told the other handlers a bit later. "He won't even eat."

They compared notes and found that all the dogs had lost their appetites, partially or totally. Some were simply slowing down as they worked. But, they agreed, the dogs *wanted* to perform well nevertheless.

"What can we do?" the handlers asked each other.

"Well," Caroline said, "I think we could make sure they get the reward they need."

Until this mission, with a few exceptions, the dogs had basically been doing wilderness work. Their reward, in training and on missions, had been bound up mostly with finding live victims. Now, abruptly, they were disaster dogs. This was the first time they had worked with large, collapsed buildings, amid relentless death, and the relative lack of success in finding human life had undoubtedly worn down their motivation.

"They've found too many dead bodies," Caroline said. "What they need is another live find. And *we* need to give it to them."

So the handlers enlisted the services of a Mexican veterinarian who had introduced himself earlier and volunteered to work with them. He owned a kennel in Mexico City and raised German shepherds, the vet had said, adding that he was interested in learning how to train them for disaster work. (Mexico had no dog teams, but this man would later put together one of the country's first canine search-and-rescue units.) He was also genuinely concerned about the health of the American dogs during their stay.

"We need to remotivate them," Caroline said to the veterinarian.

"How can I help?"

"When we get into the field, it would be great if you could go into the wreckage and hide yourself. Just to let these dogs find you."

"That's it?"

"Please."

At the first disaster site that morning, the man eagerly obliged by crawling into the rubble and hiding. One after another the search dogs went in, picked up his scent, found him, and happily alerted. Caroline was ready with a stick when Aly ran back to her, barking and waving his tail. Having gotten this necessary perking-up, the dogs were refreshed and ready to work again.

The team members were learning and creating new techniques by the seat of their pants. This latest exercise was, of course, a version of how "victims" hid themselves in the woods during wilderness training. It was also based on the fundamental concept that a search dog was playing a game in which the joy of winning was the expected result. In training, the dog was first given short problems; these were extended, or made more difficult, only when the dog had solved them. And so it went. A good handler guided her dog from success to success, each more challenging than the one before, without ever taking a shortcut through failure. That way, the dog did not become confused or discouraged but instead remained always eager.

The incident with the vet also gave Caroline a deeper realization that it was not just the hard work that gave the dogs so much stress, but also the emotional strain. In their own way, they had been heading toward burnout.

# Chapter 10

# The Factory

HOMELESS RESIDENTS THROUGHOUT THE CAPITAL had been camping outside for five days, with nothing but sheets of plastic to protect themselves from the usual heavy afternoon rain. They had created small villages of makeshift tents in parks and streets, using random pieces of wood and furniture as well as donated blankets. Some had facilities for cooking. In one encampment, someone had managed to run a TV wire up an electricity pole and get the set running. They lacked sufficient food and water, but soccer-watching continued.

"This is the Thieves' District," the veterinarian said. "If you live anywhere in Mexico City and your house is robbed, you come down here and buy back what they stole from you."

It was a poor neighborhood of tenements and industrial buildings. Families from other sections had come here to camp outside a large clothing factory where relatives, mostly young women who worked at sewing machines, had been trapped. Eleven stories high, the factory and its adjoining warehouse ran the length of an entire block. Ninety-four female garment workers had already taken their seats in the sewing rooms when the first quake struck at 7:18 A.M., causing the top four floors to give way and "pancake" down on the seven below, creating layers of crushed debris. After an upward jolt from the ground, the first floor dropped completely into the basement. The second floor was now on street level.

Thirty-five women working on the second, third, and fourth floors had managed to get out. They were injured, shocked, and dazed, but alive. That left fifty-nine others still trapped inside the squashed sewing rooms above the fourth floor.

Caroline spoke with one woman's husband, named Miguel, who had become the de facto leader of the distraught family members. "We all rushed over here, and we haven't left for one minute," he said. "We've been working with our fingernails and pure Mexican courage. If they come with bulldozers, we will stand in the way."

Miguel said that optimism had been high during most of that initial day, because people heard cries or even voices from inside. But their hopes had dropped as rescue workers periodically arrived, only to leave again. The building had been declared too hazardous; also, they lacked the tall cranes needed to carefully remove giant slabs, as well as jackhammers for smashing through concrete and creating tunnels leading inside. This heavy equipment existed, but it was being used at other locations that had higher priority.

When President Miguel de la Madrid Hurtado came through the infamous Thieves' District on a tour of quake damage, family members had pleaded with him directly. Mexico's highest official had promised to send aid, but it never arrived. The disappointment of relatives turned to horror that some of the young women might still be alive, yet would be left to die.

Hired guards, under orders from the building's owners, were barring from the wreckage all but a few hand-picked workers, who were allowed into the ground floor. Their objective was not to look for survivors but to salvage any clothing and office equipment that was still intact. Husbands and brothers of the garment workers, who were in a low social category, were able to dig only along the edges.

Day by day, the cries from within grew softer.

"The officials have abandoned us," Miguel said to the U.S. rescue team, nearly crying from desperation and exhaustion. "They don't care about the poor people. We don't want to say anything that isn't true, but we feel that the people in charge of coordinating the aid did not provide the equipment that the President ordered."

By now, the voices had stopped.

. . .

Members of the American dog team took one look at the factory and groaned inwardly.

Caroline spoke with engineers who said the tall building was so fragile and unstable that it endangered the lower, intact structures surrounding it. What was left of the factory would have to be demolished.

It was definitely an *oh, shit* building.

Aly worked on the periphery of the site with Bourbon, Sardy, and Pepper. No natural voids existed and no debris tunnels had been opened, so it was impossible to get inside. A pervasive smell of death came from the factory, but all the dogs demonstrated fairly keen interest, so Caroline and her colleagues left double markers of orange surveyor's tape, indicating that people might possibly be alive.

Radioing back to their command, they called for more help with structural assessment as well as for tools. Then, reluctantly, they moved on.

Caroline learned later that new rescue teams had arrived at the factory with tow trucks, backhoes, and excavation equipment, and cautiously began to bore a tunnel into the compacted rubble. When the precarious upper floors began to move again, though, they stopped for fear of further collapse.

The owners of the factory appeared. Family members keeping a vigil jeered at them for not having provided any help in getting more help to the site. The owners, bearing a permit from the Defense Secretariat, rushed into the now-ground-level second floor.

"Shame on you!" a woman screamed. "You don't care anything about what happens to your own workers!"

The factory bosses came out carrying files and stacks of loose documents. Ignoring the taunts and pleas, they hurriedly left the scene.

The elderly Mexican woman and the young girl were at the newsstand in the Sheraton lobby. The girl saw Aly approaching and ran into the back room.

"What's wrong?" Caroline asked.

The old woman sighed, shaking her head. "She just found out. She has lost her family. All her family."

Caroline stood wondering if it was possible to feel more helpless than she already did. "Do you mind if I go to her?"

"Of course not."

The girl was in a small storage closet, seated on a stack of newspapers. Caroline sat on another stack next to her. Aly moved closer. The girl stared stonily straight ahead.

Minutes went by. Then, gently, Caroline encouraged her to talk about what had happened. The girl spoke so softly that it was difficult to pick up her words.

"My mother . . . brother . . . cousins . . ."

Gradually, as the girl continued to talk, tears began to flow. She petted Aly and then hugged him, sobbing and gasping for breath. Caroline put her arm around the girl, whose whole body was now convulsed with grief, and she herself began to weep.

They held each other in the midst of the newspapers until their tears had spent themselves. Aly pressed against Caroline's knees. Then they emerged from the storage room and went on with their separate lives.

The phone rang. It was 2:00 A.M., so she had slept for only a few hours. A hotel assistant told her that a Mexican man down in the lobby was desperate to speak with a member of the American dog team, preferably the woman who spoke Spanish. The man would not be dissuaded.

Caroline threw on some clothes as Aly stretched but failed to move from the bed. "No need for you to come with me," she said as she headed for the door.

Miguel from the clothing factory was waiting. How he had gotten all the way to the Sheraton from the Thieves' District was a mystery. He squinted through puffy red eyes, his chin and cheeks unshaven.

"You've got to come with me!"

"Just a minute, Miguel. Please tell me—what's happening?"

"The factory! Those people sleeping out in the tents over there, in the streets, they hear voices—again!"

She listened as he frantically waved his arms and told her about the new voices. It had been several days since the quake, so the probability that any of those women were still alive had dropped to nearly zero.

"Miguel," she said in a low but firm voice, "people hear voices because they're *hoping*. They *think* they hear them, because they have hope."

"No! They hear them! They do! And the authorities, you know, they're going to bulldoze that place! They're going to wreck the building! With so many still inside! Because they don't care about the poor people. The poor people's workplaces and houses—they're the first to go."

She imagined the bulldozers that would arrive later that morning, only a few hours away, and the family members standing by as all hope for their loved ones vanished in clouds of dust.

"Okay, Miguel. I'll go up and get the team. We'll leave as soon as we can get a van."

Caroline knocked on each of their doors to wake up Hatch and Judy and Linda. "I know you guys really love me for this," she said, "but there may be life in that factory, and it's going to be torn down. It's a long shot, but we've got to try."


Dawn broke over Mexico City as the van headed toward the garment factory.

"When we were here before," Caroline said, "the dogs did act up a little. They showed some interest. But they couldn't get close enough."

"They also showed there was plenty of death up there," Hatch said. "You couldn't mistake it. The place stank to high heaven."

Miguel, who had returned to the factory, greeted them along with family members who had heard the most recent voices. Perhaps, they pointed out, the cries had come through the new openings made by rescue workers. But now the building was silent again, so maybe it was too late after all.

"It's very dangerous," a Mexican engineer said. "If you can get up to the third or fourth floors, don't try to climb any higher. Too unstable. See if the dogs alert upward. But stay on the east side of the building. Let your dog go to the other side, where most of the collapse took place. Those ceilings could fall at any moment. Let the dogs go check out the unstable parts."

Caroline shook her head. "We go *with* our dogs."

"Then walk softly. And don't touch anything structural."

A hole had been cut into the factory, through a wall inside the first floor of the clothing warehouse next door. Strangely, the warehouse had gone unscathed. Garments still hung neatly from hundreds of racks.

Linda Wallace started into the hole with Bourbon, and Caroline went without Aly to observe. Inside the factory were slides of rubble that had crashed through from the floors above. Some stairwells looked bombed out, others looked okay. Starting at the second floor, which was now at ground level, they crawled behind the dog on their bellies and then climbed up a debris slide to the third floor.

Bourbon, looking toward the ceiling, started to bark and jump up and down.

"There's definitely life up there," Caroline said, "but it's impossible to tell just where or how high."

First Judy Graham went into the hole with Sardy, the female German shepherd who had been her search partner for seven years. Hatch Graham followed her in as observer. It went unspoken that husband and wife preferred to risk their lives together.

The Grahams reappeared covered with cement dust. They had gotten onto the third level (once the fourth floor) and into a large sewing room. Sardy had gone toward the west side of the room, where a hanging ceiling had formed a kind of cave. Sardy's posture at first had indicated only death, but then she bolted under the dangling debris and disappeared.

"A minute later she returned," Judy told Caroline, "with a look in her eyes as if to say I should come with her. I stayed put. So she went back, to get to whatever she had smelled. I couldn't see her, but I heard her scratching in there. I called to her softly, telling her she was a good girl. Finally the dog came back out, her tail wagging slightly. She had that anxious look in her eyes. I'm convinced there's someone alive in there. Probably severely injured."

It was Caroline's turn to go in with Aly.

At the hole leading into the factory, the putrid odor of death was overwhelming. Hatch, volunteering to observe a gain, played doorman.

"Ladies first? Or gents?"

She smiled. "In this case, gents first."

Aly went inside as Hatch crawled behind. Caroline did the same. Then they climbed upward through the pancaked rubble, using helmet lamps and flashlights to see where they were going. The awful smell grew so strong that she thought she might pass out. On either side of her, huge rats silently stared with beady red eyes.

Aly led them up to the large, mostly devastated sewing room on the fourth floor. Despite the noise of workers outside, and the sound of pigeons cooing beyond shattered windows, it was eerily silent up there. Life in that room had suddenly stopped.

The women were gone, but everything else remained. The ancient sewing machines, obviously once arranged in row after row, were now askew. A thick layer of cement dust covered the machines as well as bolts of cloth, scissors, and fabric scraps. Rotting food was strewn about the floor, and rats had clearly foraged there. Other items, on the tables, seemed to have been preserved as if in a time capsule: half-finished sodas, cups of coffee, sandwiches, snapshots of husbands and kids, a bag of makeup next to a mirror. In one corner were stacks of children's books and reading primers.

Near a side wall of the sewing room was a huge glass water bottle, still intact, with paper cups stacked beside it.

Caroline and Hatch got to their feet and moved forward, but the water in the bottle began sloshing from side to side. They stopped. Then they cautiously took another step.

The water sloshed again.

*Oh, man,* Caroline thought, *we're in a real safe place. . . .*

Without warning Aly moved quickly but nimbly ahead, toward the west end of the room. He went as far as he could go, to where the collapsed ceiling had formed a large rubble pile beneath an overhang.

*This must be the cave,* Caroline thought. *But how can that damned hanging ceiling be holding the weight of all those floors above us? What the hell is preventing the rest of the building from coming down? Chicken wire?*

There was, in fact, a small opening between the rubble and the overhang.

Aly started inside and disappeared.

Caroline and Hatch waited.

Silence.

*Where is my dog?*

Caroline spontaneously got to her knees and, forgetting about her own safety, started crawling after her partner. She got to the cave's opening and continued headfirst, now inching along on her belly through the pitch-black recesses of a narrow tunnel. She held her breath as long as she could, then took gulps of air through her mouth to avoid the horrible stench. Aiming her flashlight up ahead, she tried to locate Aly to make sure he hadn't fallen down a shaft. A big rat scurried past her face. She continued to squirm forward. Even though she was not claustrophobic, she felt as if the building were closing in around her.

At last, in the beam of her flashlight, she saw Aly about a dozen feet ahead of her. He was digging and whining. As she approached, he began to bark at her.

"Good boy," she whispered. "What's going on?"

Without warning he bounded toward her. He grabbed the light from her outstretched hand and climbed over her body, racing back through the tunnel behind her. Unable to find a stick to reward himself, Caroline realized, he had grabbed the only available object to tell her about his live find. And now, she thought, Aly was proudly bringing the flashlight back to the open part of the sewing room, where he could share the good news with Hatch as well.

She reached for her headlamp, but it was gone. She was alone in blackness.

Crawling ahead, she came to a wall of debris and could not penetrate farther. The scent had to be coming from the other side. And earlier, the dogs had also alerted upward. So there was probably life on the west side of a floor above.

She could not turn in this tight space. Squirming again on her belly, she started backing out.

"Aly! Give me my light! *My light!*"

And, of course, he came back.

The two young women were still clinging to life on the sixth floor, which had been crushed down near the fourth. One lay at the entrance to an elevator, pinned under the heavy dead bodies of coworkers. The other was trapped between a sandwiched floor and ceiling. They were unable to move. Scavenging rats and pigeons picked at the corpses next to them. After nearly a week in the wreckage, they had reached the point of *wanting* to die.

Then the women heard the dogs barking from below and realized there was still a chance. The sound came to them as if in a miraculous dream. Dehydrated and unable to cry out, they summoned the strength to endure until a rescue team could reach them.

Later Caroline learned that the women had managed to stay alive because of frequent rain showers in the afternoon. Although pinned, they had been close enough to broken windows to be able to catch some water in their mouths.

Rescue workers wanted to bring timbers up to the fourth floor to shore up the sagging ceiling, but were discouraged by structural engineers. "If we even touch it," the engineers warned, "the whole damned thing will come down."

Members of the California rescue team finally brought a crane and had themselves deposited on the roof. They secured themselves with ropes, then rappeled down the side of the building. They went through a window into a narrow space on the crushed sixth floor. A medic managed to reach the women with water and started intravenous feedings. Other workers began the slow, laborious process of cutting and moving debris (and dislodging bodies) to free the two women without further injuring them or destabilizing the building.

After more than twelve hours, the women were lifted out through the window and brought down one by one on the crane.

The second woman seemed barely alive. She was unconscious, and the medic had difficulty finding her pulse. He bent over her, terrified that she was about to die.

Then she reached up, grabbed his hand, and squeezed it.

Miguel's wife was found dead, but his persistence had helped save two other women's lives.

Neither hearing nor seeing those women, it was Aly and the other dogs who had found them. It was they who had offered the trapped women a reason to hope and to live.

# Chapter 11

# Shakedown

THE YOUNG GIRL AT THE HOTEL NEWSSTAND, still red-eyed from crying, approached with a small object wrapped in tissue paper. Caroline tried to refuse, but the girl was adamant: *"Es para agradecer su trabajo, y un acuerdo pequeno de la gente de Mexico."* "To thank you for your work, a small remembrance from the people of Mexico." The girl stroked Aly's head as Caroline unwrapped the paper and discovered a piece of ceramic pottery. The small brown hand-painted jug was one of the few precious things from her family that the girl still possessed.

Caroline knew she probably would never see the child again. She also knew she would keep the object for the rest of her life.

*"Gracias,"* she whispered, hugging her. *"Gracias."*

"What the hell are we going to wear? What are we going to do?"

All the dog handlers and rescuers had been invited to the National Palace, where Mayor Ramon Aguirre Velásquez of Mexico City was to present a medal to each nation's team. The Americans were in a tizzy; none of them had a full set of clean clothing left.

"Well," Caroline said, "we're going over there just the way we look in the field. We'll stay dressed in whatever we're wearing. And we'll bring our dogs."

"No, no, the dogs aren't invited!"

"They're our partners, aren't they? We couldn't have done anything without them. They're coming with us!"

The diplomat's daughter was beginning to relish this encounter with protocol.

A speech would have to be made, and she was elected to deliver it in Spanish. "Listen, guys, knock on my door when it's time to go. I need ten minutes to write what I'm going to say."

Search-and-rescue units representing ten countries had gathered at the National Palace. Some handlers, notably the French and Italians, were lined up in full dress uniforms trimmed with military-style braid. Only the Americans had arrived wearing dirty work clothes. And only they had brought their dogs.

Each group stood while its team leader or ambassador gave a speech in his own language through a translator. Then Caroline walked forward with Aly, who wore his rescue vest. She delivered her remarks in Spanish.

"We are very gratified that we could come here and work with the Mexican people. We are volunteers, and this means a lot to us. But the real gratitude, and the real admiration, should go to the Mexican people themselves—for their fortitude, and for the way *they* have been working nonstop during this crisis. This is a beautiful country, and a wonderful people, and all of us hope we can come back someday, under different circumstances, and enjoy the country."

Aly basked in the applause.

An official from the American Embassy found her in the crowd. "My God, lady, you and that dog just did more for U.S. diplomacy than we've been able to do in ten years!"

They were one of the last dog teams to make the decision to leave. Caroline was all too aware of the message their departure sent to the city's residents; they were saying, in effect, that there was no more hope. It seemed too soon to abandon Mexico City while its citizens were just starting on the long road to recovery.

During five days of searching, with less than thirty hours of sleep, the full U.S. team of thirteen dogs and handlers had worked on sixty-eight separate buildings in the city. None of the handlers or dogs had been injured. Their dogs had located countless dead bodies, but surviving relatives had been grateful beyond words. The mission would have been a success for that alone.

But, in fact, the lives of twenty-two persons had been saved because of their efforts.

Waiting for transportation in the morning, they learned that Hurricane Gloria was on its way up the East Coast of the United States. Caroline thought of the kids at home and wondered if Art was already at work. Did he know about the hurricane warning? Would he be there? Linda, who lived in Maryland, had a ten-year-old daughter and a six-month-old baby at home. Suddenly their focus shifted from the plight of strangers to the possible dangers faced by their own families.

At the U.S. Embassy they asked to use the "red phone" in Ambassador Gavin's office, but were told it was impossible. Caroline dug in her heels. "We need to know our children are safe," she said. The embassy officials finally gave in. Up in the ambassador's spacious office, they used the "red phone" to call home.

An old city bus arrived in front of the hotel later that morning. The handlers and dogs piled in for the ride to the airport, followed by the Mine Safety and Surface Mines officials in their truck. Halfway there, the bus jerked to a halt. They waited in the heat until the Mexican driver finally announced the transmission had blown.

They groaned.

"But it's okay," he proudly announced, "because we still have reverse and fourth gear!"

They cheered.

Ingeniously using pieces of wire to keep the motor running, the driver started up in fourth gear. The bus shuddered forward with a long, low grinding sound. When the driver saw a massive traffic jam up ahead, he swerved onto the sidewalk rather than stop his momentum. Out of habit, Hatch jumped out to keep other vehicles from blocking the way.

A U.S. Air Force C-130 was waiting on the runway, a welcome sight, and they hurried out of the bus—only to wait again. The truck was loaded through the back of the transport plane. Then went the search-and-rescue team's gear, strapped onto pallets. At last the passengers were allowed to board.

The aircraft climbed over Mexico City toward the volcanoes, and Caroline started to relax. But moments later she and the handlers knew something had gone terribly wrong.

"Gasoline!"

The fuel line on the truck had ruptured, and the entire contents of its gas tank were flooding through the inside of the plane. The smell made them gag, so they covered their noses and mouths with bandannas. Far worse was the sight of the exposed wires in the open cargo space. A single spark could ignite the gas, turning the plane into an instant fireball.

The captain came down the stairs from the cockpit and walked toward the back. Caroline watched his expression, thinking he was obviously trained to conceal any concern and certainly would not panic. He opened the huge rear cargo door, and as the plane began a steep U-turn, they got a panoramic view of the Mexican countryside.

"We're heading back," the pilot announced. "We'll make an emergency landing at the airport. The moment we hit the ground, don't take your gear or anything. Just grab your dogs and run. Get behind the nearest hangar."

They held their breath as the plane hit the runway and finally rolled to a halt. Once outside, they and the dogs raced for shelter. There was no explosion, however, just a three-hour delay in the heat. The truck was unloaded, and all the team's gear was cleaned of gasoline. The inside of the plane had to be scrubbed.

It was night before they landed in Texas.

The Grahams, together with team members from California, stayed aboard the plane for its flight to Travis Air Force Base. Caroline, Linda, and Marian found themselves stranded with their dogs in San Antonio at the Lackland base, where they would have to spend the night.

Walking toward a military bus, they encountered two officers.

"Good evening, ladies. You're just back from Mexico?"

"Yes," Caroline said, "and we want to go home."

"Maybe you'd like to talk about your experiences?"

*Are they shrinks?* she thought.

When they got to a motel within the compound, they were told they could not make or receive calls from their rooms.

"Why not?" Caroline demanded.

It seemed that the State Department had arranged for a special team of psychiatrists to debrief them. (The two officers they had met earlier were, in fact, among the psychiatrists on the base.) The government wanted to learn if the dog handlers were mentally and emotionally stable following their experience in Mexico City. The plan was to hospitalize them—for a week!—to observe their reactions.

"We're not prisoners of war," Caroline argued as she began scheming to escape.

She washed a pair of jeans and a shirt in the bathtub, while Aly slept on the bed. If nothing else presented itself, they would run for the nearest gate and let the U.S. government make its move to stop them.

Fortunately one of the State Department's disaster psychologists was Dr. Jeff Mitchell of the University of Maryland, a pioneer of Critical Incident Stress Debriefing (CISD) in the United States. Dr. Mitchell got on the phone to Washington and argued for their immediate release.

"For one thing, if you put them in a hospital and separate them from their dogs, you *are* going to have crazy people! Number two, they need to get home. And third, they're volunteers—you can't do this to them. They're not guinea pigs!"

They were set free the next day.

Caroline, Linda, and Marian flew to their different destinations on the East Coast. The State Department had made special arrangements with the airlines; this was the first time any U.S. rescue dogs had flown as passengers in the cabin of a commercial plane. Aly wore his rescue vest aboard the flight to Newark, and Caroline settled him on the floor by her feet.

During the flight, Caroline gave him sips of water from a Sierra cup. She had made sure not to feed Aly before takeoff, to ensure his maximum comfort. When friendly crew members tried to give him blueberry yogurt, she begged off: "Thanks, but I think we'd have quite a mess if he tried to eat that."

She had to keep his tail from flopping into the aisle, the better to avoid tripping passengers and crew.

Returning from a trip to the bathroom, she saw that Aly had taken over her seat. He was surveying the scene, so now the whole plane knew he was aboard. Caroline tried to stay calm as Aly posed for a series of amateur photographers. Unperturbed by five minutes of flashing bulbs, he was ready to nap on the floor again.

After transferring at O'Hare in Chicago, she settled in for the final leg of her trip. Seated beside her was an elderly blind woman from Nebraska bound for the Seeing Eye Center in Morristown, New Jersey, to obtain her third guide dog.

"I'd like another German shepherd," she told Caroline after they had chatted for a while.

"I think this one might be too big for you," Caroline said.

The woman reached down and felt Aly's head. "My, my," she chuckled. "No, they wouldn't let me have one *this* large!"


Once home, Caroline was bombarded from all sides with the immediate needs of her family. Andrew had soccer practice, and Joanne was going to a school dance; they both needed rides. The younger ones, Alastair and Heather, were vying for her attention. Alastair could hardly wait to tell her about the horrors of his father's homemade spaghetti sauce. And, of course, Sasquatch was desperate for a hug and some play and a good long walk.

It was impossible for them, Caroline realized, to grasp what she and Aly had just experienced. The children only knew that her absence had disrupted *their* lives. Now that she had returned, their routines could get back on track again.

Caroline sighed. "Okay, everybody, I just need to take care of Aly right now. Let me get a good night's sleep, and then I want you to tell me everything I've missed."

**Caroline Anne Ruthven Gale:** The first of many passport photos.

**Just Married:** Pickles posing with Caroline and Art for wedding shots in California on May 4, 1968.

**Christmas, 1975:** Andrew, Zibo, Joanne and Jaeger.

**Buddies:** Sasquatch and Andrew.

**Schutzhund Training:** Caroline teaching Zibo to bark at the man with the burlap sleeve.

**Rewarding a Find:** Caroline, as "victim," emerges from her hiding place to play with the dog who found her.

**Finding a Victim:** Sasquatch uses his nose to locate the "missing person" during wilderness training. (RAY JONES)

**First Military Flight:** On the way to Mexico City, 1985.

**Mexico City Earthquake:** The collapsed apartment building where relatives of Spanish tenor Placido Domingo died.

**Back Home:** Caroline and Aly in 1985, after returning with the U.S. Disaster Team from the Mexico City earthquake. (STEVE KLAVER)

**El Salvador Quake, 1986:** On the top floor of a government building where Aly finds a woman still alive.

**Death Alert:** At the 1987 L'Ambience Plaza disaster in Bridgeport, CT, Aly alerts on the scent of a dead body and shows his total aversion.

**On the Scent:** Aly during exercises in 1988, before going to the Soviet Union to find survivors of the Armenia earthquake.

**Armenia Quake, 1988:** Caroline and Aly (*front left*) with members of the U.S. Disaster Response Team at base camp.

**Miracle Recovery:** A 13-year-old Armenian girl, buried for six days under quake debris where Aly alerted, is rescued alive.

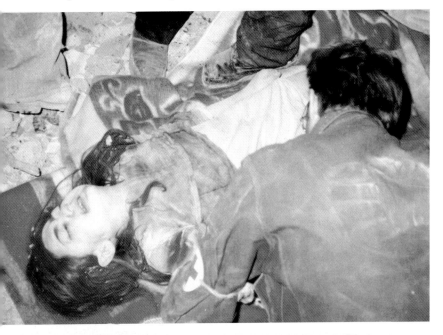

**Agility Practice:** Pascha must walk, sit, stand and turn on a six-inch-wide board that bounces with his weight.

**Disaster Training:** Caroline and Pascha in Indiana for a 1994 session with the Federal Emergency Management Agency (FEMA).

**Water Search:** Pascha on New Jersey's Raritan River, trying to pick up human scent that rises to the surface. (ED PAGLIARINI)

**Making an Alert:** Pascha shows Caroline where his nose has helped him find a drowning victim. (ED PAGLIARINI)

**Edison, N.J., 1994:** Caroline and Pascha with rescue workers where an apartment complex exploded and burned.

**Clearing Work:** Caroline follows Pascha through the Edison rubble, making sure no victims remain.

**Time Out:** Caroline and Pascha with some of their awards from the U.S. and countries around the world.
(Reinhold Spiegler)

Now, more than ever, she was grateful for Art's gentle concern and tact. He could welcome her home without insisting on hearing about Mexico City all at once.

She was in her own bed at last, but the sleep wouldn't come. She went downstairs into the study and sat on the sofa, alone, staring into the dark.

*Is Mom crying?*

A few mornings after Caroline returned, Joanne had come into her parents' bedroom and asked her mother a simple question.

"What was it like in Mexico?"

"Well, it was . . . it was . . ."

Caroline had been unable to go on. Her eyes had filled with tears. Now Joanne sat next to her on the bed, wondering what to do. She had never seen her mother looking so fragile, not ever, and it was scary.

"Whoa, Mom," she nearly whispered. "Are you okay?"

"I'm fine, honey. It's just . . ."

Joanne listened as her mother explained a little bit about the suffering and death she had seen. Joanne found the revelations more than unsettling. What if her mother had been hurt or killed? Caroline had always seemed so calm and in command of her emotions, yet now she was clearly vulnerable.

Aly seemed different, too. If possible, his bond with Caroline had become even stronger. Joanne could see in his eyes, as well as in Caroline's expression, that what they had gone through had changed them.

Caroline did not really know what the effects on herself had been. Not yet, anyway. At home, she offered the family bits and pieces of her experience but emphasized the lighter side, like Mr. Oklahoma and Hatch's traffic directing.

As for the rest, "You had to be there," she would say.

The truth was, she herself was uncomfortable talking too much about Mexico. And she had to guard against snapping at her kids without warning. Alone in the car one day, while playing a tape of Placido Domingo singing in Spanish and English about love, she burst into tears.

"It made me snap," she told Art later, "and at first I didn't even know why."

Images appeared at odd times: the partially excavated corpse of a woman, the face of a bewildered child, the factory sewing room. She heard sounds: people shouting and crying, sirens wailing, machines grinding, walls and ceilings toppling. Other senses came into play as well. She had coughed up cement dust for at least a week, a physical symptom; but when she still tasted it once in a while, was that her imagination? And those unbearable, horrid smells would come back to her as though they too existed here and now.

One small blessing was that if she had nightmares, she forgot them as she awoke.

Caroline started spending seemingly endless hours on the phone with Judy Graham and Linda Wallace. She felt the need to speak with people who had been there, to share memories and talk them over. It was comforting to know she wasn't alone and that her reactions to such an abnormal experience were, in fact, quite normal.

They discussed how, unlike the people of Mexico City, they had volunteered to be there. If the dog handlers were victims in any sense, they had been willing ones. They had gone there for a purpose. But clearly even witnesses to such a terrible disaster could pay a psychological cost.

*Is the world really such a benevolent place? Is it safe? Do I deserve to be alive when others died so randomly? Is it ever possible to control what happens? Is there any fairness? Does my life, after all, have meaning? What is it that I really want to do before I die?*

Statistics were easier: Mexico City had ended up with a total of seven thousand persons dead, thirty thousand injured, and forty thousand who had become permanently homeless. The cost of recovery would be some billions of dollars; the process of repairing and rebuilding would take years. The United States was groping to embrace its neighbor as an ally, although a visceral anti-American sentiment continued to permeate Mexico's official outlook.

"Maybe that's why the White House allowed us to go there with our dogs in the first place," Caroline told officials at a State Department debriefing, "and you people would know that better than we would. Was it a political decision to send us? Because the government wants better relations with Mexico? Well, our pledge to save lives has nothing to do with politics. Our response was an act of goodwill. We are independent volunteers, not political pawns."

And as independent volunteers, Caroline and the others would continue to go wherever they were needed. "So," Art said with a wry smile, after he and Caroline had discussed the possibility of similar missions in the future, "I guess we have a new trend."

"I guess so," she said, adding, "I *hope* so."

It was true. No matter what emotions were swirling around inside her, she wanted that pager to go off; she wanted to find herself on the next plane to the next disaster. She wanted to go back and do it again, do it even better next time. She was ready.

Mexico had given her a powerfully clear picture of how all humanity was linked by its common suffering. *We are not alone,* she thought; *we are not isolated or cut off, no matter how hard we may try to ignore each other's pain. When we watch the news about some tragedy happening to people in some foreign land, the geographical distance does not really separate us. We are part of it all, whether we want to be or not.*

It was also clear to Caroline that people who went into any kind of emergency service, not just search and rescue, could survive over the long haul only if they genuinely cared about others. If they were driven instead by ego, they wouldn't stay with it very long. The tangible rewards would never compensate for the physical and emotional price that was paid. At the same time, someone who was *too* compassionate could become psychologically drained, could burn out and be of no use to themselves, much less anyone else. The alternative was to try to achieve some sort of balance, to be both caring and functional at the same time.

Meanwhile she became busier than ever. She was still running a household and chauffeuring kids around, and going off on local wilderness searches with Aly, but now she was also attending frequent meetings in Washington, D.C., for debriefings and other kinds of government-sponsored sessions. The U.S. Disaster Team Canine Unit had become a factor in international rescue work, and, as one of its founders and leaders, she had taken on a new and larger role. She herself wanted to learn more: about structural safety and hazardous materials, to name two areas that concerned her. Technically she was an unemployed volunteer who never received a dime; but in every other respect she was a professional.

Search-dog units were now springing up all across the United States. When Caroline had begun in 1972 there had been only two groups, one on either coast, but by 1986 their number had passed forty. There were growing demands on her time for public appearances, lectures, training sessions, seminars, media interviews, and the like. The field of canine search and rescue, virtually unknown just a few years before, was taking off. And she was among those at the forefront.

*Chapter 12*

# Mission to El Salvador

"CAROLINE? WOULD YOU BE READY TO GO TO EL Salvador?"

She had just drawn a bubble bath. It was 9:15 P.M. on Friday, October 10, 1986, and Bill Dotson of Dogs-East was calling from his home in Virginia.

"Sure. What's up?"

"Earthquake."

The Central American republic had been jolted around noon by two quakes just fifteen minutes apart, Dotson told her, adding that they had registered 5.4 and 4.5, respectively, on the Richter scale. The tremors had occurred ten miles northwest of the capital city, San Salvador, bringing down government offices, hospitals, schools, and apartment buildings. Thousands were injured, thousands trapped in the wreckage.

Dotson explained that the U.S. State Department, through its Office of Foreign Disaster Assistance, was requesting an advance team of four handlers and their dogs to respond at Andrews Air Force Base in Maryland. "We have a C-141 flight at five in the morning," he said, "so we're getting in fast this time." And this time they'd be working closely with five extrication experts from the special operations division of Metro-Dade Fire Rescue near Miami, Florida, who were being dispatched to El Salvador on a separate flight.

*Five o'clock*, Caroline thought. *Plenty of time . . .*

She lowered herself into the bubble bath, but the phone rang again. She heard Art answer it downstairs.

"Caroline? For you."

Walter "Bob" Kessecker at the State Department was on the line, speaking in his unmistakably abrupt manner. She had met him at some of the Washington briefings—a balding man with glasses who had handled logistics for the military before joining State. It was not Kessecker's role to go on a mission; rather, he would calculate the equipment needed, how many people with dogs could fit on a plane, what weight the aircraft could take. She thought of him as a tough military career guy with a brain for details and a heart of gold.

"We need your passport number," he was saying, "and listen, there's a glitch."

"Glitch?"

"You have to be at Andrews by two A.M."

"*Two* o'clock? That's just four hours!"

"Can you make it?"

"I'll be there."

If she drove fast, she could just make it. She called the local service station in Bernardsville: "If I'm down there in forty-five minutes, could you give me a full tank?"

"I'm closing now, but I'll come back and meet you."

Too much to do, too little time. She had to cancel upcoming appointments and organize rides for the kids. She raced through the house while Art, speechless, watched the chaos. Joanne was throwing a fit of teenage hysteria over the prospect of being stranded without either a driver's license or her mother to shuttle her to and from various places over the weekend.

The search-and-rescue closet on the second floor contained backpacks and duffel bags with clothes and gear for every climate and situation. El Salvador would be warm, so there was no need for bulky winter stuff. She thought ahead: *Dog food, dry and moist, with instant oatmeal, vitamins, supplements, and snacks . . . passport, VHS radio,*

*special European pills for diarrhea . . . T-shirts, lightweight stuff . . .
and what else, what else?*

Aly barked and paced around the kitchen below.

She would bring the same diet for him as she had done in Mexico.
He would drink at least two gallons of water a day in the tropics. She
would not let Aly drink any water that she herself would not drink. She
would bring her own water filter this time, so she could be self-sufficient in terms of safe drinking water for them both.

Caroline loaded Aly and her gear into the Suburban, along with a
thermos of coffee. The owner of the local service station had returned,
as promised, and soon she was on the New Jersey Turnpike for the
drive south to Maryland.

*What have I forgotten? My tetanus and yellow fever shots are proba-
bly still good, and the passport's in my pocket. . . . Will I make this
deadline? Got a long way to go. Ah, to hell with the speed limit . . .*

She activated the blue light and gunned it. Her speedometer rose
toward ninety, and she gained on the trucks ahead, calling on the CB:
"Move over, please! This is an emergency vehicle!" The truckers responded and she flew past. The adrenaline junkie in her took over for
the nighttime ride.


Caroline drove through the Andrews gate at 1:15 A.M. and pulled
up outside a hangar. The C-141 Air Force transport plane was there,
but no cars or people. She got out with Aly, wondering if she had
come to the wrong place, and finally Bill Dotson showed up. She had
gotten there first, although she lived the farthest distance away.

Bill was going without a dog as an extra team leader and observer
in the field. Caroline knew him as sort of a "good old Southern boy"
whom she had met at NASAR gatherings. In the seventies he had
actually put his dog through the Swiss search-and-rescue training, and
she had enjoyed talking with him about all aspects of the field. They
had spoken frequently on the phone, sharing their similar philosophies
and trading new discoveries.

The three other team members soon arrived from Maryland and
Virginia. Caroline knew each of them from previous conferences, but
they had never worked together.

Beth Barkley, about Caroline's age and also blond, had been a professional singer. She was outspoken and took no nonsense from anyone. Her spayed female dog, Panda, was a large white German shepherd with a pinkish nose. Beth had trained her with commands in Spanish.

Next came Heide Yamaguchi, a Japanese American whose neutered male dog, Shiro, was a small white mixed breed trained, naturally enough, in Japanese. Heide was an efficient worker with lots of stamina, a solid team player.

Phil Audibert of Virginia rounded out the team with his big but gentle golden retriever, Matt, an intact male trained with English-language commands. Caroline knew Phil as a Southern gentleman who was highly educated, with a degree in political science from George Washington University—an intelligent, introspective, sensitive man who had developed great rapport with his dog.

Coming along with Bill Dotson to assist was Dr. Jeff Mitchell of the University of Maryland, the expert on critical-incident stress, who had saved Caroline and Linda Wallace from being held for observation in San Antonio. She had attended his debriefings in Washington after Mexico City. This time the State Department had assigned Jeff to act as a disaster psychologist for the El Salvador mission. Tall, with brownish curly hair and a boyish expression, he carried a camera around his neck and, like a tourist, expressed wide-eyed enthusiasm for making his first visit to Latin America.

Strike team members watched their gear being loaded onto wheeled pallets and slid through the rear door of the giant military transport plane. They boarded with an assortment of State Department engineers and experts in satellite communications. Boxed meals from McDonald's were handed out as the C-141 took off before dawn.

They tried to stretch out and sleep, but most were too excited. Caroline was the only one who had been on the Mexico City mission, so she tried to give the others an idea of what to expect. Again, she had to yell above the noise and communicate by pantomime.

A State Department official briefed them on the political situation: El Salvador was filled with poverty and long-running civil strife; there was widespread hostility against President José Napoleón Duarte and his army; and because Duarte was being supported by the Reagan administration, there was considerable anger being directed at the United States.

"The leftist guerrillas have been fighting the government for six years," the official said, "so the situation is very unstable. They've called a truce during the earthquake crisis, but don't count on it."

They landed outside San Salvador at the Ilopango military air force base at 8:00 A.M. Central American time, less than twenty hours after the quakes had hit. The team members were unaware that the base was also a center of operations for the U.S. Central Intelligence Agency. It was a crucial relay station for supplies in the CIA's clandestine support of *contra* rebel forces trying to overthrow the leftist regime in Nicaragua. The State Department was sending disaster assistance to El Salvador as a gesture of American solidarity with Duarte and to show gratitude to him for letting the CIA use his air base.

The passengers could not see outside, so Jeff Mitchell eagerly jumped up to be first out the door with his camera. He lifted his lens as the rear door opened. And then he froze.

"Ohhhh," Jeff said, gazing outside the plane. His eyes bulged as he turned back to the others. "There are guns everywhere, as far as you can see. And they're all pointed at us! I nearly took a picture of a guy shooting me! He waved his gun for me to put down the camera. . . ."

Caroline remembered how, as a child in Venezuela, she had accompanied her father to his office at the British Embassy in Caracas. It was an old building and the ceilings leaked, so during the rainy season he would sit at his desk holding an umbrella. And there seemed to be constant attempted revolutions, with opposing forces shooting at each other outside the embassy in the public square. Caroline's father would go to the window and fire his gun in the air. The soldiers and rebels below stopped shooting.

"Please quiet down!" he'd yell. "I have an important call to make, and I need to conduct it in peace! Give me five minutes! Please!"

"Hey, Jeff," she called out now, "welcome to Latin America!"

Team members and their dogs went out one by one and climbed down to the runway. Caroline felt the familiar humid heat of the tropics, and sure enough, armed Salvadoran soldiers stood twenty feet apart in a long line. She and Aly walked past the M-16s and Uzis until they were greeted by members of the U.S. Embassy and the Office of Foreign Disaster Assistance.

"Is this a war zone?" she quipped.

Young men with machine guns followed the handlers as they took the dogs to relieve themselves. They made bathroom trips for themselves as well, with the soldiers accompanying them at gunpoint to the rest room doors.

Then they were led to a pair of U.S. Embassy vans, with motors running. The vans were armor-plated. Even their thick windows were bullet-proof. *Not*, Caroline thought, *the mode of transportation we might have expected.*

"Leave your gear with us," they were told. "We'll take it in the first van and put it where you're staying. Right now we want you in the field."


Hundreds of families with children occupied the roadsides. They had slept overnight in huts fashioned from blankets, pieces of cardboard, and plastic trash bags to shield them from sudden torrential downpours. Many had built small fires to cook whatever food they had brought with them. Embassy officials said that some 200,000 *capitalinos*, or residents of San Salvador, were homeless. Outlying villages had been damaged as well. Thousands of homes in the city had been partially or completely shattered. Some of the neighborhoods most severely affected were also among the poorest. Conditions there had been miserable enough before the disaster, but now people were desperate for water, food, and medicine. The van passed citizens weeping and scrounging among the remains of their stucco homes.

The quakes had been much less powerful than the ones in Mexico City and also far less devastating. Structures in San Salvador were not so high and not as many were involved. Destruction in the downtown area was concentrated within about twenty blocks, where office buildings and hotels sat like crushed sandwiches, tilting over and resting at crazy angles. The Ministry of Planning offices were shattered. The Presidential Palace was badly damaged. Parts of the U.S. Embassy were in shambles.

More than a thousand persons had died, and ten thousand others were injured. An unknown number of victims were still missing.

Many terrified people had managed to escape in the minutes between the first and second large tremors. But most of the major hospitals had been destroyed or evacuated, so medical teams were providing emergency services and performing operations in hastily erected outdoor clinics. The square beside the damaged Social Security Hospital was filled with patients on cots inside makeshift tents. Those who were not injured waited in line for rations of water and food.

The handlers and dogs arrived at the ruins of the Rubén Darío complex of government and commercial offices, stores, restaurants, banks, a movie theater, and a clinic. Thousands had been working or shopping when the first earthquake hit. Many people had fled amid the horror and chaos, but up to 1,200 were buried either dead or alive.

One five-story office building had lost its top three floors, which had pancaked downward. Next door was another office building, totally unstable, leaning way over. A third collapsed structure was still burning, with acrid smoke billowing from its wreckage. On the corner was a bank with its windows blown out. All the sites were being heavily guarded by Salvadoran soldiers.

Leading the rescue teams that worked at a frantic pace was the Metro-Dade squad of five men, who were coordinating their efforts with Salvadoran locals, Guatemalan firefighters, and Mexican miners. The Florida men, wearing their blue Fire Rescue uniforms with patches, were led by a big, rough guy named Doug Jewett, whose face conveyed the fierce determination of a bulldog. He paused to greet the dog team and go over the priorities.

Caroline was impressed with the Metro-Dade firemen, who were all fluent in Spanish and seemed to combine the attitude of streetwise Miami with a Latin temperament. They worked tirelessly and professionally, joking and swearing, without any kind of attitude. It was their style, she saw, to get down to the nitty-gritty and work with the locals, involving them in the rescue efforts by letting them work with the tools and even training them on-site.

Doug Jewett had also been in Mexico City, Caroline learned, but she had never seen him because the U.S. team had not combined its search and rescue components. But she knew about the Metro-Dade team and had heard some good stories about them. During a tricky extrication at the Mexico City disaster, Jewett called on his radio for a special tool and was told he would have to wait for visiting Nancy Reagan to pass in her motorcade. "I don't give a damn if she passes through!" Jewett roared. "I need that tool now!" What he did not know was that his radio was on the same frequency as that of the First Lady and her Secret Service agents.

Caroline saw that Aly, having gone through the Mexico experience, seemed right at home, as if saying to himself, *Oh, I see, it's this kind of rubble again. Okay, let's go!*

They began on the burning side of Rubén Darío, where Aly stayed on the edges to avoid scorching his feet. He was still able to pick up scent through the smoke and pinpoint the location of human remains in debris that was still smoldering—which, for Caroline, reconfirmed the usefulness of search dogs at scenes of fires, plane wrecks, and explosions. She had taken Aly through a German-style test during which smoke had billowed over the track from strategically placed pots. The dog's nose had worked just fine, as it did in the smoke right now.

The handlers moved from site to site within the complex, all four dogs making live finds while identifying the location of dead victims. They used the same check-and-recheck system first employed in Mexico City: one dog alerted, the next confirmed the alert. And the handlers used surveyor's tape with the same code to mark the spots where victims were definitely alive, possibly alive, and definitely dead.

Soldiers carrying machines guns accompanied the Americans wherever they went. "You are not to pick up any papers!" one shouted at Caroline inside a collapsed Salvadoran government office, where documents were scattered around. "You are not to look at anything!"

Most of the young men were actually boys, some no older than twelve, recently recruited from the countryside to help protect the government against guerrillas. Swaggering with bravado, they swung their guns as if they were toys, no safeties on. They were also edgy and trigger-happy. Some soldiers even began shooting at random when the earth started to rumble from unexpected aftershocks. Caroline and the other searchers tried not to transmit their own fears to the dogs, who had been taught to ignore sudden loud noises.

The four American handlers left the Rubén Darío complex that afternoon as two separate teams. Caroline and Beth followed Aly and Panda into the Casa Presidencial office building and climbed over debris toward its roof. The dogs showed increasing interest.

"Over here," Caroline said.

Aly was alerting toward the center, excitedly pawing and scratching downward. Panda did the same from a side angle.

They marked the location with three strips of tape and made their way back down to find the Salvadoran government engineers.

"It's our feeling that people are alive in there," Caroline said, making sure they understood the urgency.

She and Beth moved on.

They spoke to the manager of the badly damaged Gran Hotel San Salvador, the American owner of which was still missing. He had gone into his office to make a telephone call just before the quake hit. He might have been trapped as he sat behind his desk.

The hotel's upper floors were reasonably intact, but the entire building was tilting at a forty-degree angle. The owner and others feared missing would be down in the lower level, where the front lobby had been. That section had been utterly crushed, so the second floor was now almost at the level of the ground.

Caroline and Aly climbed inside with Beth and Panda as Jeff Mitchell followed them. They worked their way upward in semidarkness. Workers with heavy equipment out front were trying to move concrete slabs with a bulldozer that made the rear section sway with every jolt. Caroline looked at Jeff, who had turned pale.

"I'm getting seasick," he said.

"Me too, but I'd like to get over to the elevator shaft."

"Really? Why?"

"That would be the best scent source, because it funnels everything."

"Caroline, we're rocking. . . ."

But she continued toward the shaft, where Aly suddenly cringed. Beth came over with Panda, who also backed away.

"Someone's down there," Caroline said, "but not alive."

The swaying continued as they worked their way toward the front again. They climbed out a second-floor window to the relative safety of a debris pile.

Live victims at Rubén Darío were still being evacuated in the early evening. Caroline and the others followed their dogs through newly opened shafts or tunnels, reconfirming their original live finds and pinpointing the likely location of each survivor more exactly. They had to quit searching because of a curfew the government had imposed throughout San Salvador, but the actual rescue efforts would be allowed to continue through the night. The Miami Metro-Dade crew had brought out thirty-two persons alive so far.

The handlers—exhausted, filthy, hungry, and triumphant—were taken to the Hotel Presidente, a five-star operation, which had a policy of not permitting dogs. "We're not staying here unless they're with us," Caroline said.

An embassy official negotiated with the manager, who finally relented. "If you go out to walk the dogs," he said, "take them into the rear garden. Don't go out the front of the hotel. It's too dangerous. You'll be either kidnapped or shot."

Caroline was grateful that the hotel still had running water. She bathed and fed Aly, and then showered, changed, and went back down to join the others for dinner. The hotel's luxurious atmosphere was in utter contrast to the disaster scenes outside, where life-or-death events were still unfolding. Reporters from around the world obeyed an unspoken rule that the hotel was home base, where no interviews were conducted.

Aly seemed to be feeling fine after she returned from dinner, maybe because of his success that day. Caroline took him downstairs, then through a back door and outside to relieve himself in a garden near the swimming pool. She noticed that the surrounding wall had barbed wire on top.

"*Aly, mach dein Poop-Poops,*" she said.

Caroline spent two hours in the room purifying water for her and her dog to drink the following day, pumping it into an old thermos jug that held five gallons. They would need all of it.

When she was finally dozing off at three in the morning, a loud noise awakened her. She assumed it was an aftershock, but then a bright spotlight swung past the window and she saw a low-flying military helicopter.

"It's okay, Aly. Back to sleep . . ."


Among the earthquake stories in the morning paper was one about a large Catholic school that had been totally destroyed. Students from kindergarten to eighth grade, which was about the highest level most children in El Salvador achieved before leaving school, had been in classrooms or eating lunch in the cafeteria. Hundreds had died and many others were still unaccounted for, but no dog teams had been directed to the site. The thought that some children might be trapped alive made Caroline's blood race.

"We need to go to this school," she told an embassy staffer at the hotel. "These are children!"

"There *is* no school."

Anger rose in her throat. "Look, I'm not stupid. I read Spanish, and it's right here in the paper!"

The school was operated by nuns and lay teachers, who had also been trapped. Heart-rending photographs showed parents screaming over their children's bodies, which had been lined up on the pavement outside the wreckage. There had to be hundreds more victims inside.

"It's in a district that's not friendly to Duarte."

"And *that's* why we're not trying to save those children? Are you serious?" *Welcome,* she thought, *to the politics of search and rescue.*

The Duarte government had been determining where the Americans could search, the embassy staffer told her.

"So far," Caroline said, "our efforts have been restricted to the business center. It's been all government-type, upper-class people, the establishment. What about the outlying areas that were affected? What about the other neighborhoods where people surely need our help? Why aren't we allowed to go to any of the surrounding villages? To the poorer suburbs?"

"Security reasons."

Fresh anger had risen against the Duarte government because of the army's aloof behavior during the crisis. Few if any of its fifty thousand soldiers had been sent to assist rescue efforts. They had not dug through rubble or helped extricate victims. Many had simply leaned on their rifles and looked on.

Such an uncaring attitude, on top of the disaster itself, could only raise the level of hostility toward those who ruled a country of impoverished slums. Half of El Salvador's population was out of work or marginally employed. The leftist guerrillas could count on fresh recruits for their tireless campaign of hit-and-run war against the government.

"The school is off-limits," the embassy staffer said, "but we'll find out what happened there and let you know."

"Please," Caroline said.

"It's an international ant heap," someone at the Rubén Darío site remarked. In Mexico City, there had been so many areas to cover that the rescue teams had spread out across the city. Here, they seemed to be fighting for space on the same pile of rubble.

Members of the Swiss team, arriving on the second morning, made their entrance still drinking beer from the plane. Except for two women they were macho males, swaggering with arrogance because of their stature as the most experienced search-and-rescue unit in the world. For many years the Swiss had been pretty much the only game in town, so to speak. Supported by their government, they regarded themselves as professionals, not mere volunteers, and clearly it was difficult for them to accept any other foreign team as an equal. They reminded Caroline of the boys at the Swiss Embassy in Turkey who had enjoyed beating her up on the soccer field when she was a girl. Perhaps they had grown up to come here and taunt her again.

One of the Swiss females was a brawny young woman who looked as though she worked on a farm and was used to carrying big bales of hay. She climbed onto the rubble, threw her German shepherd over both shoulders, and marched into a shaft cut through the debris. The Americans promptly nicknamed her Brunhild after the character from Wagner's opera.

Then came the French. The Italians showed up. So did the British. And a dog unit from Belgium appeared. The result was far more canine power than was needed to search the few downtown areas designated by the Government.

"An international traffic jam," someone else remarked.

"What are *you* doing up here?" a Swiss dog handler shouted at Caroline as she followed Aly across the rubble. "You don't know what you're doing! Get off! I am now going to search!"

Caroline glared at him.

"Look at these stupid American women," the Swiss guy said to his partner in German, not realizing that Caroline could understand him. "Their dogs probably don't know water from piss!"

She buttonholed the leader of the Swiss team after climbing back down. "Excuse me," she told him in idiomatic German, "but you have a man up there who needs his mouth sewn together!"

The American dog handlers and the Metro-Dade crew continued to coordinate smoothly with the Mexican rescue workers, whose rugged, down-to-earth *topos*, or miners, would stop at nothing to help save lives. Caroline knew some of these "tunnel rats" from having worked with them in their own country the year before.

Otherwise the mass confusion among national teams grew wilder, and tempers flared as members argued over whose dogs were better-trained and which rescue methods were more effective. The turf war escalated when the Swiss declared they were the "elite" unit and demanded that Salvadoran officials remove the Americans from the Rubén Darío site. Doug Jewett and his Metro-Dade workers furiously declared they would "personally and physically" toss the Swiss off instead. When Doug got mad, he got mad.

"This should not be happening," an observer declared with understatement.

The Swiss weren't the only ones acting hostile. Caroline asked the Italians if the Florida rescuers could borrow an acetylene torch, but their team leader gave her the finger along with a stream of Italian obscenity. Caroline retorted with some gutter Italian that made his mouth fly open.

The Americans and British, on good terms, found space on the garbage-strewn pavement to sit together eating sandwiches of white bread and bologna provided by their embassies. Crowds of citizens looked on. Many of the children, who seemed to be orphans or street urchins, were so obviously hungry that Caroline and the others could not bear to eat in front of them. They wound up giving away their food.

They were still resting on the sidewalk when a shiny black car from the Japanese Embassy pulled up next to them. Japan had just started to get into search-and-rescue work, so it had sent five observers to El Salvador strictly to study the work of others and take notes. The observers came over to greet their embassy's shiny car, from which emerged a Japanese hostess wearing a kimono. She set up a table with chairs on the dusty sidewalk, in front of the starving Salvadoran children. She covered the table with a white cloth and brought out china plates, bowls, glasses, and napkins, creating five place settings. The Japanese observers accepted hot towels with formal bows, then took seats to be served a traditional six-course meal of exquisite Japanese food with green tea.

The Americans and the British stared in wonder. The hungry Salvadoran children watched, salivating. Rescue workers continued to drag bodies from the wreckage nearby; dirt and the stench of death filled the air. The Japanese team members, oblivious to it all, lifted their chopsticks and ate with gusto.

# Chapter 13

# Street-level Politics

ALL FOUR OF THE AMERICANS WENT BACK TO THE Gran Hotel early the next morning. New tunnels and shafts had been opened into the building. Heide and Phil worked their dogs near the swaying rear of the hotel, while Caroline and Beth discussed how to get beneath the crushed front lobby. Beth and Panda went in first, through a shaft leading to a steep eight-foot drop into the basement area. Four Mexican miners lowered Panda to the bottom. Beth crawled behind her dog through narrow spaces to the boiler room, where Panda reacted upward. The animal lowered her tail and backed away as Beth followed with a light, unable to see much in the blackness. But her dog had indicated that at least one dead body was above them on the first floor.

The miners lifted Panda back up the steep shaft, and Beth followed.

Caroline started toward the basement to see if Aly would confirm Panda's alert. She used her hands and feet to brace herself as she climbed down the eight-foot shaft, while a Mexican miner below reached up and caught her. She didn't want Aly jumping down and injuring himself, and so Phil and the miners lowered Caroline's heavy German shepherd from hand to hand. She might have allowed Aly to jump down if she had done so, but she would not let him try any feat that she herself did not perform.

The miners joined her in the dark boiler room, which was filled with water heaters, air-conditioning machinery, and large pipes. The lobby and first-floor offices were above. As Panda had done, Aly whimpered and backed away. Caroline looked up, shining her flashlight, and saw fresh blood dripping from the ceiling.

Then she realized Aly was pacing around as if wanting to leave, and she knew he sensed the coming of an aftershock. The steep shaft would hardly be safe, so she aimed her light around to find another exit.

Before she could see any alternative, the tremor arrived. The ground shook, and it seemed that the hotel might fall into the basement on top of them.

*Oh, shit, here we go . . .*

She crouched next to a wall with Aly and the miners until it was over. The new dust in the darkness made it even more difficult to see. Caroline focused her light and realized that the shaft had collapsed. Their escape route was blocked.

She used her radio to reach the others outside, concealing the urgency she felt.

"Hey, guys, we're still down here, but we can't get back out. I can't even see. We may have to get the Metro-Dade guys or somebody to pull us out of here. Otherwise we're fine."

She bent down to find Aly, but he was gone.

"Where's my dog?" she whispered to the miners. They didn't know.

She saw that part of the ceiling—the spot from which blood had been dripping earlier—had come crashing down. Was Aly under a new pile of debris? The panic went through her like a shock wave.

*"My dog! Where's my dog?"*

She and the miners slowly waved their lights around.

"Aly? Aly? *Hier, Aly!* Aly!"

Silence.

Minutes went by. She knew that dogs could see better than people in the dark, and that their hearing was far more acute, so maybe he was using those senses—in addition to his incredibly accurate nose—to make his own way out. But then, at last, she heard him returning.

"Aly?"

His face appeared in the beam of her flashlight. She saw that his wide-eyed expression was eerily human. He barked at her as if to say, *Come with me!*

"He's trying to tell me something," she told the miners. Then she addressed the dog directly. "What have you got? Show me."

Aly started off. Caroline followed, the Mexican miners trailing. The dog moved around and over rubble, then into a tunnel. She crawled behind him in the blackness. They continued at an upward angle for several minutes. Then, up ahead, she began to see daylight.

It was a hotel room. She got to the window and realized that Aly must have taken her to the other side of the building and up to the second floor, which had dropped to just three or four feet from the ground. She stepped onto the balcony and called to the workers outside.

"We're over here!"

She and Aly jumped down and climbed over rubble to solid ground, where she sat and put her hand against him. Then the gravity of what had just happened to them hit her, and she started to shake.

"Thank you," she whispered. Her eyes filled with tears. "Thank you."

Aly wagged his tail, then sat beside her. She put both arms around his neck and hugged him to her. He turned and licked her face.

Members of the Swiss team at the central downtown site were increasingly disturbing the coordinated rescue efforts by dog teams, engineers, miners, medical personnel, excavation workers, and local diggers. They moved some rubble without warning at one point, causing a debris slide that pinned a Guatemalan worker's leg and trapped some Mexican miners.

Finally the site coordinators walked off in frustration and disgust. The Americans and all the teams from other nations followed. The Swiss, taking over, worked their dogs in a few shafts, but then started training some inexperienced members of their team in the use of various rescue tools.

"And meanwhile," Beth cried out, "victims are dying in the rubble!"

The Swiss dogs added insult to injury by lunging at people, so they had to be tied to fences when they weren't searching.

The French, exasperated, packed up and left for home.

The Americans went to the partially destroyed U.S. Embassy to meet with State Department officials on how to deal with the Swiss and restore a semblance of harmony to the rescue effort. The rescuers' armored van was given a thorough going-over at the gate by bomb detectors, while the handlers themselves were subjected to body searches.

"We're Americans!" someone shouted. "We're down here to help! Why do you have to put us through that?"

The answer was that some U.S. marines had been killed in a San Salvador restaurant a few days before, so American military personnel were extremely hesitant to trust anyone.

Caroline used the embassy meeting to bring up the topic of the school that had been destroyed. The U.S. officials finally admitted its existence: "Well, there *was* a school, but it's been razed to the ground."

The handlers were silent.

"Show it to us," Caroline said at last.

Salvadoran soldiers accompanied the American team to a poor neighborhood, where they saw that the school had indeed been bulldozed. It had been four stories high, but there was nothing left in the flattened area any longer except for a few walls at the edge of a cement foundation. To the side were some piles of rubble, but most of the debris had been carted away. Still standing intact was a statue of the Virgin Mary.

Caroline and the others could not speak. She was sure that the dogs could have made a difference. It seemed all too clear that the internal politics of El Salvador had caused some of those children to die needlessly. How many could have been saved? How many had still been alive when the building was razed?

The bulldozers had left no evidence.

Caroline was interviewed on the street by a Salvadoran television crew, causing the U.S. Embassy to decide that she and her colleagues from the States had become prime targets for antigovernment guerrillas. Salvadoran soldiers henceforth would act as personal bodyguards wherever the Americans went.

"How do you tell the good guys from the bad guys?" Caroline asked her protector, a young soldier with an Uzi.

"The bad guys wear sneakers."

"Oh. I see . . ."

She watched as Jeff Mitchell's bodyguard went with him when he walked over to a crumbled building and aimed his camera. The soldier promptly pushed the muzzle of his machine gun into the side of Jeff's neck. Then came the loud click of the safety being removed. Caroline rushed over, yelling in Spanish, until the soldier moved his gun away. The color slowly returned to Jeff's face.


The crowds were becoming ugly.

People were desperate over the fate of their loved ones and wanted positive results from the searchers, nothing less. Their anger was rapidly growing. They watched sullenly as rescuers dug through wreckage. Caroline had noticed that many people in El Salvador, of Indian descent, had a way of remaining unexpressive—stone-faced, you could say—when confronted with trauma. But now some actually booed and hissed when a team emerged empty-handed.

Caroline, thinking of the children who had died at the school, demanded to be allowed to visit other locations.

"There's a covered market that apparently collapsed, and maybe you should go there," a U.S. Embassy staffer named Sean said, "but it's in a very poor district, a slum area, and it might be dangerous. A lot of drugs and prostitution. The residents hate Duarte, and they're anti-American. If you insist on going, I'd better come with you."

He strapped two small guns to his legs and lifted his machine gun. Caroline and Aly followed him aboard the armored van as Bill Dotson joined them with Phil Audibert and his dog, Matt. A Salvadoran soldier came as well.

They rode through sections that seemed successively poorer.

Thousands of refugees had streamed out of the capital in recent years, fleeing unemployment and civil war, into dozens of surrounding neighborhoods. Caroline had heard about one crowded area called Comunidad Modelo, which was tucked along the edges of a canyon. The quakes had caused part of a mountainside to crash down on the community, leaving several dead and hundreds homeless, but no soldiers from the nearby Salvadoran army base had come to assist.

Most of the poor neighborhoods and villages had no leverage with which to get basic services from the government. The people were angry at Duarte for doing nothing to help them, but most were hesitant to express their opinions publicly. Others had been punished or killed for speaking out in the past. But many more would wind up favoring the rebels if the government kept ignoring them.

The van rolled to a halt, and Sean told the Salvadoran soldier to stay there so it wouldn't be stripped in seconds. Sean also handed one of his guns to Bill as the group hiked through garbage-strewn alleys to the *mercado*—a large enclosed market where a series of food stalls had collapsed. Possibly some customers or vendors had been trapped in there. The stench of meat and vegetation rotting in the tropical heat was overpowering.

Sean turned to Caroline. "I want you and Phil to wait out here with the dogs."

He and Bill carried their weapons into the market. Caroline stood there as a crowd began to gather. People were coming from everywhere. They moved closer and closer. Their faces were grim and even hostile.

Caroline kept Aly on-leash. He seemed tuned in to her growing uneasiness, glancing up at her with a certain look in his eyes that she knew meant his patience was running out. He was going into what she called his "protective mode," probably because she was transmitting her own fears to him. He stood there with his muscles growing increasingly tense, ears cocked forward, as the angry crowd seemed about to become a mob.

"What should we do?" Phil whispered.

"I don't know," Caroline said under her breath, "but I'm going to do something—and fast."

She faced the mass of unfriendly faces. People were staring coldly at the small American flag on her shirt. Several stray, hungry dogs circled as if they wanted to take on Aly, who was trying his best to stay calm. It seemed that only his presence was making them stay back. His eyes darted around and he watched every movement. But the crowd continued to move in around Caroline and Phil.

Caroline glanced at a small boy in front and stooped so her face was at his level. She had to hurry but avoid making any threatening move. Reaching out and smiling, she gently took the boy's hand. He hesitated.

"Come meet my dog," she said in Spanish, and finally he stepped closer. "This is Aly."

The others watched as the boy petted him. Aly nuzzled against the youngster's face. Caroline raised herself and spoke loud enough for people in at least the first several tiers to hear her.

"I was born in Chile. I'm a *Latina*. I'm with an international rescue team, and we're here to help. Are there any people missing that you know of? Because if there are, then we will search for them."

She kept on talking, her facial muscles beginning to ache from the tension. She could feel the sweat running down her back.

"I know what it's like, because I'm a mother myself. I know how terrible it must be to lose people. What can we do to help?"

A man spoke up. "What do they pay you?"

"Nothing."

"You must make money from this, no?"

"No. We're volunteers."

"You mean you're not paid?"

"That's right."

"How can you leave your husband and children to do this work?"

"Because," Caroline said, "we care about other people."

They were silent, eyes searching, as if trying to absorb the possibility that someone had come all that way to help them for no ulterior reason. These people, so desperately poor even before the earthquake, had lost what little they had possessed; and, Caroline thought, any U.S. financial aid to the Duarte government and the Salvadoran army could mean nothing to them. But this personal contact with an American citizen on their turf was different.

A middle-aged woman in the crowd stepped forward. "We know there are some dead," she said flatly. The others nodded, apparently regarding her as a local leader. "Their bodies are underneath a wall that collapsed. They need to be removed."

"We'll make sure to get that word back," Caroline said.

"We need water. We have no good drinking water. Everyone is going to get sick."

Caroline knew that people in slums like this one did not have running water from pipes in the first place. Usually the women trudged up hills with big jars on their heads to fetch water pumped from wells.

"Your pumps were knocked out?"

"Yes. And with the flash floods, our gullies, where people wash their clothes, have become polluted. But people are starting to use that water for drinking."

"I'll get that information back to the authorities."

"The officials won't listen. They don't care about us."

"Perhaps, through our embassy and the international groups here, we can see that something is done. We'll try."

Bill and Sean emerged from the collapsed market. They were covering their mouths and gagging. Sean curled his finger around the trigger of his machine gun as he approached the crowd, but Caroline gestured for him to put the weapon away.

"It's okay, Sean. Just back off. I'm handling it."

"So far as we can tell," Bill said, "there are no victims in the market."

"Let's go," Sean said, watching the crowd. "We're getting out of here."


The armored van stopped at a park overlooking a mud slide caused by the quake. Caroline walked among the trees and bushes and realized that here, at last, was a chance to go to the bathroom in peace. There had never been any privacy downtown, especially for a female, so team members would stand around her holding up a blanket. Here was an opportunity to be alone.

"I'll be there in a minute!" she called to the others. "I'm just going into these bushes!"

She ducked behind the foliage and unzipped her jump suit, which was actually a military surplus outfit with multiple pockets, while Aly stood guard.

Then, without warning, he bolted from the bushes. Caroline glanced around, but could no longer see him. He would have taken off like that only if there had been some emergency.

*Oh, my God*, she thought, struggling to get back into the jumpsuit. She had its sleeves on, but now the zipper was stuck. She pulled and pulled, but it wouldn't move. She raced from the bushes, still tugging at the zipper, then stopped and held her breath. Aly was growling at four Salvadoran soldiers, who were focusing on him through their gun sights. They held their fingers tensely against the triggers.

"Don't shoot!" Caroline yelled in Spanish.

The four guns were aimed at Aly's head.

"*Perro de rescate!* This is a rescue dog!"

Slowly the guns came down.


Representatives from each national team were summoned to the prime minister's office. The Salvadoran government promised that the Swiss, who did not attend, would be expelled from the country if their inappropriate procedures and failure to cooperate with other teams continued. President Duarte went to Rubén Darío and personally returned control of its search to the Metro-Dade crew. Aftershocks had caused the top floor to slip and crash over the edges of the building, making it tougher to get through shafts leading into the wreckage, so heavy equipment was brought in to help with the delicate removal of concrete slabs.

The exhausted Miami men had accepted lemonade from a street vendor, so now some of them had the runs. Luckily Caroline had brought her European diarrhea pills, which she began dispensing to help them recover.

A newly coordinated rescue effort was launched. Caroline translated as workers from the different countries started to exchange ideas and training tips. The Americans worked in tandem with the British and even the Swiss, who had begun to cooperate. One of their dogs would go in and come back out, then a U.S. dog would repeat the search in the same place.

A Swiss handler even complimented Aly. "Nice dog," he said, and Caroline did a double take.

Many of the European dogs, to Caroline's surprise, had been trained to give "bark alerts" when finding the scent of live or dead victims alike. She explained that U.S. dogs were not trained to alert in any special way; rather, they were allowed to exhibit spontaneous changes in their body language and excitement level, leaving it to the handlers to interpret this natural communication.

"Fascinating," the Swiss handler said. "So how *did* your dog alert in that tunnel?"

"Well, he expressed revulsion—"

"Yes, yes! Mine had the same reaction!"

"—and so I knew he was alerting on death."

"Ah! I see!"

Caroline and her teammates decided that evening to ignore the Duarte government's curfew and keep working all through the night. It was their fifth day in El Salvador and, the U.S. dog handlers agreed, they were down to one chance for a final push before all hope of finding more people alive was gone. She volunteered at 10:00 P.M. to return to the Hotel Presidente and pick up food and coffee, while the rest of her team continued to work with their dogs on the site to confirm and reconfirm each alert. She and Aly, with two bodyguards, went by van for twenty minutes in darkness through San Salvador's eerily deserted streets. Not a car, not a soul, was in sight. The bodyguards, guns ready, were visibly nervous.

"Why is no one out?" she asked.

"The curfew."

"I know. But people aren't even outside their own doors."

"No one goes out after dark," the guard explained. "That's when you get killed."

A couple of hours later, back at the search site, Caroline lay down on the pavement, making a little space for herself amid the dirt and glass. Jackhammers were blasting new tunnels into the wreckage as she rested her head on Aly. She closed her eyes despite the shouting of workers and noise from heavy equipment and generators. Caroline and her dog, ignoring the searchlights and swirling cement dust, both fell asleep until a touch on the shoulder told her it was time to search again.

An embassy official called a halt to their work later that morning. George Shultz, the U.S. Secretary of State, had just arrived, and they would be taken to meet him. Some of the Metro-Dade workers were furious at the interruption. "We're here as people, not politicians, so why do *we* have to go?" they grumbled. But eventually all the members of the U.S. team stood lined up in a crowded square near Rubén Darío to file past the Secretary and shake hands with him.

They were being shipped home that day, so emotional scenes took place with volunteers from other nations. They realized during the hugs and goodbyes that, despite all their differences, the teams had become a global family whose members had shared an indelible experience.

"Instead of flying out of Ilopango air base," Bill Dotson said, "we have to go to Comalapa Airport. It's an hour and a half from the hotel. And we're leaving right now."

They boarded the usual van, with the dogs and all their gear, and were soon on a highway in the countryside. They stared through the bullet-proof windows at lush tropical vegetation and jagged volcanic peaks, remarking that it was breathtakingly beautiful. The road was deserted, however, and they noticed that the guards were growing extremely tense.

"What's wrong?" Caroline asked a guard.

"This is not a safe road. All along here, the guerrillas ambush people. Constantly."

Caroline turned to the others and spoke in English. "Well, it seems this is no area for a vehicle to break down."

A C-5A military plane, the largest flying carrier in existence, waited on the runway like some giant steamship. Their van was stopped at the gate, however, and the guard refused to let it pass. The handlers and dogs waited, roasting in the heat, while their driver and the guard argued back and forth. At last Caroline climbed over the gear to the front, near the driver's window.

She addressed the guard in Spanish. "Sir, I realize you're trying to do your job, but do you mind if I use your telephone? I want to make a personal call to President Duarte. He knows we're supposed to leave on that plane." It was, of course, a total bluff. She hadn't the slightest idea how to call El Salvador's president. But they were rolling through the gate a few minutes later.

*"Muy bueno,"* one of the bodyguards told her. *"Muy bueno!"*

This airport also was being guarded by soldiers with machine guns. The C-5A was being refueled, so the team had to wait for two hours, baking under the tropical sun. Then they carried their gear from the van and placed it in a row on the runway.

A contingent of about thirty U.S. government personnel arrived to share the plane ride home. Some were members of the State Department, and others were Secret Service agents who had guarded Secretary Shultz during his stay in El Salvador. The agents declared that all the dog handlers—despite the fact that they too represented the United States—would have to be searched.

Their duffel bags and backpacks were opened one by one as the agents went through everything. Caroline grew angry at the indignity of having to watch as they pawed through her underwear.

"Can you believe it?" she said. "We're U.S. citizens!"

They were in the air at seven o'clock that evening, without having eaten anything or even had coffee since early that morning; but there was no food on board for them, so they passed around some granola bars. Caroline watched as the Secret Service agents carefully opened their packaged dinners of roast chicken, vegetables, and rolls, which they ate without any thought of sharing. Another indignity.

She herself was beyond hunger, even beyond exhaustion, and her blood sugar was getting low. She felt nauseated. Her ears hurt, and it seemed that the vibrating noise of the plane had been joined by the sound of blasting jackhammers. She made a mental note to check if she and Aly had suffered any hearing loss.

She lay on the floor and rested her head on Aly, who was already sleeping, and closed her eyes.

The sun rose as Caroline passed through Baltimore on her way back up the East Coast. She called Art on the car phone, waking him up to say she was on I-95. Her own voice sounded like a distant echo. Art reminded her that Andrew was expecting them for parents' weekend up at the Hotchkiss School in Connecticut.

"Oh, God. When do we have to leave?"

"Well, today's Friday. We should go this afternoon."

Caroline took care of Aly first. She hated to leave him so soon after a mission, but he was given a hero's greeting by Joanne, Alastair, and Heather, and they would be home, with Palmira, to pay attention to him. Meanwhile, Caroline went over every inch of Aly's body to make sure she had not overlooked any cuts or bruises or signs of illness. He did not seem to have lost weight, but the vet would check that later during a thorough examination. Caroline parted the hair of Aly's fur, inspected his pads and his ears; she gave instructions for him to have plenty of food, water, and rest, along with his vitamin supplements.

Satisfied that he was healthy and unharmed, she took the longest shower she could remember. Then, after shoving her dirty clothes into the washer, she drove into downtown Bernardsville. "Do something, please," she said to the hairdresser. It took three more washes to get out the dirt. At home again, she took a bath. Her knees had been bruised and cut from crawling. She had worn gloves while searching, but scrubbing all the grime from under her fingernails was impossible. Her nails were torn; she used polish to cover as much damage as possible. She had dressed and packed another bag by the time Art drove home from work to pick her up.

Aly was nearly asleep on a blanket in the kitchen as she bent down to pet him. He wagged his tail. And then she was off to the hills of northwest Connecticut.

"So," Art said, "tell me about it."

"Well," she began, "it was . . ."

Caroline paused. Her eyes closed, and the next thing she knew, Art was trying to wake her. He was saying, in a gentle voice, that they had arrived.

On that fall Saturday morning, the Hotchkiss campus was peaceful as Caroline strolled with her husband and their older son past the old red-brick buildings. Art had gone there, and now Andrew was a student at the school. The three of them were joining other parents and students for brunch. Caroline had spent the prior week in dirty T-shirts, coveralls, a hard hat, and work boots. Now, as if in a dream, she was wearing a string of pearls, a skirt, stockings, and high heels.

Over brunch, she socialized with the other parents, but offered information about herself only when asked. Even then, she kept it to a polite minimum.

Her mind drifted to the Gran Hotel, where Aly had discovered an exit for them to escape from the boiler room. The hotel's American owner had been found dead, where the dogs had indicated. The total figures weren't in, but there was no doubt that the American canine team had helped to save nearly forty lives. . . .

"So what have *you* been doing, Mrs. Hebard?"

She refocused, turning to the woman who had spoken. "Well, I just came back from Central America."

"Oh! A vacation?"

"Well, not really . . ."

Later she joined Art and Andrew for a hike up in the nearby wilderness, and it was healing for her. She thought back to the evening before, when they had taken Andrew out to dinner. Caroline had tried to keep from lowering her head onto the plate in front of her. How, she had wondered, do you go in a single jump from earthquake aftershocks and guns and falling cement and dead bodies in El Salvador to a parents' weekend at a posh Connecticut prep school?

In the motel room at two in the morning, she sat up in bed. Cold sweat poured down her body. Utterly confused and panicked, with no memory of where she was, Caroline tried to collect herself.

*Where's my dog? Where's the nearest exit? Who the hell is this guy in bed with me?*

# Chapter 14

# Water Search

*ARTHUR DEAR,*
*Went to Trenton for a search. Back whenever.*
*Use the frozen pasta or the chicken. Don't forget*
*Alastair has a school play tomorrow night.*
                                      *Love, Caroline*

Traveling light and moving fast, Caroline raced home after each mission and resumed the running of her household.

"Art and the kids are totally supportive," she told a member of Northeast Search and Rescue, a new unit she had formed with co-leader Bruce Barton of Stroudsburg, Pennsylvania. "They accept what I do and I think they're proud of me, but I know that my rescue work often disrupts their lives. When I come back from a search, they don't want to hear about what I've seen and done. What they want is to get their routines back on track.

"So I have to block out what I just went through and fall back into the role of mom. I've learned to keep the other side of my life away from them. I think, psychologically, they feel safer not knowing about any of the risks I take. And I never force it on them."

These days it was increasingly her pager that summoned her, and she joked that it felt like a leash around her neck. When the beeper went off, pulling her away, she was off to meetings, debriefings, training sessions, and, always, more searches. Random notes in her calendar for the remainder of 1986 recorded part of the story:

Oct. 25:     Dog handler meeting
Nov. 6:      Search near Bloomsburg, PA
Nov. 7:      Search in Trenton, NJ
Nov. 9:      Training in Chester, NJ
Nov. 10:     Search in Scranton, PA
Nov. 14:     Search in Hazelton, PA
Nov. 17:     El Salvador debriefing in Washington, D.C.
Dec. 6:      Search in Tobyhanna State Forest
Dec. 12:     State Department conference

The search near Bloomsburg was for an eight-year-old boy who had wandered away from home. Hundreds of officers and volunteers had combed nearby woods and fields for two days. Then the police called Caroline, who arrived with Aly on the third day. They began at the spot where the boy had been last seen, and Aly showed some interest, apparently following a scent pattern, but Caroline could see that he had not yet become really enthused. Aly then led her down to a riverbank. He walked upstream along the edge, stopped, sniffed, and began barking toward the water.

"Do you have a boat?" she asked.

Officials at the scene, skeptical, expressed their doubts by laughing and joking:

"Does your dog walk on water, too?"

"Can Fido scuba dive?"

Caroline sighed. "No," she said politely. "But if you just get us out in a boat, we'll be fine, thank you."

They brought a rubber raft with a motor. Caroline sat up front with Aly. When they had gotten to the middle of the river, he leaned overboard and barked. He reached his paw out of the boat and scooped at the water as if trying to dig through it.

"I think we need a diver," she said.

Still incredulous, rescue workers used a pair of yellow buoys to mark a fifty-foot section on the surface where Aly had barked continuously. Then a police diver went down between the buoys to comb the bottom. He discovered the boy's body ten minutes later.

The police and rescue workers scratched their heads. The dog's performance seemed unbelievable.

Had he been lucky?

Had he really known what he was doing?

If so, how?

In fact, Caroline and Aly had become pioneers in the virtually unknown field of canine water searching. She had become intrigued back in the seventies, during the early days of search and rescue, when Zibo was trying to find a lost hunter and showed intense curiosity at the edge of a swamp. His wilderness training had been geared to finding missing persons strictly on land, but search volunteers went farther into the swamp and eventually discovered the hunter's submerged body.

Was it possible that a search dog could consistently find victims of drowning? Did Zibo actually have the ability to pick up human scent that was rising through the water? From what depth?

Caroline and other dog handlers from different states began to share their experiences in order to build evidence. They communicated frequently, comparing notes, and Marian Hardy of Dogs-East in Maryland began developing a data base to consolidate their information. She and Caroline started to devise an actual training procedure, and Caroline put both Zibo and then Sasquatch through it. After Aly's arrival in 1984, Caroline continued to refine her methods. Water searching was still in its infancy two years later, but she felt it was now coming closer than ever to being a science.

What the handlers had understood at the outset was that odors are stored, filed, recognized, and interpreted in the brains of all animals, including humans. But compared to a human brain, much more of a dog's brain, fully an eighth of it, is devoted to smelling. And not only the brain is involved. A dog has many more olfactory or receptor cells in its nose than any person does. A human nose might have 5 million smell-receptor cells, but a German shepherd's nose has more than 220 million. By that yardstick, a dog's power to pick up scent is forty-four times as powerful as that of a human being. And dogs process the information their noses receive in a somewhat different way, so that a dog's sensitivity to certain molecules may be up to thousands of times greater.

The dog handlers learned, from scientific studies unrelated to search-and-rescue work, that the body of a drowning victim releases invisible skin particles (with their accompanying vapors) and secretions (oils and gases). These, being lighter than water, rise from any depth until they eventually go all the way up to the surface. Once they break through into the air, the particles form the narrow point of a widening scent cone. And a trained dog, identifying the cone, will follow it back to where its scent is most concentrated on the surface of the water. Depending on variables related to depth, current, wind, temperature, and so on, the dog's alert is an accurate guide to the location of a drowning victim below.

Caroline never actually taught her dogs to alert on the water, nor did she guide them to alert in any specific manner; instead, the dogs reacted naturally, and she learned by observing them. Mostly they bit the water or pawed at it, whining and barking.

Training began by first making Aly feel at ease around water and by swimming with him. Then she began a series of exercises from shore, rewarding him initially with a treat or toy for each success. First, a helper held him while Caroline ran into the water and submerged herself, using a mask and snorkel. When the helper let go, Aly jumped in and found her. Next, the helper took him out of sight while Caroline submerged herself again. Now Aly had to use his nose to produce the same results. Once released, he rushed right in and found her again. After that, she stayed with Aly while the helper played victim in the water. The humans' roles were reversed, but to the dog it was still the same game.

She also got Aly accustomed to small boats. Then, as training progressed, she took him out on one in which the bow rode close to the water. (If the boat had a motor, it was best if it did not emit copious fumes that might confuse him.) This time the helper was a scuba diver who had submerged himself; when Aly alerted, the diver came up and gave him his reward. She kept increasing the diver's distance from the boat, as well as his depth, and soon she herself did the rewarding when Aly alerted.

The only catch was that Aly began outsmarting her by recognizing bubbles on the surface indicating the scuba diver's presence below. She could tell by the angle of his head when he started to "cheat" by using his eyes instead of his nose. To counter that, she replaced the diver with human hair inside a stocking. After it was submerged, oils from the hair broke the surface, and Aly reverted to smelling his way to success.

She found on their first actual water searches that many factors came into play. Witnesses to drownings can misjudge distances amid the distortions caused by water and light; bodies in rivers or lakes can be moved by currents or snagged by fallen trees; layers of cold water, called thermoclines, can trap bodies and scents deep below (although a boat's motor might break these layers); strong eddies, whirlpools, and low-water dams are not only dangerous but can keep bodies trapped; in tidal regions, a body partially underwater keeps moving; heavy algae in lakes can trap scent below the surface; and so on, with seemingly endless variations.

Aly sometimes would follow scent in the water by walking to the boat's bow or stern, and once in his excitement he actually jumped overboard and started swimming in circles around the alert spot. After that, Caroline started bringing a harness and leash on water missions—especially for situations involving floods or heavy pollution, in which he could lose his life unless she was able to haul him back aboard quickly.

(Aly was not the only one whose life could be endangered. One time, using a canoe in winter, she forgot to bring his stick reward with her; when Aly alerted, he nearly knocked her overboard trying to grab the paddle for his trophy. She never forgot his stick again.)

On large lakes or other bodies of water, she learned, it was wise to bring three dogs to cover different sections. If one dog alerted, the other two could then confirm. She advised against dropping a buoy until the second and third dogs gave their alerts, because they might be crafty enough to use the buoy as a marker. Instead, she felt, spotters should be placed strategically along the shore, with binoculars, to triangulate the drowning site. When all three dogs had alerted without any visual aids, the buoys could be floated.

Such work demanded intense concentration, so Caroline made it a rule to keep Aly confined to the boat no longer than thirty minutes at a stretch. She brought him back to shore and played with him for about fifteen minutes before going out again.

And when he did find a drowning victim, Caroline made sure to have someone hide onshore so she could give him a "live find" before they left the scene. Aly had feelings, too, and while he was always glad to please her, he did not enjoy finding death any more than the human searchers did. While using her dog's unique abilities to shorten the terrible waiting and uncertainty faced by anxious families, she made sure to do so with respect for *his* emotions, too.

In a town called Fort Hunter in upstate New York, a trickle of water known as the Schoharie Creek was normally so low that a person could walk right across it. But in early April 1987, heavy rains swelled the Schoharie so much that it developed swift currents and reached flood stage. Murky brown water roiled and thundered by at 64,800 cubic feet per second—a rate likened by state power authorities to that of Niagara Falls.

One hundred and ten feet above the Schoharie was an imposing structure known locally as the Thruway Bridge, which spanned not only the creek but wooded areas on either side of a ravine, carrying traffic 450 feet across. It had stood there for thirty-three years, but on the Sunday morning of the flood, its concrete pilings began to collapse under the strain, and two mid-sections of the bridge broke away.

Authorities could not know immediately that four cars and a tractor-trailer, containing a total of ten people, had tumbled one by one into the roaring waters below. But by the end of the day divers were able to locate two cars and recover three bodies from inside them. It was probable that other vehicles were under the water, trapping more victims, and maybe some bodies had been swept downstream; but clearly there would be no survivors. Before asking divers to take additional risks, officials wanted a more definite indication of what else was under the still-raging current.

The sheriff's department, aware of Caroline's work in other states, summoned her late that night. She and Aly arrived at dawn the next morning.

In the gray morning light, the remaining high, teetering sections of the massive bridge jutted partially over the rushing water far below, where tons of fallen metal and concrete had created a series of dangerous rapids. Adding to the mess were pieces of debris that had been carried downstream from summer homes farther up the valley; as Caroline watched the water, she saw a refrigerator tumbling on its way toward the Mohawk River farther downstream.

She knew that the cold water was probably preventing the rapid decomposition of any bodies, so fewer oils or gases would be coming up. And before those fewer scent particles even broke the surface, the force of the current would disperse them over a longer distance. As water searches went, this one would be more difficult than usual for even the best-trained search dog.

A more immediate problem was the obvious danger of getting out there in a boat. Caroline nevertheless agreed that she and Aly would join a member of the dive team aboard an inflatable rubber craft with a motor. The vessel would have to be launched downstream of the bridge—for safety reasons, as well as to give Aly a better chance to pick up the oncoming scent—and would then have to make its way back up toward the collapse point, where submerged vehicles were likely to be.

The boat was surprisingly stable, holding three people and a dog with no trouble, so the only task was to just hang on. But when they were out on the swiftly moving water, the pilot said he wasn't sure if the engine had enough power to head upstream against the river's treacherous current.

The scuba diver looked at her. "Aren't you scared?"

"I can't afford to be. If I'm afraid, I'd be telegraphing that to my dog. And he wouldn't be able to work effectively."

"He'd be able to sense your fear?"

"Sure. And he'd smell it, too."

"Well," the diver said, "*I'm* scared to death."

Aly was concentrating. He hung his head over the boat's prow, nose toward the water. Then, closer to where the bridge had collapsed, he barked and reached down to paw the surface.

"There are bodies down there," Caroline said.

"This is amazing," the diver said after Aly had indicated several other spots. "Are you sure he's right?"

"Yes. But I'd like to try one more thing, just to have him reconfirm."

Later, at her request, Caroline and Aly boarded a strange-looking flat vessel known as an airboat, whose 300-horsepower engine drove a large propeller for easy maneuvering in rapid current. The airboat took them to the edge of a small island below the bridge and dropped them off. They walked around to the island's tip, where Aly alerted upstream toward the same areas of water as before.

"Good going," she told him.

With the information Aly had given her, Caroline was able to tell officials that more than one body still needed to be recovered from the Schoharie.

Members of the state police, descending upon the scene by noon, declared that they were now in charge. Other volunteer dog teams from Northeast Search and Rescue had arrived to join Caroline and Aly, but the state troopers angrily rebuked the sheriffs for having called in any outsiders in the first place. The two law-enforcement agencies squared off, trading accusations.

It was the start of a turf war.

The troopers set up their own command post on the riverbank, complete with five portable toilets. Caroline gratefully headed for one of them. Of all the details involved in her work, the "pee factor" held special hazards. On this occasion, as often was the case, she happened to be the only woman among the rescue personnel at the scene. All the male divers, state troopers, sheriff's deputies, investigators, and other dog handlers could turn their backs and surreptitiously relieve themselves, but for Caroline there was literally nowhere to go. Here at last was an opportunity, however, so she put Aly on a down-stay and started for one of the bright green doors.

"Hey, you!" the trooper in charge shouted at her. "This is state police property!"

Caroline turned around. He was wearing a nifty regulation hat with a wide brim, a full uniform, and shiny boots. "Excuse me," she said, "but why can't I use one?"

"This is a state police command post."

*Okay, buddy,* she thought, backing off several feet down the bank. There she stopped and watched, waiting for the officer to leave his post. Instead, he himself walked over to one of the toilets and went inside. Caroline saw her chance. Turning to Aly, she pointed to the door and told him, with an intense expression on her face, *"Pass auf"*—putting him on alert to keep the trooper at bay.

Aly bounded to the door of the portable toilet and stood there growling and barking. When the trooper began to open the door, the dog's deep-chested response was so menacing that he quickly closed it again.

"Good boy," Caroline whispered, suppressing a grin. "Good boy."

Then came the trooper's plaintive voice from inside. "Ma'am? Could you call off your dog?"

"Well, there's a condition."

"Ma'am?"

"Yes?"

"I could *arrest* you for this."

"I could also get *you* into some trouble," she replied cheerfully.

Aly barked again, as if to emphasize her point.

"Let's make a pact," the officer said.

"Truce?"

"Truce."

Aly stood guard proudly as Caroline exercised her hard-won right.

Later she took Aly for a walk downstream. If people had been swept out of their vehicles, he might pick up their scent from shore. Two miles from the command post, at an eddy close to shore, Aly became excited. He bounded into the shallow water to grab something with his teeth, then came out proudly holding the truck driver's log, which had been carried all that way downstream by the muddy current.

Caroline and Aly left for home that night. It took another three days for the swollen creek to become safe enough for the police divers to risk an extensive underwater search. After more than a week, they ended up discovering the seven remaining victims—all of whom had been trapped inside their vehicles—in the exact locations where Aly had given his alerts.

# Chapter 15

# The Edge of Burnout

THE CALL CAME ON AN EVENING, LESS THAN TWO weeks after the Thruway Bridge collapse.

L'Ambiance Plaza in Bridgeport, Connecticut, was about half completed when its concrete and steel had come crashing down at 1:17 P.M. on Thursday, April 23, 1987. The complex was to have contained more than two hundred apartments in a pair of thirteen-story buildings, connected by an entranceway and an elevator shaft in the middle, with a five-story parking garage below.

Construction workers using the lift-slab process had begun by erecting steel columns to the planned height of the twin buildings. At ground level, they had been pouring concrete into molds to create huge floor slabs reinforced with meshes of steel cables. They hoisted the slabs by hydraulic jacks placed on the I-beam supports and locked each floor, weighing many tons, into position with steel joints.

As workers were continuing this process, one of the huge jacks may have failed, overloading the joints and causing adjacent I-beams to buckle under the pressure. Or it might have been that the temporary braces on the sides of the steel columns could not hold the weight of the concrete slabs; when those slabs began to slide, the locking devices would have ruptured. Whatever the reason, one of the giant steel columns suddenly snapped.

The explosion and release of energy made it seem to those on the construction site as if a bomb had gone off. Then came the deafening, thunderous roar of nine layers of the building collapsing and crashing like a house of cards, burying workers under twisted steel girders and shattered concrete.

Seventy-one men were on the job, which covered a site of nearly two acres. Some workers jumped clear of the steel frames, and others fled just in time. Forty-three escaped, eleven with injuries. Most of the twenty-eight trapped victims probably had been caught down toward the center of the building, where they had gathered with their lunch boxes just before the catastrophe.

Caroline and Aly arrived in a cold drizzle the next morning with Bruce Barton, coleader of Northeast Search and Rescue, as overhead. Two additional volunteers with their dogs were on the way. She and Bruce reported to the command post, which had been set up in one of the construction trailers.

The workers on the scene already seemed near the breaking point from grief, anger, tension, and confusion. Several hundred anxious volunteers, all wearing hard hats, were sifting through sixty-foot-high mounds of tangled wreckage for any signs or sounds of life. Six cranes were crowding the air above to carefully remove rubble in relatively small, car-sized hunks, to prevent everything from shifting and crashing onto possible survivors.

The crushed bodies of thirteen workers had been brought out so far, but that left fifteen still missing.

Caroline learned that the construction workers were part of a tightly knit community of Italian, Hispanic, and Portuguese families. Fathers were searching for their sons, sons for fathers, brothers for brothers. Although firefighters and emergency-service crews from Bridgeport and surrounding communities were on hand, the workers themselves had virtually taken over the site. This was a family matter, and they meant to be in charge.

Behind the police lines, reporters and photographers congregated. A few were attempting to bribe rescue workers to lend them their outer clothing, so they could sneak disguised into the site; some were arrested. Others were paying a thousand dollars per day to residents of nearby row houses so they could survey the site with high-powered lenses from the rooftops. Construction workers and police officers shouted angrily at TV crews taking footage of distraught relatives.

"These people want respect," an officer yelled at a cameraman, blocking his access. "Can't you give them a little respect?"

Amid the tension, leaders of the different trade unions involved were squabbling. Labor bosses drove up in shiny limousines bearing kegs of beer, vats of lobster bisque, and other gourmet items for their union members on the site. Finally the command-post leader stomped over and said, "Look, the food is fine, but get the booze out of here!"

Mayor Thomas Bucci of Bridgeport arrived with a structural expert. They climbed into a crane-lifted cage that took them up for an aerial view of the scene, forcing all work to stop.

"What does he think this is?" rescuers complained. "A campaign stop?"

Workers booed the mayor.

"Get that thing down!" a construction foreman shouted, motioning with a swift jerk of his hand toward the crane operator, who started lowering the cage. When the mayor stepped out, he tried to explain that he had gone up there hoping to understand what might have caused the tragedy, but the angry foreman turned and walked away. The other workers broke into applause as the mayor left.

Caroline and Bruce had been assigned to the Connecticut State Police K-9 Unit, which already had its own dogs at the site.

"You people are on standby," the chief said. "If I need any volunteers, I'll let you know."

"Fine," said Caroline, who recognized the signs of territorial jealousy when she saw them. She turned to Bruce and added, "Let's get our dogs out of here."

The cold rain was coming down harder, so they took shelter in the lobby of the nearby AT&T building. After nearly an hour, Caroline could not bear waiting any longer. It was early afternoon when she walked back to the site with Aly to get a closer look.

She saw, to her astonishment, that a state police K-9 officer was heading into the wreckage while keeping his dog on a leash. He was breaking one of the foremost rules for using search dogs at a disaster scene. It was dangerous for both handler and dog to keep the animal restricted that way. It also prevented an air-scenting dog from being able to go wherever his nose led him.

Then she noticed another officer, a big man with a thick neck, trying to work his beautiful German shepherd. The dog, clearly inexperienced and insecure, was hesitating. "Go on in there!" the officer shouted, pointing to a void. "Go on, go on, go on! Get the hell in there!"

And with that, he kicked the dog's rear end with his boot.

Caroline exploded inside. She stomped over to the K-9 chief, trembling with rage. "How *dare* you let someone like that handle a dog?" she said. "I will *not* stand by and watch any cruelty to an animal!"

She walked off before he could reply.

The police dogs lacked experience at disaster sites. They should have been allowed to proceed freely but did not have the training to do so safely. They were patrol dogs, accustomed to remaining on-leash while tracking criminals and to being released only when it was necessary to bring a fleeing suspect to the ground. The dogs were working on-leash at L'Ambiance Plaza simply because that was how they'd been taught to work—not to mention the fact that if they attacked someone, the state police could have a liability suit on their hands. To further guard against that risk, the whole site had to be cleared of workers each time the patrol dogs were deployed. When that happened, they were met with jeers from impatient rescue workers and family members.

Caroline went back to the K-9 commander. "Can we work *our* dogs?"

"Well, we'll see."

"Look, this is ridiculous," she said, and proceeded to explain why.

The commander listened, then said, "Okay, okay. Bring your dogs."

It was late afternoon when Caroline and Aly finally climbed over the rubble. They came to an opening that possibly led down toward the section where construction workers had gathered with their lunch boxes just before the collapse. The state officers came over with their weary patrol dogs on leashes.

"Now," the chief told Caroline, "you and your dog will follow these police officers and their dogs into this hole."

"What's the point of doing that?" she said, unable to conceal her dismay. "You only need one dog to search and another to confirm."

"Those are my orders."

Caroline clenched her teeth. *This is a complete waste of time*, she thought.

The patrol dogs filed over a plank and into the void. She and Aly followed them. They could walk upright most of the way, but then came a narrow section where the officers had to bend over and squeeze themselves through. In such close quarters, the patrol dogs began to snarl at each other. At last, however, the group came upon a half-crushed body. A man's head, part of his torso, and one arm were hanging out of a wall of rubble. His skin had turned a purplish color, and his eyes were open.

"Aw, Jesus, look at that," an officer said.

"Oh, God!" another exclaimed.

"Damn!"

*Like a bunch of kids at a sideshow*, Caroline thought, seething with frustration. She brought Aly out of the tunnel, and soon the officers emerged with their exhausted police dogs as well.

"Look," she told the K-9 chief, "our dogs are trained for this stuff. But they need to be allowed to cover the total site. They can work without hampering any other part of the rescue effort. They can give us a very good idea of where other victims are. And we'll know whether they're making live or dead alerts."

The commander did not answer.

Retreating again to the sidelines, Caroline saw that on top of everything else, the state police were pushing their dogs far too hard. It was taking less than forty-five minutes for each patrol dog to become nonoperational. Their pads were being cut, and they were getting stressed to the breaking point. One after another, the patrol dogs literally shut down, absolutely refusing to work anymore. They had reached burnout.

Caroline and Bruce told the commander they'd be there if and when the state police needed them, and left the site.


The call to return came at two in the morning: "We need the dogs." It was still pouring outside, so she scrambled into her foul-weather gear and they hustled back over to the scene, where activity continued with the help of generators and lights. At the command post the K-9 chief asked Caroline how her dog worked best, and she replied, "Well, it would be good if he could get as high as possible on the rubble." She knew that at nighttime, the scent would be drifting upward.

So Caroline and Aly were elected to ride in the bucket of a crane to get to the very top of the massive debris pile.

Aly was unperturbed as they were hoisted up in the rain. He climbed out of the bucket and stood beside her. Men below them were moving debris all over the site; as Aly started to sniff for other human scents, Caroline looked around to find a way downward toward the center.

"*Such und hilf*," she told Aly, pointing, and right away he picked up some scent and went to where a huge metal I-beam was slanting downward at an angle into a debris hole. He took a tremendous whiff, and before she knew it, he had disappeared.

*Holy God*, she thought, *that was a real reaction!*

Caroline knew the next step was to follow him into the dark hole.

"Hey, guys, I need that hole illuminated. I've got a head lamp, but I want more light, okay? My dog has disappeared down there, and I don't know where he is at this point."

Some extra lighting was brought up, and Caroline climbed onto the I-beam. She slid down, literally on her rear end, into the tunnel. Then she saw Aly. The two of them were now actually inside the wreckage—alone, surrounded by tons of precarious debris—and he gave her a look as if to say, *There are bodies down here, and I don't like it one bit!*

Everything they had experienced together over the years let her read the message on his face and in his body language. Aly had found death, no question about it. He was pawing and whining and actually turning away from the scent with a look of utter distress. They could go no farther anyway, so Caroline praised him and gestured for him to start out. He did so with no trouble, and then she planted her hands and feet on the I-beam and moved like a spider back up the steel girder to the top of the site.

Two workers lifted Aly and carried him off the debris pile as Caroline made her way down. That, in Caroline's mind, was another demonstration of her dog's special character—in this case, his willingness to be handled by strangers without complaining.

As dawn broke, a young woman arrived at the edge of the rubble, where rescue workers still labored. Shivering in the rain, she stood directly across the street, wrapped in a yellow blanket. Her face was puffy and red, her expression grim. The crowds of onlookers were gone, for now, and the street was otherwise empty.

Caroline, working with Aly, had seen her there before. She knew that the young woman was scanning the busy scene for any small sign of hope that her husband would be found. The woman stayed for a while, then left, returning to the high-school gymnasium two blocks away where other family members were keeping vigil.

They were being kept like prisoners in there, Caroline felt when she paid a visit. The press was being held at bay, which was probably a good policy, but the psychological environment seemed awful. There were no psychologists or social workers to provide counseling and personal intervention, so the victims' families had no means of identifying their emotions, much less expressing them. Anxious relatives sat on bleachers or metal chairs, huddling in nervous circles, their faces drained. Some napped on Red Cross cots. Others picked at a hot buffet. A priest circulated from group to group, urging people to keep praying. It was the only thing they could do.

More rescue units had arrived from various parts of the country, including New York, Florida, and California. Among them was the

Miami area's Metro-Dade crew, led by Doug Jewett, who greeted Caroline as if it had been just days rather than six months since they'd worked together in El Salvador. "I know this dog," Jewett told the state K-9 commander, referring to Aly. "I've seen him work. You don't have to worry about people being on the site with him. He'll be fine."

The K-9 commander nodded. "I've noticed," he said.

Also on hand were specialists with infrared cameras to detect body heat. Some had brought ultrasound listening devices attached to long cables in order to pick up traces of human life deep inside the wreckage. One group was using an unusual form of radar which had been developed by the military during the Vietnam War to locate tunnels built under the jungle by the Viet Cong. Now this "ground radar" was producing a chart that showed a series of black and white rippling effects indicating the levels of debris at L'Ambiance Plaza, with the white areas representing open spaces that rescue workers might use as they crawled the other volunteer dog handlers were being put up at a nearby hotel. She and Aly burrowed their way through.

To Caroline this was the start of a trend toward using modern technology at disaster sites in a massive way. "They're all bringing their new toys," she joked, but the equipment fascinated her. No resource should be overlooked, she felt, so long as the operators didn't get in each other's way. As it was, with eight cranes swinging high over the rubble, it seemed that an air traffic controller would come in handy as well.

Aly, using his low-tech nose, had reconfirmed all the alerts he had made earlier. Caroline drew a sketch of the wreckage site to show Doug Jewett and local rescuers where Aly and the other dogs had indicated victims were most likely to be located. The search dogs had given no sign that anyone was alive, and markings of orange spray paint on pieces of mangled wreckage, or ribbons tied to exposed rebar, signified where they had detected death. But the rescue workers refused to give up hope.

Whenever needed, members of the carpenters union built makeshift walkways and bridges, erecting them rapidly with tremendous courage and skill. At times all activity ceased and everybody watched, in hushed silence, as someone—a "tunnel rat" from Miami or a construction worker—risked his life by slithering through an opening, hoping to find someone alive. But, invariably, the man would come back out shaking his head.

The worst fears of the missing workers' family members were being slowly confirmed. With agonizing regularity, each of the fifteen missing men was added to the death toll. The final figure would be twenty-eight.

If they had accomplished nothing else, the dogs' assistance had enabled the searchers to find the remaining dead up to two weeks earlier than would have been possible otherwise. As Caroline drove home with Aly, she felt grateful that they had been able to help shorten the nearly unbearable period of time relatives had to wait to learn the truth.

But she also looked ahead. The experience had deepened her conviction that dogs sent to disaster sites needed to meet the highest standards of training and qualification. And it had made her more dedicated than ever to raising those standards. To do anything less, she thought, would be a disservice to the victims and their families.

She vowed to call the chief of the Connecticut K-9 team and have a chat. Maybe they could find some common ground. It was not unlikely, after all, that they would meet again.


Caroline and Hatch Graham, working from the East and West coasts, respectively, had labored mightily to put together the first International Disaster Dog Symposium, under NASAR sponsorship. Nicknamed "Response '87," the five-day event at a hotel in Orlando, Florida, drew eight hundred members of canine search-and-rescue teams from around the world. Here was the beginning, at last, of a global network bringing together dog handlers from many countries to share techniques, formulate standards, get to know each other better, and prepare to coordinate efforts in future disasters.

Other nations sending representatives included Canada, Costa Rica, Guatemala, Hong Kong, Japan, Thailand, West Germany, and the United Kingdom. The Swiss, still feeling above it all, did not attend, and the Italians sent word that they could not afford the trip.

The foremost objective of the conference, as conceived by the organizers, was "to save lives and reduce suffering" by promoting the use of search dogs. The barriers to that goal included "dogs not being used because of politics and religion; inability to function because of hostile environments, language barriers, inadequate equipment; not meeting standards or expectations; lack of education by others concerning how or when our dogs can be used; and not enough financing for the U.S. team and many of the others."

On the last evening of the conference Caroline received an urgent call from one of the dog handlers who had been with her and Bruce Barton at L'Ambiance Plaza.

"I haven't been able to sleep," the man said. "I'm having nightmares." He mentioned other signs of his shaky emotional state.

"Just hang in there," Caroline said. "I'll get you some help."

From her hotel room she phoned Jeff Mitchell, the disaster psychologist, and asked him to find a qualified counselor who lived near the distraught handler.

"Don't worry, I'll take care of it," Jeff said. Then he asked her, "Are *you* okay?"

"Me? I'm fine."

"You sure?"

"Well, you know, it's just so busy," Caroline told him, meaning it. "Maybe when this all finishes, I'll just collapse."

She hung up, suddenly feeling exhausted. Doubts about her own emotional state began to creep into her mind.

*El Salvador, Schoharie Creek, Bridgeport—and now this symposium, all back to back, without letup. Maybe . . . maybe I'm* not *okay. . . .*

Caroline shrugged off such thoughts and went downstairs to receive a NASAR award for her work in search and rescue. Governor Thomas H. Kean of New Jersey had written to congratulate her, adding, "I thank you for devoting your time and energy to such a worthy cause. New Jersey is fortunate to have individuals like you who do so much to make our state a safer place to live."

She addressed the conference, ending with the theme that each person should be trained to work with specialists in all the other phases of search and rescue. "We can't put blinders on and think that because we're dog handlers we don't need to know anything else," she said. "Disaster work is search *and* rescue. We are only one of the tools.

We've got to acquaint ourselves with heat sensors and other special detectors, with jackhammers and hydraulic tools. We need to know about structural safety, hazardous materials, medical treatment, search management, and critical-incident stress. And we need to start having drills with all these components, to see how each of us fits into the whole picture. We must never stop learning, especially about our dogs. I cringe when I hear someone say that he or she is an expert. No one is an expert in this field!"

Later that night, she walked Aly in a grassy area behind the hotel. When they returned to the parking lot, she suddenly stopped. Aly waited, as if sensing her emotions.

*I'm not in control anymore.*

Tears were building, but she refused to let them out.

One of the British handlers, who happened to be outside as well, saw her and came over.

"Hi, Caroline," he said.

She could barely respond.

"Is something wrong?" the other handler asked, concerned.

"I—I think my nerves are shot," she said, her voice shaking.

They sat on the curb of the parking lot. Caroline tried to speak, but tears overwhelmed her.

"I wanted so badly for this conference to be a success," she sobbed.

"It *is* a success," the British handler reassured her.

"I feel like there's just been so much on my shoulders," she confessed, and she talked about the stress of going on so many missions while having to organize the symposium. But that wasn't the only problem. The call from that one handler had triggered something deeper. On top of the time pressures and the emotionally draining nature of search-and-rescue work, she was trying to excel in two very different aspects of life. On the one hand, she was fiercely independent, strong-willed, and determined to give her all in search and rescue. On the other, she was a wife and mother, and felt a strong desire to give her all to her family as well. She was putting enormous pressure on herself to be perfect in both parts of her life. As she talked—and cried—that night, she began to wonder whether she had been trying to prove something. She knew it was a question she'd have to come back to and explore further, but right then it was a tremendous relief to drop the weight of such a double burden and allow herself to be vulnerable.

She had been talking—and occasionally crying—for two hours when her pager went off. Grateful to get away from these thoughts for a while, she went to find a phone. The next morning she flew to Pennsylvania with Aly for a wilderness search.

The next dog to arrive in the Hebard household was a huge German shepherd, five years old, named Max, whose owners were moving to an apartment in Manhattan. Clearly the dog would be too much to handle there, so Caroline volunteered to try to find him a home. Max came to stay with the Hebards—temporarily, they thought—and because he was wild and uncontrollable, they started calling him Mad Max.

Caroline called a young paramedic named Trevor, who had been wanting to get into search and rescue. "Do I have a dog for you," she said, adding truthfully, "This is a magnificent animal!"

Trevor came over to the Hebard house, where Max was waiting, and he liked the dog right away. Max was, in fact, a beautiful German shepherd—even if he did weigh a whopping 110. Trevor loaded him into his truck and went home. About an hour later, however, he reappeared with Max.

"I can't handle him," Trevor said. "I mean, he's *too much dog!* He's also got this thing he does—he turns and turns in the truck, going crazy! I think he's got a screw loose. He sits there looking at his tail and suddenly starts chasing it in circles, and the whole truck shakes!"

Part of the problem was that no one had played with Mad Max as a puppy. He had been left alone a lot, so chasing his tail had become his entertainment.

"Okay," Caroline sighed, returning Max to one of the pens in back of her house, where Aly and Sasquatch lived. Two days later, at dinner, she said to Art, "Don't worry about Max. I'll find a home for this guy."

What Art said next surprised her. "No, I really like this dog. Let's keep him."

"Really? You mean it?"

"I've started doing some obedience stuff with him," he said with pride.

Art had always been good with the dogs, but he spent long hours at the lab, where he was now engaged in work on superconductivity, so he had little time to help with care and feeding. But these days, when he went out for walks, he brought Max with him. He and the big dog had formed a connection. Max would race ahead and then return to nuzzle him with affection, going back and forth that way all during their outing. Without conscious effort, Mad Max had become Art's dog.

When Caroline took Max out, she would always use a leash because he was so powerful and unpredictable. And one evening that winter, when her husband was still at work, she was walking with Max and the kids up toward a nearby schoolyard where, although they didn't know it, a television soap opera was filming some action scenes. "Look at all those lights up there," she said as they started up the driveway of the school. At the same time, within a split second, Mad Max pulled the leash out of her hand. A hundred and ten pounds of dog went racing away at full speed. She ran after him, yelling, "Max! Max! *Hier! Hier!*"

It turned out that he had cornered a skunk. As Caroline made a flying leap to tackle Mad Max, who was barking madly while the skunk was trying to break away, the TV producer came running down the driveway, screaming, "What are you doing? You just ruined a whole scene! Now I have to reshoot all of this!"

"My dog wants to do battle with a skunk," Caroline replied. "So stand back unless you want to stink."

The producer was furious but backed off, muttering, "Do you know how much money you cost me?" and "Stupid woman!"

After getting Mad Max back to the house, Caroline put him into the pen. Both of them were reeking from the skunk. Still outside, she took off her fire company jacket and stripped off most of her other clothing, shivering in the cold. Upstairs, she stepped in the shower to clean herself off, using vinegar to get rid of the skunk smell. With fresh clothes on, she raced outside and drove into town to the pharmacy, thankful that it was still open. From previous experience, she knew what worked best to get the skunk smell out of the dog's fur.

"How can I help you, Mrs. Hebard?" said the pharmacist.

"Well," she said, "I need a case of Summer's Eve douche."

Behind the counter the man's eyes widened. Caroline glanced around and noticed that a woman who attended the church where Art sang on Sundays was staring at her as if thinking, *What on earth is that crazy Hebard woman up to now?*

"Oh, no," Caroline hastened to explain. "It's for one of my *dogs.*"

The pharmacist and the woman goggled. Without another word, the pharmacist went to find what she wanted.

Back home, Caroline washed Mad Max with the douche to take the odor out of him. She also used the douche on all her clothes, followed by a second wash in vinegar. She grinned as she worked, thinking of the reaction she'd gotten in the pharmacy. *Hey, it works,* she thought with a shrug.

Caroline didn't train Mad Max for search and rescue, because he was too old, but he was a sweet dog and his devotion to Art continued. When her husband worked in the vegetable garden, Max was always with him. Or else he was in the swimming pool they had built in back of the house. If someone had left the gate to the pool area open and the big dog happened to be out of his pen, he would not hesitate to seize his chance. "Here he comes," someone would say as Mad Max became a blur of muscle and fur racing headlong toward the pool. More often than not, he used the diving board, catapulting into the air and landing with a tremendous splash that caused a miniature tidal wave. All in all, a terrific dog.

There was no letup, throughout the next year, in the work Caroline was doing to help develop and advance canine search and rescue. In March 1988 she flew with Aly to Guadalajara, Mexico, to attend an emergency management workshop. Her talk, called "Disaster Dogs and the Integrated Urban Disaster Team," was the workshop's feature presentation. She later spent a month in Australia, teaching water search methods, but she was forced to leave Aly at home because of that country's quarantine regulations.

On a trip to Europe in September that year, she and Bill Dotson watched the search dog trials in Germany. In France, at the invitation of the French dog team, Caroline conducted courses and shared training methods. Making notes for a report to the Office of Foreign Disaster Assistance, she observed that all of the French dog handlers were required to pass a test to obtain the government certification they needed to work. She herself was decidedly against overburdening the search-and-rescue field with bureaucracy, though she did urge that the qualifications for all volunteers who went on missions be raised and standardized.

Caroline wound up that trip in Switzerland. Every major town throughout the country, she found, had its own dog training site, including agility courses and piles of debris with built-in holes and tunnels. "Met some familiar faces," she wrote in her report, referring to members of the Swiss team who had been in El Salvador, "and managed to erase any past conflicts."

On the morning of Thursday, December 8, 1988, Caroline was in her fund-raiser mode. She had driven with Aly to Allentown, Pennsylvania, to meet with public-relations people for the Alpo pet food company, which was now the official sponsor of the U.S. Disaster Team Canine Unit. She and coleader Bill Dotson, who had driven up from Virginia, told the PR staff that the team desperately needed financial support to help its volunteers pay for basic equipment. It cost each dog handler about $5,000 to get "field-ready," with backpack, boots, sleeping bag, tent, portable stove, compass, and other supplies. And that didn't include the expense of maintaining a dog with everything from food to veterinary services and immunizations.

Upgraded hand-held radios were at the top of Caroline's list. It was critical for dog handlers inside dangerous buildings to be able to communicate quickly and clearly to those outside; in foreign disasters, where conditions were usually chaotic, it was often a matter of life or death to reach structural engineers, rescue teams, medical technicians, and others as fast as possible. A modern high-band radio, small enough to clip onto one's belt, cost about eight hundred dollars.

Caroline viewed her public-relations work as a necessary chore. "It would be a godsend if the American public knew how much we need help," she said. "Most of our groups have tax-exempt status, but I don't think many people are even aware of us. The average volunteer can't really afford to be field-ready."

"We need to get more exposure for your team," the PR people said. "You need to be more visible."

The irony was that the search dogs got plenty of publicity whenever their services were actually used. "I guess what we really need," Caroline remarked ironically, "is another disaster!"

Two seconds later her beeper went off.

# Chapter 16

# Disaster in Armenia

HER PAGER SHOWED A WASHINGTON, D.C., PHONE number, and Caroline recognized the number for the Office of Foreign Disaster Assistance. It was as if she had called *them* with that flippant remark about needing another disaster. Aly had gotten to his feet in the conference room; he paced back and forth, watching Caroline's face. He knew the sound of the beeper and that it caused excitement in her. Bill Dotson and the PR people fell silent as she called back.

Now she heard the voice of Bob Kessecker, logistics officer for OFDA's Operations Support Division, speaking to her from the State Department.

"Caroline, are you ready to go to Armenia?"

"Armenia?"

"Didn't you watch the news this morning?"

"No, Bob, I left home early. I didn't want to wake Art up by turning on the TV."

"Well, there's been a big earthquake. We're working right now with the Soviets to get you people visas and arrange to fly a team in."

"What sort of ETA are you talking about?"

"We're not really sure. It's still all in limbo, but we need you to be ready."

"I'm in Allentown with Bill Dotson. We need to go to the Poconos and do a homicide search around noon today. Do we have time for that?"

"Yes, I think so. Give me your car-phone number."

She gave Kessecker the number.

Now Caroline told the group what she had just heard. The quake had struck Armenia the day before, but no one at the Allentown meeting had heard anything about it.

"Maybe I'm jinxed!" she said with a rueful laugh, while a rush of excitement went through her. Then she sobered. "I think we'd better go and do this homicide search right away."


Caroline drove down out of the hills, listening for any news from Armenia. Bill was following in his car. They had gone up into the Poconos, to a house in the woods, where she and Aly had helped police confirm that the victim's body had been buried some weeks beforehand in the basement. It had taken Aly just a few minutes to react with disgust and then scratch at a section of concrete floor, indicating the presence of human remains. Only the dog had been able to pick up traces of the scent, which had otherwise been trapped. The officers thanked her. Now they could extricate the body and charge their suspect with murder.

A news bulletin about Armenia came on the radio in Caroline's Suburban. Thousands of people had died instantly, and thousands more were buried in villages and towns across a vast area. Soviet President Mikhail Gorbachev, in New York City to address the United Nations, had canceled the remainder of his trip and sped to Kennedy International Airport. His flight was taking him first to Moscow and then to Armenia, where the death toll was being estimated at more than fifty thousand men, women, and children.

As Caroline drove through the leafless trees and green pines of the wintry Pocono Mountains, she wondered whether the United States would really send help to the Soviet Union—to the so-called Evil Empire, as President Reagan had called it. And would the Russians *accept* American assistance?

Her car phone rang. She hated using it on narrow, winding roads, and she was already so pumped up that her driving had become erratic, so she pulled over. Bill swerved to park behind her.

A three-way conference call ensued. Bob Kessecker was on the line from Washington, along with the head of the Swiss rescue team from Europe. The Swiss, having mobilized quickly, were already at the Zurich airport with their dogs. Caroline and Bill were instructed to pull together a U.S. team. They would leave from Kennedy the following afternoon.

Kessecker had promised government supplies for the mission, but Caroline decided to bring her own. She went through the search-and-rescue closet, bringing out a warm sleeping bag, a heavy-duty tent, her water purifier, and a small portable stove. She would also take a portable radio, a hard hat, gloves, boots, a flashlight, a compass, a thermos, emergency medical supplies, and layers of winter clothing.

Then she drove down to King's, a local grocery store, and got them to donate two hundred dollars' worth of freeze-dried and other nonperishable food as well as aspirin, lip balm, tissues, and toilet paper, plus oatmeal, snack food, granola bars, and candy that could be handed out to survivors. And she grabbed some sanitary napkins, which doubled as excellent compresses for wounds. At home she stuffed everything into her backpack and a single brown duffel bag. No matter what the State Department brought in the way of supplies, Caroline and Aly would be totally self-sufficient, capable of surviving independently for ten days.

Bill manned the kitchen phone, while she used the one in her Suburban outside, and they made calls up and down the East Coast to line up handlers. The Alpo folks got in touch to say they were donating a two-week supply of dog food for the team. They would also send a limousine to bring Bill, Caroline, and Aly to the airport.

It was 2 A.M. by the time they had rounded up a team of eight handlers, six of them women, with their dogs. Caroline was the only member who had been to both Mexico and El Salvador for those earthquake disasters. Bill, who had been with her in El Salvador, would be going to Armenia without a dog to act as "overhead." The plane would stop at Dulles, so Bill's wife would be able to drive from Virginia to meet him there with his gear. Beth Barkley, another veteran from the Salvadoran mission, would be joining the current team with Panda, her white German shepherd.

The others were first-timers in terms of experience on international missions. It was a giant leap from finding missing persons in the wilderness to encountering mass destruction and suffering, especially in a place that was totally foreign to them. Of necessity, the handlers were from the eastern part of the country. Caroline had worked with each of them on local searches, but there was no way to know how they would do on this trip. Now they were going to be thrown together for the first time and dropped into Armenia during a catastrophe in the middle of winter, and how they would work under those stressful conditions could not be predicted.

"We're not a team yet," Caroline said, "but we're going to *make* ourselves a team."

Their dogs would include Aly and three other German shepherds, a Rottweiler, a golden retriever, and two black Newfoundlands.

The upstairs conference room at the airport Hilton was crowded with State Department people and medical personnel. Reporters demanding interviews waited outside. There was so much clamoring that Bob Kessecker, in constant phone contact from the OFDA office in Washington, D.C., arranged for a news conference with Bill and the dog handlers. After they fielded general questions, they joined others bound for the Soviet Union at a briefing by a Federal official.

"What we're facing in this mission is so staggering that it's almost beyond comprehension," he said. "This is the first American relief flight. We'll be going to northwestern Armenia, in the Caucasus Mountains. That area is home to nearly a third of Armenia's three point three million people. The earthquake had a destructive magnitude of six point nine on the Richter scale, and the damage is concentrated in an area eighty kilometers in diameter. It struck at eleven-forty-one A.M., when children were at school and workers were in factories, which accounts for the high number of deaths. The Soviets tell us that the earthquake killed or injured as many as a hundred thousand people—"

There was a gasp.

"—and more than half a million are homeless. The hardest-hit places are Leninakan, Kirovakan, Stepanavan, and Spitak. The latter, a town near the epicenter with twenty-five-thousand inhabitants, was totally destroyed. To put it bluntly, Spitak has been erased from the face of the earth. It no longer exists."

Now there was stunned silence.

"We'll be concentrating on Armenia's second-largest city, Leninakan, where much of the population of two hundred and ninety thousand is now homeless. Eighty percent of the houses, apartments, services, and industry has been destroyed. Virtually all of Leninakan's hospitals and medical facilities are gone. Up to twenty thousand of the injured are being helicoptered or motored to Yerevan, Armenia's capital and largest city, seventy miles away. Roads and railways have been severely damaged, and telecommunications are out everywhere.

"This is a calamity," he added, unnecessarily.

It was near midnight when they boarded a heavily loaded Boeing 727 jet chartered from Trans Air. Clearly, the government wanted to avoid a military transport for this first flight in, but the handlers discussed the rumor that the plane was occasionally used for CIA operations.

The first stop was Washington. Among those waiting to join the flight was Julia Taft, head of OFDA. Her presence seemed to verify the mission's humanitarian and diplomatic significance to the U.S. government.

"We're making history," she told the reporters who had gathered at Dulles Airport in the early morning. "This is the first time the Russians have asked for help in a disaster from the United States, so it represents a new level of trust between our countries. It's a special opportunity for us to reach out and work with the Soviet Union."

Doug Jewett arrived with an advance team of six other workers from Metro-Dade Fire Rescue. They greeted Caroline, to whom they had become familiar figures, and she felt grateful that these experienced men would be in Armenia to back up the efforts of the search dogs. Others from Florida, as well as firefighters from Fairfax, Virginia, would be following soon aboard a military aircraft.

The plane's total complement of forty-two passengers comprised the initial strike force of what would be the biggest U.S. relief effort in the U.S.S.R. since World War II. As coleader of the canine unit, Caroline was one of twenty-six disaster-relief specialists aboard. The group also included six trauma experts, a shelter specialist, and three representatives of Armenian-American groups.

Among the doctors were Hank Siegelson, an emergency-room physician from Atlanta; James Dugal of Illinois, an expert trauma surgeon; and Robert Gale of Los Angeles, a UCLA bone-marrow specialist. Dr. Gale had gone to the Ukraine two years earlier to treat victims of the nuclear accident at Chernobyl. His experience working with the Soviets would be an asset.

The explosion and partial meltdown of the Chernobyl reactor had killed thirty-two people and spewed radiation that eventually circled the globe—even as Soviet authorities tried to keep the full extent of the disaster secret. But now they were communicating their country's plight quickly and fully. Health Minister Yevgeny I. Chazov had been bluntly open: the "terrifying arithmetic" in Armenia was such, he said, that "delaying help by each hour means that of every thousand persons concealed under debris, twenty more will die." People were still calling from the ruins, he added, "but every hour those screams are becoming quieter."

And Yegor Yakovlev, editor of the weekly *Moscow News*, would soon be even more frank in his own written commentary: "For the first time, perhaps, in our history, we are not afraid to admit we need help—really huge amounts of help—because we cannot cope alone. We always pretended that socialism was so perfect, and so superior to capitalism, that we needed no assistance from abroad. So this is a basic change in the way we see ourselves and the way we see the world. We at last recognize that realism must prevail, that human lives count more than false pride."

. . .

The strike force left Dulles at 3:30 A.M. Saturday, Eastern time, less than three days after the quake, to begin its thirteen-hour journey of eight thousand miles. Because the plane did not have large fuel tanks, it would have to hop and skip across the globe, landing to refuel in Newfoundland, Ireland, Frankfurt, and Belgrade. Aly and the seven other dogs traveled with the human passengers in the main cabin, which was also packed with 4 three-thousand-gallon water tanks as well as smaller ones, medicine, blankets, tents, hard hats, protective masks, plastic sheeting, leather gloves, and—in the event they would be allowed—hand-held radios.

The handlers had brought their own portable communications gear, but all the high-band radios had been confiscated by the State Department. "If you take that kind of equipment in," officials had said, "the KGB will accuse you of being spies. You'll be arrested."

"You want us to go in there," Caroline had shot back, appalled, "and literally have no communications? What if someone needs help? What if we need rescue assistance right away? What about our ability to communicate with other foreign teams?"

"Sorry," they had told her, "but that's the situation."

The briefings continued during their flight.

"This region has been torn by ethnic violence between Armenians and Azerbaijanis, and the Soviets already had about fifteen thousand soldiers stationed in the area, based in Yerevan. Obviously the earthquake has exacerbated an already difficult situation. . . ."

"One thing to avoid is any offer to trade goods on the Soviet black market. . . ."

"Health hazards include hypothermia, frostbite, and other cold-related injuries. Hepatitis A and B are the most hazardous risks at this time, so we recommend you be careful of local food and water and touch the dead bodies as little as possible. . . ."

Having lived in Turkey, which bordered on Armenia, Caroline was asked to speak to the group about some of the cultural shocks they might encounter. "Women in this area are second-class citizens," she told the female dog handlers. "Plus the men may be shocked to see you running around wearing pants and jumpsuits. Don't be surprised if they follow you around, thinking you're an easy target."

An Armenian-American doctor spoke about the close-knit, religious culture they would find: "They are like the early Christians, and similar to those of the Greek Orthodox faith. So if you find an icon or anything like that, don't try to take it as a souvenir. It would offend them deeply."

The plane went into its final landing approach. It was just before dawn as they circled over Yerevan, capital of the Armenian Soviet Socialist Republic. This city of 1.5 million had been virtually untouched by the quake. Caroline gazed down and saw that Russian tanks, stationed there because of the civil unrest, lined the streets.

The airport runways seemed barely lit as they finally descended. Everyone belted up and waited for touchdown.

But the plane abruptly swooped upward again.

"We've had to abort," the pilot announced, "because a Soviet transport is on the runway assigned to us."

He had not seen the parked plane until the last moment; no one had told him it was there.

Now they were in a holding pattern.

Below, the airport was a scene of absolute chaos, the result of a massive airlift from North America, Europe, Asia, Australia, and the Middle East, bringing tons of rescue equipment, medicine, food, and clothing to the relief effort. During the past two days, Soviet engineers had been working frantically to lengthen the runways, but the international traffic jam was causing confusion and delays. The planes were arriving with over $100 million in assistance from seventy-three countries, including more than two thousand rescue workers.

Their landing had been delayed by an hour. Now young Soviet soldiers, gathering around fires along the runway to keep warm, stared with curiosity as the plane taxied past them. Caroline, seated next to Julia Taft, looked out the window. The Russian soldiers smiled and waved, until a superior raised his arms and apparently ordered them to stop. Then, like mischievous kids, the soldiers sneaked little grins and gave surreptitious hand signals as signs of welcome.

The passengers waited while Soviet officials examined their visas and inspected their gear. As they disembarked on the runway, the early-morning temperature was below freezing. Some of the soldiers came over and greeted them with hot tea, digging into their pockets to hand out cookies as well. They also offered to guard the U.S. search-and-rescue gear that was being piled on the runway.

Caroline and her teammates brought their dogs into the airport building, where Julia Taft desperately tried to reach the U.S. ambassador in Moscow by phone. No official delegation had greeted them. There were none of the expected directions from the Soviet Ministries of Foreign Affairs and Health. They would need transportation across a mountain pass to the stricken city of Leninakan.

"Gorbachev is about to arrive," Julia said, "so we're not going to be allowed out of the airport for a while."

The nightmare for the Soviet leader had been compounded by another tragedy when an emergency relief plane from Moscow, landing near Leninakan, had collided with a helicopter and crashed. Its Russian passengers, nine crew members and sixty-nine servicemen, had been on their way to help victims of the earthquake. All had been killed.

Caroline and the other Americans watched as a motorcade sped a grim-faced Gorbachev past the airport crowd to his waiting helicopter.


They were crammed into an old, rickety bus, which Julia Taft had found for the seventy-mile trip northwest. An ancient heater was noisily running up front. Caroline sat with Aly as they bumped over narrow, icy, rutted mountain roads. Beside the road the ground dropped off into sheer cliffs. The driver faced a steady stream of oncoming relief vehicles that were bringing survivors from Leninakan to hospitals in Yerevan. He kept swerving to avoid each car or truck that passed in the opposite direction.

"My God," someone said as the passengers flinched, "they make *three lanes* out of these little roads up here!"

Then came a plateau. Its barren landscape reminded Caroline of the Anatolian Plain, in Turkey, which she had seen many times with her parents as a little girl.

It was late afternoon as they approached the outskirts of Leninakan. Freezing rain and sleet fell from the clouds; the air was gray with smoke and dust, and mud was all around. It was stuffy inside from the heater, as well as from all the passengers and dogs, so several windows had been opened. The light, Caroline thought, seemed funereal. And she recognized the powerful stench of death.

Already they were seeing the signs of destruction. They gazed out the windows at pile after pile of rubble, one larger than the other as the blocks continued. The streets were jammed, not only with rescue vehicles but also with cars whose drivers were either arriving—for whatever personal reasons—or trying to flee. This vast industrial town almost looked as if it had suffered a nuclear attack.

Caroline looked out one side of the bus, then the other, at thousands of darkly clothed, homeless survivors wandering aimlessly over and through the devastation. Some were by themselves, while others held hands. Others, obviously exhausted, huddled around small fires in the freezing drizzle. Many carried whatever belongings they could hold. No one seemed in a hurry. It dawned on Caroline that there was nowhere to go. Some were dressed warmly, but others had little to protect them from the bitter cold. All were hollow-eyed, expressionless, dazed, in shock. The ghostly wanderers were everywhere. Every time the bus turned into a new street, there were more.

The bus moved slowly, bumping over congested roads that were cracked with deep ruts and holes. Caroline saw people roaming across twenty-foot-high mounds of broken concrete, pausing to dig into the rubble with their bare hands. Some were desperately searching for victims, while others seemed resigned to picking up small items of significance from what had been their homes. One woman was lifting up a doll.

The passengers on the bus had exclaimed at each new sight of devastation, but they fell silent as the blocks of horror went on and on. Caroline noticed that the blank-faced citizens outside seldom spoke or made sounds. She heard occasional whistles from police officers or soldiers, and the motors of trucks or tractors moving debris, but among the thousands of survivors there seemed to be a quiet that was unreal, eerie . . . terrifying.

Someone remarked that it had been thirty-six hours since they had left Kennedy Airport. Four days had passed since the earthquake.

The hands on the clock tower in Leninakan's central square were frozen at 11:41 A.M. That was the moment when, without warning, a rumble from the earth had shaken the entire city and caused most of its buildings to collapse like accordions. From an epicenter up north near the Armenian-Georgian border, seismic waves had traveled downward and outward, leveling more than fifty towns and villages while damaging a hundred others. When the tremors blasted through Leninakan, citizens must have felt as though time itself had stopped.

From the bus window, Caroline began to hear more noise, and she wondered whether the terrible scenes she had witnessed had at first caused her simply to ignore the noise around her, making the city seem silent. The square was filled with other vehicles. Military men shouted through loudspeakers. Gun-toting soldiers roamed everywhere.

Shots were fired. The people being fired upon, someone said, were looters.

And everywhere they looked were coffins. Coffins were stacked on street corners. Coffins were piled in empty lots or fields. The crude wooden boxes had red or black markings, according to some sort of code, perhaps indicating male or female. And there were smaller coffins. The sight of the little boxes stacked together pulled a thought from Caroline's subconscious mind:

*The children! Where are the children? Among all the masses of people we have seen, the children have been missing! We've driven miles through town and we've seen none! Where are the children?*

A command post for the U.S. strike force was set up on the second floor of the local KGB building, an older structure that had survived the quake. Julia Taft and others from the State Department would also be sleeping there. Caroline helped to carry one of the portable but heavy water tanks up an old wooden stairway. In the hall, Soviet soldiers zealously guarded each door as the Americans went by with their gear.

The Swiss team was in a nearby room, so Caroline went to see its members, most of whom she knew.

"Our dogs are beat," the Swiss handlers said. "They've been finding nothing but death. We're pulling out tomorrow."

*My God*, Caroline thought, *we just got here!*

She learned that eighteen thousand victims had been pulled from the wreckage in the immediate aftermath of the city's collapse. The first foreign teams, the French and the Swiss, had arrived within the critical seventy-two-hour window in which rescuers generally had the greatest chance of success. Even so, many of those extricated had died soon afterward from injuries, shock, and exposure to the cold, exacerbated by the lack of adequate medical facilities. It was not difficult to understand why the Swiss were disheartened.

Caroline returned to the room where the Americans had gathered. "Okay," a Miami firefighter was saying, "now that all our government bigwigs are situated here with the KGB, how about us peons? Where do *we* get to spend the night?"

The promised tents and other supplies from the U.S. government had not arrived. They were on another plane, a C-141, with additional Miami rescuers and a ten-man contingent from the Fairfax County Fire and Rescue Department of Virginia.

Caroline, who could speak some rough-and-ready Russian, was recruited (along with Bob Gale, who was more fluent) to find temporary lodgings for the American team. Brusquely taking charge, Gale told her to leave Aly in the bus with the other dogs. She followed him into a waiting KGB car and they were off.

Squeezed between a pair of agents in the backseat, she was nearly crushed by these heavyset, grim-faced men, whose bull necks and beefy shoulders seemed to be a KGB trademark. The car jockeyed through traffic until they came to a park in which military-green Soviet tents had been erected on the grass amid the trees. The large encampment was now a tent city for homeless survivors.

One of the agents leaped out and, using his authority, swiftly requisitioned one of the huge tents for the U.S. disaster team. "You will stay here tonight," he said. Then he jumped back into the car and sped away.

Caroline stayed with Gale to make sure the tent would not be commandeered by others. It was a well-constructed tent, with insulation, that could accommodate fifteen people. She could stand inside and walk around, as in a large room. That night it would have to sleep eight handlers and eight large search dogs, along with Bill Dotson and seven Miami rescuers. Caroline decided to keep her own tent on standby.

It was still raining as she and Gale stood in the early-evening cold, waiting for the rest of the team. Armenians from the other tents came bearing tea, bread, and expressions of gratitude. One man kept clasping his hands to show friendship and repeated in English, "Reagan—Gorbachev!"

An older Armenian man, who had been strolling through a park when the quake hit, said he had been forced to "play God" in deciding which victims to try to save. Sometimes he had had to pass by the sounds of people pleading for help, because there was no way of getting to them, and go to anybody who might have a chance.

He told them that he had walked up to wreckage piles and often seen no one, though he had been able to hear their voices. It had seemed, he said, that "the ground was crying for help."

For three days there had been no cranes or heavy equipment, he said—three days! And it took so much time to get just one person loose. Mothers and fathers had pulled frantically on their children to free them, but sometimes the child would go into shock and die. The screaming had been everywhere, and buildings had continued to topple through the day. As the hours went by, the cries had become weaker and fewer. Every hour more had died. And then the ground was silent.

Now the man asked for understanding. "Please do not think we are indifferent to our dead and wounded. Nearly everyone here has lost someone. I myself lost my sister, but I am grateful to know she died instantly, without too much suffering. I cannot cry. We still have to find our people, alive or dead. We have much work to do. Later there will be time, too much time, to cry."

He offered an Armenian saying: "God gave suffering to the tree, and it broke. God gave suffering to the stone, and it broke. God gave suffering to man, and he survives. That is what makes us special and great."

Caroline noticed that about sixty men and women were keeping vigil next to the encampment. They were gazing across the street at the smoldering wreckage of a collapsed building, about a hundred yards away. Smoke was billowing upward in the freezing drizzle. She walked over to the group to inquire about it. The building—what remained of it—was an elementary school in which four hundred children had been seated at their desks in classrooms.

Fifteen had gotten out.

The quake had hit just four minutes before their 11:45 A.M. recess period.

*Just four minutes later,* Caroline thought, *they all would have been playing outside in the schoolyard.*

"*Ryebyonka!*" Caroline heard the parents saying over and over. It was Russian word for "child."

Now the old, rickety bus pulled up with the remaining members of the American team. The grief-stricken parents, seeing Aly emerge with seven other dogs wearing rescue vests, immediately assumed that help had arrived. They swarmed toward the handlers and even grabbed their arms, while the dogs watched as if to make sure there was no threat to their handlers.

"*Ryebyonka!* You *must* find our children!" they demanded, pointing to the burning wreckage.

"My child is in that school!" a mother screamed.

Caroline knew how quickly grief could turn to rage. Amid all the shouting and crying, she conferred with her colleagues in a huddle. "Listen, we're going to have a riot on our hands if we don't do *something.* We don't want the dogs to burn their feet, but we have to make at least a show of searching."

She and the other handlers took their dogs across the street and worked around the edges of the hot rubble. The four-story building had been prefabricated, made of partially reinforced concrete, much of which had crumbled to dust. The fire had spread through wood flooring, desks, doors, books, papers, and whatever else inside that could have been ignited. There had been no water to fight it.

It was difficult to get very close, but as the parents watched, Caroline brought Aly with her onto the burning rubble, taking extreme care to see that he didn't step on anything too hot. She whisked him through the heat and smoke before moving off the site again.

In her mind, the handlers had been obliged to make a conscious effort to show they cared. Psychologically, the parents had needed to see this. Turning them down had not really been an option.

And the effort did serve to placate them, at least somewhat, although Caroline knew that no one could have survived in that school. Many of the teachers and students would have been crushed to death in the collapse. Then, if the fire had not killed most of the others, the remaining victims would have died from smoke inhalation. She knew, but did not say, that none of the 385 other children in there was alive.

But the parents were still surrounding their tent, besieging them, at midnight. It was impossible to sleep. Caroline finally made her way outside in the bitter cold and rain. She faced the distraught men and women, and using her limited Russian, said, "Look, I'm sorry, but we've been traveling a long time. We're exhausted and so are the dogs. In order for them to really work well, and also for us to function, we absolutely have to have a little sleep."

Members of the crowd nodded and slowly walked off.

In the dark tent again, Caroline groped toward her sleeping bag. Aly was sprawled right next to it. Every inch of space on the ground was taken up by the sixteen team members and eight dogs. Each dog was covered by a blanket and each slept beside its handler. Somehow she managed to fall asleep.

# Chapter 17

# Praying for Miracles

"WHERE'S CAROLINE? WHERE'S DOTSON?"

Someone was aiming a flashlight around. She groaned. "Yeah?"

"You guys are needed back at the KGB building. The other rescue teams have come in. We need to bring them over here."

She shone a light at her watch. It was three in the morning. Pulling on some clothes and leaving Aly in the tent, she joined Bill and they started trudging half a mile across town through frozen mud. It was an even eerier scene now, with bonfires burning in the darkness, debris everywhere, and coffins piled all over. Some were partly open, with bodies in them. The entire city was quiet. Homeless survivors huddled around the bonfires, and Caroline could see the flickering silhouettes of others who were still roaming on top of the wreckage, digging for loved ones. The stark absence of children in their midst contributed to an atmosphere of emptiness and hopelessness, of palpable gloom. The future, in this desolate place, was gone.

They were stopped by some soldiers wearing flak vests and carrying AK-47's or other automatic weapons. The officers reminded them that because of previous civil unrest, Armenia was still under martial law and that the Soviets had imposed a curfew from midnight to five in the morning. Caroline and Bill were warned that no one was allowed on the streets without proper authorization and identification, and violators could still be arrested or shot without warning.

At the headquarters, they discovered that the newly arrived rescue workers from Florida and Virginia had simply gone to sleep in their bus. Caroline and Bill looked at each other. "I'd love to strangle the guy who called us out here," she said as they walked back in the subzero cold.

It was near dawn in the cold tent. Caroline noticed that the water jugs had frozen solid overnight. She shoved them into her still-warm sleeping bag so that they would melt. Aly would need plenty to drink along with his morning meal. She rummaged through her duffel bag to find packets of instant oatmeal and hot chocolate, along with the little stove she had brought.

Bill opened his eyes and watched. He whispered to her in his Southern drawl, "Where did you get the fuel for that thing?"

She smiled. "I smuggled it onto the plane."

"You did?"

"Well, I figured we weren't going to get any fuel once we got here, so I brought my own."

Bill was clearly enjoying this. "Caroline, that's illegal!"

"Hey, Dotson," she said, lighting the stove, "illegal or not, we can have a hot breakfast."

They rode in the old bus, whose heater made it difficult to breathe, through streets gridlocked with military and emergency-rescue traffic. It was a mile and a half back out to the Leninakan airport. Tons of American medical and relief supplies had been piled and stored on a muddy field next to one of the runways. The rescue workers who had arrived during the night were busy setting up a "permanent" U.S. base camp there—much to the annoyance of Caroline and the other dog handlers, who were eager to start searching right away.

The OFDA officials had brought in lightweight summer tents, ideal for the tropics. There was no insulation to keep out the extreme cold; in fact, they had been purchased originally by the State Department for use in Africa. The tents could sleep eight people, but in this case each would accommodate four handlers and four dogs, plus gear, with cots for the humans to sleep on.

Caroline's tent would keep her warmer, but she didn't want to isolate herself from the team, so she staked a claim to one of the cots.

Aside from their vests, the dogs wore no special clothing, because their fur coats protected them in the daytime, or at least whenever they were moving around. But when night came again and the dogs slept for hours in one place, the handlers would have to wrap them in extra blankets to keep them warm enough.

The tents had come in cardboard shipping cartons, which were used creatively by the rescue workers to fashion a communal outhouse. But their architecture was based strictly on the male perspective: The makeshift toilet had no door, and its wide opening looked out on the main approach runway for Soviet planes and military helicopters. The female dog handlers had to sit there in the glare of the lights, facing the pilots.

With their base camp finally in place next to the airfield, the handlers and dogs were taken back into Leninakan later that morning.

The devastation went on and on, but Caroline noticed that the oldest buildings were generally still standing. The vast majority of the destroyed structures were newer, and more shoddily built. These had toppled in piles of dusty fragments. Their concrete, mixed with volcanic rock, was so light that it literally had shattered and disintegrated upon impact.

*Pravda*, the Communist Party paper, later blamed the inadequate buildings on the regime of Leonid Brezhnev, whose eighteen years in power had ended in 1982. "Practically everything constructed during those years of stagnation collapsed," *Pravda* reported, adding that high-rise buildings of that era seemed to have contained more sand than concrete. They had gone up without even I-beam supports, despite repeated warnings by seismologists. The paper said those responsible could face criminal charges.

The Swiss had told Caroline that the wreckage was so tightly compacted together that few air pockets had been created, so even if trapped victims had not been crushed, they probably had been unable to breathe. Most had probably suffocated or succumbed to injuries and freezing temperatures within a few days. Perhaps thousands of bodies would never be located, and even when they were, it would be dangerous and difficult to remove them.

*Did we get here too late?* Caroline wondered as she tried to push away a growing sense of despair.

Meanwhile the current Soviet government was being criticized, by the country's own media, for lack of preparedness and organization. Even now, not enough heavy cranes were available. Rescue workers were smashing up or down through the fragile concrete with picks, shovels, and hatchets.

Aly was working hard. But he was alerting over and over on the presence of hidden dead bodies. At the same time, being unable to get very far into the crushed buildings, he seemed frustrated, and expressed it by barking, pawing, and looking over at her as if to say, *What the hell is going on here? Why can't I go any farther?* She too found it frustrating, and often he seemed to know it. *I understand*, the expression in his eyes told her. Then he would come over and bump gently against Caroline's legs. *So why aren't you doing something now?* was the message she got from each of his impatient bumps.

She felt that his emotional as well as physical endurance was being tested as never before. The rescue crews were carefully moving chunks of debris to create new holes; when Aly went into one and alerted, she would peer in with her flashlight to see if the bodies were visible. Despite the cold, which was slowing the rate of decomposition, the stench made her reel backward; but she knew that for Aly, whose nose was so much more sensitive, the impact must have been shocking and overwhelming.

So she began working him in twenty-minute spurts, broken by ten minutes of downtime to rest. During those breaks he lay down on the pavement, at her instruction, but the air was so cold that she couldn't let him stay in that position too long. He might stiffen up and be unable to continue. She kept giving him water from her Sierra cup.

Drinking it helped to relieve his stress, while also preventing his nose from drying up and losing much of its scenting power.

The handlers also took turns hiding, to perk up all their dogs by giving them occasional live finds.

Caroline remembered the constant clamor of people in Mexico City insisting they heard the voices of victims inside the rubble, and it was the same here, although the religious Armenians had been reduced mainly to praying for miracles. All that most survivors really wanted was to retrieve the bodies of their loved ones and give them proper burials.

Whenever a body was recovered, all work stopped. People stood in silence until it was placed in the waiting coffin and carried away.

Caroline kept seeing Christmas decorations or children's toys amid the ruins.

A man walked along carrying the bodies of two children, one over his shoulder and the other under his arm.

A private car drove down the street with a coffin strapped to its roof.

As crushed bodies were being brought out of one building, Caroline looked down and saw a carton of fresh eggs in the wreckage. Not one had been broken.

Leninakan was still without fresh water and food, and the city had no communications. And now light snow was falling, making it slippery and dangerous for the dogs and handlers.

Temporary shelters and field kitchens had been erected to accommodate up to 300,000 of the 700,000 homeless Armenians, but many people refused to use them. Instead they sat around fires in front of their former homes, vowing to prevent the wrecked houses from being bulldozed before they could retrieve and bury their dead. Meanwhile, Soviet authorities were planning to evacuate more than 50,000 women and children from all the different stricken areas of Armenia.

As Caroline stood with Aly, watching the body of a little girl being carried out on a stretcher, she wondered at the ability of the people to go on. One of the search dogs licked the dead girl's face, trying to wake her up.

All around Aly, amid the human suffering and the odor of diesel fuel and the pervasive presence of death, were the sights and sounds of stray Armenian dogs running in packs. Because of his training, Aly was not perturbed by the noise of soldiers shooting at the wild dogs that night to keep them away from the tents and the food at base camp. Caroline kept his orange vest on him, trying to make sure he wouldn't become a target.

The handlers were still without their own radios, but the State Department people had a few, which were being allotted to selected dog teams or rescue crews. The British, setting up camp next door, had brought a portable setup for satellite communications. The Canadians came in, too, and also put up tents near the runway. Someone had thought to bring an American flag, which was soon flying high in full view of the airport's Soviet military garrison. Team members now called their campsite the U.S. Hilton. When the British and Canadians followed suit by hoisting their own flags, it seemed that a small international community had been created on Soviet soil.

Some of the soldiers, who had volunteered to guard all the supplies being protected under a tarp in the muddy parking lot, also came bearing firewood for the central campfire. It was the only source of warmth. The campfire doubled as a cook station; someone had made a grill by punching holes in metal suitcases that had contained medical supplies.

Most of the hospitals in Leninakan had been destroyed, reducing treatment conditions to the most primitive level. As a result, many of the injured either walked or managed to be driven up to the airport campsite to receive care. Doctors stitched up wounds or performed operations right there.

It was hard to imagine ever feeling warm again. And yet Caroline knew she was one of the lucky ones. She and the other dog handlers had brought, as usual, all their own survival gear; they had trained in the cold and had learned to carry their own thermal underwear, down jackets, and thick socks. But the Metro-Dade firefighters, who had been supplied in Florida with flimsy, lightweight clothing, were absolutely freezing.

In only a few places had Aly barked excitedly, tail wagging with joy as he found a stick to throw around. And in those few places, Caroline learned later, the rescue teams had brought people out alive. But mostly he was indicating the corpses with his usual whining-and-digging alert, showing less enthusiasm as time went on. All too often, his ears went down and his tail drooped as he tucked it between his hind legs. He gazed sadly at Caroline as if saying, *When will this end?*

But now, in yet another collapsed building, Aly and three other dogs showed definite interest where some local people felt there was life. His barking was not exactly joyful, yet he was being persistent. To Caroline, that meant someone below the rubble, inside a void, was still alive—but probably badly injured or near death.

The Virginia and Florida firemen faced a delicate and dangerous task. Removing debris from the top could cause internal shifts within the structure; in turn, those movements could suddenly close the life-saving void and crush the victim. But the firemen had no other choice. So these experienced rescue workers slowly and carefully pulled away chunks of rubble to create a tunnel, shoring it as they moved downward. After nearly five hours, they heard moaning and crying. And then they saw that a woman, about sixty years old, was trapped up to her knees in heavy wreckage.

She had been saved by a refrigerator. It had tipped over at an angle above her, creating an air pocket and shielding her from the rest of the falling debris. But now the rescuers saw, to their horror, that she was also being pinned by bodies. She had been stuck there with the corpses of her daughter and granddaughter directly against her for five days and nights.

The firemen decided that before they could free the woman they would have to remove the bodies. Now they began digging, cutting, breaking, and sawing pieces of debris, praying all the while that the heavier slabs would not crash down on them and the woman from above. With generators and portable lights allowing work to proceed far into the night, the rescuers finally realized that the woman's throat was being pressed by the leg of her dead granddaughter. The woman, semiconscious, could hardly breathe. Crawling downward with them was Jim Dugal, the trauma surgeon from Illinois, who determined that the leg would have to be amputated before the woman could be dislodged. To make it possible for him to perform the operation, rescuers had to hold him suspended in the rubble. Dugal had just finished when he accidentally kicked the temporary jack that supported whatever remained of the structure. The huge pile of wreckage started to shake. The firemen quickly took over again. They lifted the woman up through the tunnel and carried her out of the rubble. The rest of the building shuddered down behind them in a cloud of cement dust.

It had been a ghastly ordeal, traumatizing the rescuers, some of whom wondered aloud if saving the woman's life had been a blessing or a curse to her. She had lost all her family members; her daughter and granddaughter had died on top of her; and, the surgeon said, both of her own legs would have to be amputated above the knee.

Mercifully, the woman had passed out. The horror she had endured was unimaginable. The expression on her face would haunt the rescuers for the rest of their lives.

The crumbled buildings were always packed with crowds of grieving survivors. At times, unable to dig, they sifted through the rubble to retrieve whatever belongings they could find. They collected trinkets, religious articles and statues, pieces of beautiful carpeting, anything connected with their lost loved ones below. As people huddled and shivered around open fires, military vehicles kept driving through. Officers loudly honked their horns at the homeless, waving for them to get out of the way, and soldiers with billy clubs often felt compelled to move people aside forcibly. But at other times, Soviet army trucks arrived with apples and cheese and loaves of bread, and people would rush forward, arms outstretched.

Caroline tried to share her rations with local people, but more often it was the Armenians who wanted to give their own meager food to the searchers. Their gratitude seemed way out of proportion to what the rescuers could do.

"Thank you for being here!" they exclaimed. "Thank you for saving our city!"

Caroline remembered her father saying, "You must never say no to an Armenian," so when they pressed a piece of bread or a hunk of sausage into her hand, she always took it.

"We didn't think you knew we existed," a man said.

. . .

Even though all the foreign teams were operating with a total of 219 dogs throughout Leninakan, complete search coverage was impossible. The damage was so spread out that Caroline did not see most of the handlers and dogs from other countries. She met up, however, with the Czechoslovakian team at a destroyed paint factory.

"Nobody is alive in there," said one of the Czech doctors, who spoke excellent English. "But there are bodies."

"I'm concerned about the chemicals and other hazardous materials," she told him.

"I am, too. We have no way of testing the air quality inside the building. There have been ruptures of pipelines and tanks. I don't think we can commit our personnel in there."

"Or our dogs," she said.

Caroline knew she could not risk Aly's life by sending him into a place with toxic fumes. As well, some of the gases could ignite. Paying attention to the safety of her teammates, dogs and handlers alike, was part of her responsibility. So they made what the Czech doctor called a "very painful triage"—assigning the paint factory a low priority in the search effort, to maximize the overall effectiveness of the rescue work.

They walked away.

Despite the general lack of heavy equipment, some of the Soviet tanks were being used to pull away debris with chains, causing structures to collapse even more. Caroline watched one tank that was about to doom any chance of finding people inside the place—alive or dead—but, fortunately, the tank broke down before that could happen.

And some tall cranes, currently being used at apartment buildings, were posing other dangers. The safe procedure was to stop operating them when the dog teams were searching, simply because the cranes might drop something on them. But when the waiting survivors became frantic, rescuers often forgot that precaution, forcing the handlers to go in with their dogs while the cranes swung huge chunks of concrete over their heads.

"Listen," Caroline told the Armenians at one site, "it's very dangerous for us to work under a moving crane. Please give us ten minutes to get on and off with our dogs."

But by that time, people had become caught up in a kind of numb frenzy. And they were angry—at the earthquake, at the disaster-relief process, at the government—to the point where they no longer cared about safety.

So the handlers tried to work their dogs beneath the cranes. But suddenly a piece of concrete being lifted broke in half and came crashing down near Aly, barely missing him. "That's it!" Caroline yelled, shaking with fear and fury, as she pulled her team off the site.

It was early morning when Caroline brought some of her team back to the wreckage of an apartment building that was listing to one side and threatening to fall over. The dogs had shown extreme interest the day before, and she had reported that to the rescuers. During the night, trying to sleep in the tent at base camp, she had been unable to get the building out of her mind. She had vowed to come back.

Workers had created a new, small passageway down into the basement area. Aly went to the opening of the hole, took one whiff, and shot inside, disappearing from view. Caroline's first instinct was, *Where my dog goes, I go!*

She shimmied down a five-foot drop. It was pitch black, but she could hear Aly barking with excitement. Then she saw him in the light of her head lamp. He was digging and scratching.

He climbed back out to get his stick reward. And as Caroline started up, eager to tell people the good news, she got to the opening and suddenly confronted a pair of eyes staring at her through thick spectacles. It was Fred Krimgold, a structural engineer from Virginia Polytechnic, whom she had first met at the L'Ambiance Plaza collapse in Connecticut. After that they had met up again in Maryland, when they had shared the podium as speakers on search-and-rescue topics.

Fred, who seemed like an absent-minded professor rather than someone geared to disaster work, had one overriding structural philosophy: "Safety, safety, safety!"

Caroline's reply: "Take calculated risks!"

Now, together in Armenia, they were face to face at the opening of this one small debris tunnel. Fred, obviously alarmed, leaned down to address her with an ominous, chastising tone in his voice. "Caroline, what are you *doing* down there?"

"Hey, Fred," she said, climbing out, "I've got a live find!"

"No, no," he said, "it's too dangerous!"

"My dog is so positive, though. Someone's alive in there!"

"This building is *not safe*, Caroline!"

"But we were over here yesterday, before that hole was made, and even then the dogs showed interest."

Because of the lack of radios, she had not known that Fred and other engineers had come back since then. After the hole had been opened, they had declared the building to be too dangerous for search-and-rescue work. But Caroline had returned in the morning without knowing that. And when Fred heard that she had gone back there, he rushed over, only to find her climbing out of the hole.

"You shouldn't have been in there," he said.

"Can't we do *something*?" she pleaded.

"Too precarious. There are no internal supports."

Aly was having fun with his reward, a piece of wood that she had tossed into the air for him to catch. And now, as the team was being summoned to another search area, Caroline found herself unable to move. Soon a bulldozer would come to raze this place, flatten it to the ground. For her, this moment was the hardest of all. She and Aly had been on the brink of saving another life, only to be forced to accept that nothing would come of their efforts. Nothing, that is, but certain death for the victim or victims inside.

Caroline learned later that Fred Krimgold's warnings had been accurate. Two French firemen went into the same debris hole and tried to reach the victims. As they were tunneling farther inside, part of the structure collapsed on them. Both rescue workers were badly injured. Caroline figured they had been notified of the hazards, but, knowing the French, she also figured they would have taken the risk. When she found Fred again, she thanked him for saving her life.

That same afternoon, she heard from teammates that a thirteen-year-old girl was about to be brought out of a collapsed apartment building after being trapped for six days. Aly and other dogs had given "possibly living" alerts. After the handlers had conveyed the messages from their dogs, Armenian rescuers carefully moved enough wreckage to form a tunnel. Soon they heard the girl's voice from within. She was covered by debris and surrounded by the bodies of her grandmother and brothers and sisters. Now, after a prolonged effort to free her, there was almost unbearable anticipation and excitement. A crowd had gathered, along with photographers and reporters. And Caroline, who happened to be searching with Aly at the adjacent building, came over to watch.

Members of the crowd wept and prayed as she was carried out on a stretcher and examined by doctors. The girl's uncle and father, the only other surviving family members, were reunited with her and cried with simultaneous joy and sorrow. Doctors rushed to examine and treat her. Still conscious, she was suffering only from a few broken ribs, and complained merely of a sore throat. Undoubtedly the psychological impact of what she had experienced would be enormous, but all her vital signs were in order and she would have her life. No one could believe she was in such remarkably good condition after being buried for nearly a week.

One reason she had made it, Caroline thought, was that her body had been acclimated to the cold temperatures. And she was not a scrawny or sickly girl. Beyond that, survival seemed to depend on each person's mental as well as physical makeup. The will to live depended on the individual—you had it or you didn't. And the girl must have had it.

Saving this one life, Caroline realized, was reason enough to have come with Aly to Armenia. He and the other dogs had all shown enough initial interest for local people to start trying to uncover her. The Miami and Fairfax crews had come in to do the final extrication. It had been a total team effort, all aspects working together. If miracles were in short supply, this had been one of them.

She and Aly came to another building where the Miami and Fairfax crew asked Caroline to send him through a hole that needed checking. There were bodies inside, one of which was that of a baby. But possibly there was also someone still alive. There was no way to extract the corpses, however, without using heavy equipment. Only a dog could get in safely to discover whether life existed.

Aly was slowing down and nearly burned out, but when Caroline pointed to the hole, he obeyed without complaint. She aimed a light as he continued inside and stepped over the body of the baby. She crawled in part of the way, watching him push past a human arm dangling from the tunnel's ceiling. Then he started backing away. When he reached her, Caroline retreated with him out of the hole.

Caroline turned to the crew chief. "We'll try it again."

She told Aly gently to go in once more. Again he obeyed, confronting the same obstacles, and again he backed out. Now he looked up at her with eyes pleading for mercy: *No, not another time! You're pushing me too far!*

"I'm not going to force him," Caroline told the rescue crew. "It would be terribly wrong for me to do that. He's already gone through enough. We'll bring in another dog."

Some Swedish dog handlers had been standing by, observing. Now one of them approached and addressed her in English. "I want to compliment you on the way you treat your dog. You did the right thing by him just now. If you had forced him to go back in there, he'd never work with you again. It's obvious that he loves you, but he'd never have trusted you again."

Those were the two main ingredients, she thought: trust and love.

Aly could not handle encountering so much death for much longer. He was also getting stressed by the crowds of people who yelled and gesticulated as they ran toward Caroline. His protective instincts would kick in, making him glare at the offenders or, if needed, growl at them, and so she would have to calm him down. In addition to being protective of Caroline, he glared or growled at strangers who got close to the team's bus or tried to touch any member's gear. Just as he did back home, Aly displayed a sense of what was his personal property and took responsibility for its safety.

When they could, Caroline and the other handlers took their dogs out to the nearest muddy field to play ball with them. It was another way of helping them break through the unending grimness.

But the hours were longer than usual, so the dogs, who normally needed to sleep on and off during the day, were becoming exhausted. And the cold air was so penetrating that even with his thick coat, Aly was shivering. At one point an Armenian woman came over with a blanket and draped it over his back. Then she gave him a blessing.

Aly was dirty, smelly, cold, fatigued, depressed, and probably confused. At the same time, he took it all in stride and followed Caroline no matter where she went. He did get some rest and warmth in the bus as they went from one site to another, but that was it. Then, after disembarking, she treated Aly as if he was an athlete—walking him around and helping him limber up before asking him to climb over more piles of debris.

As soon as they got back to the campsite at night, Caroline wrapped him again in wool blankets. There was no way of cleaning him, though. All the dogs, not to mention their handlers, would have loved a shower or bath. The smell of death clung to skin, clothing, and fur, but nothing could be done about it.

Among the American search dogs, Aly stood out as a royal figure just as he had done in Mexico and El Salvador; but in Armenia there was a greater number of dominant male dogs. Caroline had wondered how they would get along in the close quarters of the campsite and in the tent, but it turned out that all these dignified dogs simply ignored each other—or, to be more accurate, they refused to make eye contact. If Aly approached one of the others off-lead, there was no aggression. Instead, both lifted their heads as if to say, *Yes, we know, we're both dominant.* One looked to the right and the other looked to the left as they passed by.

*Like two champions or kings,* Caroline thought.

There was no friction even when two dominant dogs sat together on the bus. They would lie down, inches apart, but never turn or even glance at each other, preserving their separate dignities. It appeared to Caroline that these dogs actually realized they were in the work mode and had no time or energy to spare establishing which one was more dominant. Their serious behavior exuded a sense of mission.

# Chapter 18

# Exodus

FOR THE HUMAN MEMBERS OF THE U.S. TEAM, EX-treme fatigue had become the norm. At the airport camp, loud transport planes and helicopters landed and took off all night long. The team had already reduced their sleep ration to five hours, but most hadn't really slept at all. The aircraft made the ground shake; their landing lights glared through the tents.

Everybody had developed upper respiratory problems and was rasping and coughing in the bone-chilling rain, sleet, and snow. Most of the team, according to the doctors who checked them at the tent, probably had bronchial pneumonia. Caroline's cold tablets and cough syrups were already gone, most having been handed out to the local people. She had saved the serious stuff for last, but there were precious few antibiotics left.

On a slightly less urgent level, one of Caroline's prize possessions was lip balm. Brushing her teeth was a luxury. Going out to the makeshift cardboard outhouse, facing the runway in the cold, was to be dreaded. Changing clothes in this weather, especially at night, was a chore mostly to be avoided.

The Soviet soldiers still appeared nightly with firewood and joined the rescue teams around the campfire. They brought homemade vodka, which was too strong for anyone but themselves. Caroline and others watched Bill Dotson take a swig of it, and for the first time anyone could recall, the rugged Virginian was rendered speechless.

The soldiers also brought Armenian brandy, which went down more easily. They expressed curiosity about President-elect Bush, Michael Jackson, football, hockey, Mike Tyson. Some wore baseball caps and sweatshirts given to them by the Fairfax firefighters. As the American volunteers and the Soviet officers tried to communicate, KGB agents kept coming around to investigate. Caroline came to recognize one, named Ivan, who spoke German and French. She cheerfully called to him in German, "How are you, Ivan? Did you give us a good report to the KGB?"

The grim-faced agent stared back at her until, despite himself, he smiled.

Leninakan's nickname, the soldiers said, could be translated into English as "City of Jokes and Laughter." "Yes," someone replied, "jokes and laughter to keep you from going insane."


The experience of Armenia had become a blur. At some point during the fifth day of searching, Caroline was on the bus when she became dizzy and feverish; she nearly passed out. By the time they got back to base camp, Caroline had to admit to herself that she was definitely ill. Instead of leaving the tent to go stand by the fire with the others, she crawled into her sleeping bag. Aly lay down next to her cot. She was burning up with fever.

One of the Russian officers who came to the campsite looking for her was told, "Oh, she isn't feeling well." He went to his barracks to get something, then marched back and said, "Which tent is she in?" Nobody wanted to tell him. The others were being protective, but he absolutely insisted, so one of the handlers finally relented.

Caroline glanced up as the officer walked in. She saw him reach into a huge pocket of his heavy coat and pull out a crystal wineglass. He pulled a bottle of cognac from another pocket and filled the glass to the brim. Caroline watched him through glazed, feverish eyes. She stank and felt like hell.

"You must drink this in one gulp," the soldier told her.

"*Nyet!*" Caroline replied.

"*Da!*"

The man was not going to leave until she had downed it. She took the glass and drank, thinking, *Oh, my God,* as she felt her insides burning from the alcohol. Then she passed out.

In the morning Caroline realized that she had slept through the entire night for the first time, never even hearing the low-flying, thunderous aircraft. She found herself well and fully functioning, ready to keep searching.

"That was a great home remedy," she remarked to her colleagues, laughing, "but not one I'd recommend on a normal basis!"

The exodus from Leninakan had begun. People were streaming away to live with relatives in other Armenian towns or villages across the countryside, or they were finding their way to the newly constructed shacks outside the city. Thousands were leaving by truck or bus or even on foot. In the central square, Soviet officials used loudspeakers mounted on cars to call for women and children to evacuate the city. Able-bodied men were instructed to remain behind to help with demolition. The streets had become slurries of mud mixed with the slime of a nonfunctioning sewer system. Citizens stood in the muck in long lines for soup, rice, bread, and—if they were lucky—shreds of beef.

Rumors flew around Leninakan that the Soviets were going to take all the surviving Armenian orphans and farm them out to families across the U.S.S.R. If the rumor was true, the Armenians feared, the next generation would be so scattered as to become invisible. The Armenians were on the verge of rioting.

People also protested the rush to tear down unsafe buildings and bury the dead quickly, to avoid the spread of disease. They screamed with sorrow and rage over the bulldozing and the burial of unidentified bodies in mass graves.

The foreign teams were disappearing, too. Julia Taft was on her way back to the United States. "The hope of finding any more survivors is gone," she told reporters after touching down in Moscow en route to Frankfurt. "At some point, you have to stop."

When Caroline and the other dog handlers knew they were leaving soon, they wrestled with guilt over having to abandon people whose lives had been changed forever by their country's tragedy. There had been very few live finds—the sixty-year-old woman, the thirteen-year-old girl, and a few others who had been rescued by different foreign teams. It was clear, after six days of searching, that their official function was over. Aly and the other dogs deserved to go home.

The Americans decided to leave all their tents, blankets, and other supplies for the Armenian people, whose indomitable spirit, after so many centuries of struggle and now this tragedy, seemed larger than life itself. They told some students who had come from Yerevan to help, "We don't want the military grabbing this stuff. We don't want looters to get it, either. We want *you* to be in charge. We want you to see that those who need this stuff will get it." Otherwise, they felt, people involved in the Soviet Union's rampant black market would grab the American supplies for themselves.

At dawn on day seven, Caroline appeared live on television with Ted Koppel, who interviewed her via satellite from his *Nightline* studio at 11:30 P.M. New York time. For the telecast, she and Aly stood next to Mike Tamillow, battalion chief of the Fairfax County Fire and Rescue Department, as they listened to Koppel's voice in their earphones and responded to his questions.

It was snowing and becoming much colder, and Armenians by the hundreds of thousands faced the worst of winter without homes or possessions. Television viewers were given glimpses of the stacked coffins, crushed buildings, rubble piles, cranes, dump trucks, and other sights of the catastrophe, but it was impossible for Koppel's audience to feel the shroud of numbing gloom that covered the shattered city, affecting everyone with a profound melancholy. It was impossible to convey the foul odor of death, the pervasive smell of exhaust fumes, and the vastness of the devastation and horror.

Julia Taft came on the program, live from Frankfurt, and said that the homelessness situation, worsened by the freezing temperatures of a rapidly advancing winter, was out of control. "But everybody is pulling together," she said, citing the international contingents of handlers and dogs, the rescue teams, the Soviet and Armenian officials, the survivors, and everyone else who had joined in "an enormous collaboration of humanity" to help ease the pain.

"What can *we* do?" Koppel asked as Caroline and Mike stood in the midst of one of the century's worst nightmares.


Armenians came with eggs and bread and other foodstuffs in order to make them a big breakfast on the day of their departure. They clasped Caroline's hands and kept offering her pieces of cheese, but she nearly fainted whenever she tried to eat it. The cheese reminded her of the smell of dead bodies. "Never say no to an Armenian," she told herself again as she kept inching backward, shaking her head and feeling herself turning green.

The firemen decided to make a big pot of "stew" with all their leftover MRE's, or Meals Ready to Eat, as their military-style rations were called. They threw in canned soups, canned corn, canned spaghetti, canned stew—and whatever else edible was lurking in their gear. It was the most disgusting mishmash Caroline had ever seen, bubbling on the makeshift grill over the fire.

Now a grandmother with two little kids came over to the American camp. Caroline and the others felt they were too smelly, dirty, and scruffy to greet anyone properly. But the firemen decided to offer their concoction to the pair of Armenian kids. The look on the faces of those two children was priceless: They obviously felt it was the most awful-tasting stuff they had ever encountered. But they kept eating the firemen's horrid stew—whether out of hunger or out of politeness, Caroline couldn't tell—while trying to conceal their reaction.

"Do you realize," Caroline told the firemen, unable to control her laughter, "what you've done for the reputation of American cooking?"


At about noon they boarded one of the buses for a return trip to the capital city of Yerevan. They were all fairly numb during the ride back over the mountain pass, but entering that beautiful city in the midafternoon, they felt as if they were in a dream.

They stopped at the university, dropping off more goods for students to distribute to survivors. Then they were taken past opera houses, theaters, art museums, and other cultural landmarks to a magnificent hotel in the central square.

The dog handlers were escorted by hotel employees into the basement, where they were shown a giant shower stall used to wash off the horses that pulled the carriages outside. "You must wash and disinfect your dogs," the handlers were instructed. They did so, unable to prevent themselves from being soaked as well.

Before they could get to their rooms, they had to receive the keys from women stationed on each floor. The women seemed to Caroline like female jailers sitting there. Whenever the handlers left the hotel, they would have to give the keys back to them. As the team members were being shown up to their rooms, they were told, "We don't have an exact time as to when you're going to be flying out tomorrow, but the mayor of Yerevan and other Armenian officials want to give you a dinner tonight."

Caroline and Aly shared a room on the fifth floor with Pat Yessel of Pennsylvania and her dog, Rubble, the team's lone golden retriever. The room was small, but it had a bathroom with hot water. Pat showered first, then Caroline. Each woman joyfully scrubbed herself. Then they put all their dirty clothes into some garbage bags that Pat had brought and sealed the bags tightly, to block off as much of the smell as possible.

Wearing the only clean clothing they had left, they went outside to walk Aly and Rubble.

Soviet tanks and military people were everywhere, because the government was expecting protests against the initial disorganization and slowness of the disaster response. Caroline and Pat were walking along with their dogs when two men approached them. "You are staying at the hotel? We would like to come up to your room."

Caroline listened, amused at the whole idea of being propositioned amid the tanks and soldiers, then told the men in broken Russian that she was going straight to the soldiers to report them. The two men turned and fled.

. . .

In the hotel lobby she ran into Dr. Hank Siegelson of Atlanta, whom she had not seen since the international flight from New York. Hank had stayed the whole time in Yerevan to work with hospital staff as survivors arrived from Leninakan and medical equipment poured in from around the world.

"Caroline," he said, "you've got to come with me. Can you leave Aly in your room?"

"He's dead tired," she said, "so I'm sure he'd appreciate being allowed to sleep."

"I've got to show you this hospital, where some of my patients have been."

At Hank's request, Caroline went down the hall knocking on doors to collect any leftover antibiotics and vitamin pills from her colleagues. It was early evening when they finally got outside.

"Now, Caroline, we're going to do *this*." He stuck out a thumb in the classic hitchhiker's gesture.

"Hey," she said, laughing, "you've got to be kidding!"

"Forget public transportation. We'd never get there," he said, guiding her into the street. "Okay, *now*!"

Caroline put out her thumb. Within seconds, a shiny black car pulled up in front of them.

"Here we go," Hank said. "We've got the KGB again."

The door opened, and Hank shoved her inside with the agents, who had the regulation thick necks and heavy overcoats. He gave them the name of the hospital.

"*Da!*" the driver said.

Using a few Russian words, Hank explained that he was a doctor and that Caroline was his assistant.

"*Da!*"

They rode in silence to the hospital.

Inside, they went up to a floor where doctors had been working on a nineteen-year-old girl suffering from crush injuries and pneumonia. Overnight, Hank learned, they had mishandled things by treating her with steroids.

"She died," a nurse said.

Hank was so overcome by shock, grief, and anger that Caroline thought he might fall apart. "These primitive conditions here . . . ," he said through clenched teeth, fighting back tears.

Pulling himself together, Hank led the way to a higher floor of the hospital.

"There's a man up here I want you to meet," he said. "He was the principal of a big school in Spitak, one of the towns that was completely destroyed."

The school had comprised students from the early grades up to the highest. When the first hard shock of the earthquake had hit, the principal had made sure that all of them immediately got out—all, that is, except for two, who had not been able to flee in time. When the principal had gone back into the building to try to find them, a doorway collapsed on him and crushed his entire rib cage.

The principal, a slim man in his fifties with thinning hair, was wrapped in bandages so completely that he looked as if he had been placed inside a straitjacket. Nevertheless he greeted Hank and Caroline with a wonderful, warm smile, and she was struck immediately by his eyes. They were luminous, shining with a special kind of gentleness. It seemed to Caroline that she was gazing into his soul.

"Look at this," Hank exclaimed. "Modern medicine says that when a person has multiple broken ribs, you *don't* immobilize the rib cage, or else the patient will get pneumonia. But that's exactly what they *have* done!"

Hank glanced around, then motioned for Caroline to watch the door. He quickly pulled up the principal's nightshirt and loosened the bandages. He explained the situation to him in sign language, with Caroline adding a few Russian words whenever she could. They gave him the supply of antibiotics and vitamin pills.

"Put them under here," Hank said, lifting the mattress to demonstrate. He put his finger to his lips. "Don't let anyone know," he said, telling the principal when to take the pills and how often, as Caroline translated.

The man smiled, glowing with both inner courage and gratitude.

The ward downstairs was filled with people who had been critically injured, many with broken bones and large, infected wounds. A great number of others were suffering from crush syndrome, a common occurrence during earthquakes. As Hank explained it, the person's severely crushed muscles released an enzyme that impaired the kidneys and, in turn, hampered their ability to filtrate blood. Eventually the body wastes built to a fatally toxic level. That was why so many countries had been sending expensive dialysis machines, each of which could handle several patients with kidney failure.

But there was one problem that modern medicine was helpless to treat. Many survivors, comprehending how few of their friends and relatives remained alive, stopped eating or sleeping. Some had already committed suicide in their hospital beds. Others suffered from what they described as "heartache"—a condition that, in fact, often led to cardiac arrest. They were dying, literally, because their hearts were broken.

In charge of this ward was, unbelievably, a dentistry student. He seemed to take an instant dislike to Caroline.

"You're American," he accused.

"*Da.*"

"You are from the press?"

"*Nyet,*" Caroline said.

"You are here to spy?"

"*Nyet!*"

"She works in a hospital," Hank told him. "She's with the ambulance. And she's with me!"

They were ushered into the doctors' lounge and were offered some tea. A nurse came in, clutching bags loaded with pills from foreign shipments, and spoke to Hank in rapid Russian while Caroline tried to understand what she was saying. The nurse held up one pill container after another.

"Well," Caroline translated, "she's sort of saying, 'Eenie, meenie, minie, moe.' "

Hank shook his head. "Jesus," he whispered.

They sat in the lounge and began sorting the pill containers. Some were labeled in German or French, others in English. Hank handled the English ones, while Caroline translated the German and French. They divided everything into separate piles, taking nearly two hours to complete the job.

After Hank made a phone call, the U.S. government sent pharmacists who spoke either Russian or Armenian aboard its next relief flight.

The hotel bar was crammed that night with reporters and TV crews from around the world. By the time Caroline and Hank had returned from the hospital, the mayor's farewell banquet had already begun and most of the food had already disappeared. After taking Aly out for a walk, she had left him up in the room to join Hank and the other Americans at the crowded bar. Now she noticed that a young woman, who had been with a group of French reporters, was coming over to their table.

"Are you from the United States?" she asked in accented English.

"Yes," Caroline said. "We all are."

"Do any of you speak French?"

"I do."

"Could I speak with you?"

"Of course."

The young woman took a seat and started to pour her heart out. She worked for one of the big French magazines. The Armenian earthquake was her first foreign assignment. On top of that, she had never been to a disaster scene. She was with some veteran reporters who, whenever she expressed her horror, dismissed her by saying things like, "Well, you should have seen what it was like in Ethiopia," or brought up some other scene of death and destruction they had covered.

"They keep saying, 'You should have seen this, you should have seen that,'" the young reporter said, "but what about this disaster right here? Have they no feelings left?"

*The other reporters have no empathy,* Caroline thought, *and no idea of how deeply she's been affected.*

"I'm going home tomorrow," the young woman said, "and I know it's nearly Christmas. I know my children are expecting me to put up a tree and to celebrate with them, but I've just seen so much horror here that I can't do it. I can't face even *thinking* of Christmas. What I *am* thinking of is quitting as a reporter."

Caroline recalled Jeff Mitchell's critical incident debriefings. The young woman needed a chance to vent her feelings, all of them. She kept her talking for the next two hours, their heads almost touching, as they leaned together in the noisy, smoky bar.

The return flight from Yerevan took more than twenty-two hours. They finally touched down at Andrews Air Force Base on Sunday morning, December 18. Stepping off the Boeing 727, Caroline saw that a huge crowd was on hand to give them a heroes' welcome. Among the well-wishers were members of the Armenian Relief Society's local chapter, with banners—WE ARMENIANS THANK YOU—and baskets of traditional cookies and string cheese from their homeland. Team members who lived near Washington, D.C., were welcomed by their families with hugs and laughter and tears.

Caroline had no one there. She was starting to feel a little sorry for herself when Jeff Mitchell burst from the crowd.

"I'll be your substitute family," he said as she returned his hug.

Then she faced a battery of microphones and questions from reporters, with Aly standing at her side on the airfield. She felt exhilaration and numbness and fatigue all at once, along with a sinking feeling that no words might come.

"It was very difficult to leave," she said, "but the courage and warmth we encountered is something I have brought back with me. . . ."

Inside, her thoughts were somewhat different. *We have returned from a journey into hell, if you must know, and we carry with us the personal knowledge that the people of Armenia are still there, still going through it. We are back home, but it's not over for them. It goes on, right now, and it will go on and on. Could we have done more? Should we have demanded to stay? Well, no; we did what we could do. . . .*

*Now we are supposed to get on with our lives, as before, but this experience has changed us forever. The tragedy of Armenia will remain with each of us. Our perspective too has changed. Never will life's daily problems or obstacles seem quite so large as they once did. The example of the Armenians—their incredible fortitude, stamina, resilience, endurance, and faith, despite such unspeakable loss—stays with us, as a reminder to be grateful for whatever we have.*

". . . And last but not least," she was saying, "we are grateful to these magnificent dogs, which made it possible for us to save lives."

In a nearby airport building, she and the others went through informal debriefings on the spot, with Jeff delivering what Caroline jokingly called his "usual song and dance" about emotional fallout. "You must remember," he told the returning team members, "that your families won't really understand how you feel." He also talked to relatives, telling them that the volunteers had "been through a lot, so their behavior might be a little erratic for a while, and you should understand that."

Caroline's family, her other life, was waiting at home.

It was less than a week to Christmas Eve.

## Chapter 19

# Search and Rescue Comes of Age

THE REPORTERS AND TV TRUCKS HAD BEEN camped outside the house for two days. Art had chased them away at night, but they kept coming back. And requests for interviews had been pouring in from newspapers, radio and TV stations, and magazines. Joanne, who was in her last year of high school, had answered the calls and written down all the names and phone numbers.

"You'd better start paying me, Mom," she said with a smile, but meaning it. "I've become your press secretary."

Caroline washed her clothes and bathed before finally speaking to the reporters outside. How did it feel, they asked, to be a hero?

"The people of Armenia are the heroes," she said. "There's no glory in search-and-rescue work. It's nasty, dirty, tiring, emotionally draining. It was wet and muddy and freezing over there. I've got a lousy cold, and real fatigue. It's not exactly happy work. No glory."

And she used the occasion to look ahead:

"In disaster situations, time is life. The standards of organized response must be raised. Precious hours and minutes can't be wasted. Mobilization and management must be swift and efficient or lives will be lost. And more joint training is needed, so we can work effectively with other international rescue groups."

As other interviewers arrived, she excused herself to take Aly to the vet. He had been shaking his head and scratching at his ear, leading her to conclude—correctly—that he had gotten an ear infection. The vet put him on antibiotics.

At home Aly continued to rest, but Caroline made sure not to ignore him. She had told the other handlers, "Our dogs will want to sleep awhile, but we have to remember that they've been with us twenty-four hours a day for more than a week. It would be a big mistake to suddenly shut the dog in his pen after that and see him only once a day. He'd feel abandoned. On the other hand, he's not ready for an obedience test either. Take walks with him, play ball. What the dog needs is a gentle weaning process."

Aly was six, now, and still strong, but the Armenia trip had really aged him beyond his physical years. Overnight, it seemed, his muzzle had become much grayer. His puppylike enthusiasm was gone.

Caroline herself felt drained, but there was no downtime before switching to her role at home. Her family had already put up the Christmas tree, but she still had a lot of shopping to do. When she went to buy gifts at a mall, it required an enormous emotional effort to get into the shopping spirit. Amid all the tinsel and glitter, she kept thinking of Leninakan and the Armenian children who would not see this Christmas or any other. It was important to Art and her own children, however, that their holiday traditions continue as usual. And so, in a quieter way, they did.

Right after Christmas, the canine team sponsor, Alpo, rented a small plane to fly Caroline and another dog handler to Washington, D.C., to meet with President Reagan. Leaving Aly at home to recuperate, she joined forty-five other U.S. disaster team members—physicians, firefighters, dog handlers—at a White House reception. Reagan entered the room and shook hands with everyone. Caroline stood with Julia Taft as the President read his remarks.

"Ladies and gentlemen, thanks to people like you here today, the Armenians have not had to face this tragedy alone. You conveyed what was truly a universal message, one for us all to remember at this time of year, that every life is infinitely precious, a gift from God. So whatever our race or religious faith, we are all one people on this earth. And in times of suffering, in the face of natural disaster, we are drawn by our common humanity to help one another to join in a great brotherhood of man. The lesson for this season is to love one another, and that's something you have shown in a very real and important way."

Caroline continued to receive awards throughout the spring and summer: the Heroine of Mercy award from Holy Trinity Apostolic Church in Cheltenham, Pennsylvania; the Unsung Hero award, sponsored by U.S. Senator Bill Bradley; and recognition as an outstanding citizen by New Jersey governor Thomas Kean.

It was heady stuff, to be honored this way, but Caroline reminded herself that she was, after all, simply a person who had been lucky enough to find an outlet for her energy and drive in working with dogs. And she reflected on how so many of the dedicated people she had met around the world had become her friends. There was, in fact, a global community of caring people, and Caroline was moved by the realization that she had become part of it. Each person was just a single individual, but when hundreds, thousands, millions came together, the power of their spiritual energy was unlimited.

Eighty-eight canine search units were operating across the United States by the spring of 1989, as opposed to only two when Caroline had started in 1972. They had a total of more than four hundred members, and while their level of training varied, the majority were people who genuinely cared about saving lives.

The dog handlers, mostly independent spirits with strong egos, were from all walks of life. Sixty-five percent of the U.S. volunteers were female. "Women tend to be very good dog handlers," Caroline told one audience. "Part of it is because we also raise children. And to raise and train a dog, you need the same consistent fairness." Because most of these women also held jobs, the dog units required that they have an agreement with their employers allowing them time off for "humanitarian missions" without being penalized.

As the field had grown, so had the need for rapid communication and coordination, and Alpo decided to sponsor a nationwide toll-free number through which local fire, police, rescue, and emergency groups could be put into contact with the nearest available dog teams. The company also supplied Caroline and Bill Dotson with Skypagers so they could be reached anywhere within the United States and Canada.

"If there's an earthquake in another country," Caroline told the media, "our State Department will call us out immediately through the Office of Foreign Disaster Assistance. But if an event occurs here in our own country, there's been no national system by which authorities can find qualified canine teams. Precious hours could be lost. I hope the new number will change that."

As part of her leadership in the growing national and international search-and-rescue movement, Caroline was invited to the headquarters of the Central United States Earthquake Consortium (CUSEC) in Memphis, Tennessee, for the April opening of its new seven-state training center for earthquake preparedness. Bill Dotson joined her and helped in the effort to raise participants' awareness of the U.S. Disaster Team Canine Unit. And Alpo's public relations firm sent a representative from Allentown, Pennsylvania, who arranged an exhibit including photos and videotapes of dogs at work.

Caroline was daydreaming of being out in the wilderness with Aly when an officer from a local sheriff's department entered the demonstration area. He stopped, looking at the pictures, and pointed to one of Aly.

"Do you mean those dawgs actually search out people in the water?" he said in a wonderful drawl.

"Yes, they do," Caroline said.

"Don't leave," he said, and ran out. The next thing Caroline knew, he was back. "We got ourselves a bridge collapse, and we need you. Now."

She and Aly and Bill were bundled into the sheriff's car along with Nancy Kippenhan, the PR representative for Alpo, who was suddenly getting a taste of real-life emergency work. Soon they were speeding ninety miles an hour over back roads, finally arriving near Covington, Tennessee, fifty miles north of Memphis, where a bridge carrying northbound U.S. 51 over the rain-swollen Hatchie River had collapsed.

The bridge, eight-tenths of a mile long, was fifty-five years old. A ninety-foot chunk of the two-lane highway had fallen into the swirling water. Five cars and an eighteen-wheeler had plummeted into the river right away; three smaller bridge sections, weighing up to a hundred tons apiece, had then crashed on top of the vehicles, which contained eight victims.

After two days, specially trained state police divers had recovered seven bodies. Still missing was a local farmer, Adrian Jones, age twenty-six, who had been returning from a visit to his mother in the hospital. His relatives kept vigil, but by now the divers were exhausted and rapidly losing hope of finding him. A new downpour had hampered their efforts.

Caroline and Aly joined one of the divers in a little flat-bottomed boat. As they headed upstream against the ten-knot current, the water was so dark they could see nothing. The visibility underneath, the diver said, was absolutely zero. It was also windy. Aly hung his head over the side, trying to catch a human scent from below. They repeatedly crossed the river until, abruptly, he began to whine. At the same time he leaned out to bite and paw at the water.

"He's really hitting hard!" Caroline said.

They made two more runs. Each time, Aly dipped his head and whined, repeating his alert in the same spot. Moving his paw back and forth in the water as if trying to scoop it up, he seemed to be saying, *I'm going to dig this person out of there!*

"With the current and the wind here," Caroline said, "we've got something definite within a twenty-foot radius."

"Well," the diver said, indicating the high water and hazardous currents, "we've got to wait for this to subside a little before we can go down."

The search was temporarily suspended.

Caroline was back in Memphis the following day when searchers, using a metal detector and a dragging hook, located a blue Dodge in the exact spot where Aly had alerted. Divers went down and pulled the body of Adrian Jones out of his car as his relatives, gathered on the bank, hugged each other and sobbed. Their anxious wait by the side of the river was over.

The Tennessee bridge collapse and rescue efforts made national and even international news, partially because Nancy Kippenhan had been there to publicize them. Aly became a hero, his exploits celebrated especially in the local press. Caroline later received letters from Southern law enforcement officers who had become believers in the value of search dogs after hearing about Aly's work.

More worthwhile to her than anything, however, was a handwritten letter from the mother of Adrian Jones:

Dearest Caroline and Aly—

You don't know me or I you. But its been bearing on my mind to let you know how thankful I am for coming to help locate my darling son Adrian Jones. I don't know how to thank you, it don't help the hurt. I thank God and you for finding him. I was in the hospital with pneumonia. I hope you don't think I'm crazy writing you. But it stuck in my mind all the time. I wish I had a way of helping you all out. Maybe by the help of God some day. He was my baby son at 26. I don't know if you have been through this or not. I hope not. I hope you never do. Well I'll let you go.

And may God bless you and Aly. I can't thank enough.

Mrs. M. Jones

Another handwritten note to Caroline came from Julia Taft, who had stepped down recently as director of the Office of Foreign Disaster Assistance. The two women had come to like and admire each other as a result of the Armenia mission.

"Public service is the nation's highest calling," Julia wrote. "Your father made his contributions and you are making yours, by helping rescue victims of disaster. It was a pleasure in my public service to do it with you."

In addition to the changes at OFDA, there were new players on the domestic scene. The Federal Emergency Management Agency (FEMA), founded a decade earlier, was becoming increasingly involved in national emergencies from earthquakes to floods to tornadoes, and its presence was bringing a new level of organization to disaster relief within the United States. Caroline's first encounter with FEMA came during the aftermath of Hurricane Hugo in September 1989.

She had been in Wisconsin, teaching at a search-and-rescue canine school, when she was summoned by the Virginia Department of Emergency Services. The caller was Ralph Wilfong, whom she had met during the Armenia mission. Virginia, responding to the Carolinas as a sister state, had requested dog teams to help search for hurricane survivors. So Caroline rushed with Aly to the Minneapolis–St. Paul airport, where they were given a wild ride aboard an electric cart—its driver beeping the horn loudly to get the crowds to move aside—all the way to the gate for a flight to Dulles. At dawn the following day, they joined Bill Dotson and six other dog handlers aboard a C-130 to Charleston, South Carolina, where members of a local volunteer fire department drove them to the command post, located inside a huge warehouse.

About sixty desks, each representing a different agency or organization, had been set up in this space, which seemed as large as a football field. There were, of course, people from the American Red Cross and the Salvation Army. Bureaucrats from FEMA were helping people fill out disaster-relief claims. There were various military groups, including units of the U.S. Army, the Marines, the Coast Guard, and the National Guard. The departments of Commerce and Health and Human Resources were represented, too.

Caroline thought back to the Johnstown flood in 1977, when she and Zibo had worked mainly with local fire departments. To say that things had changed since then was an understatement. Now she could see that the future promised more and more layers of official supervision—and, perhaps, confusion—in the burgeoning search-and-rescue field. Only time would tell how the nation's volunteer dog handlers might be affected.

Hugo had churned through the Atlantic, passing several hundred miles east of Barbados, with winds of about a hundred miles an hour. It had gained in force, ripping the heart out of Guadeloupe, roaring through the Virgin Islands, and cutting across the tip of Puerto Rico. Before it left the eastern Caribbean, twenty-five people had died and more than fifty thousand were homeless.

Charleston had braced itself as a warning had been issued for the East Coast of the United States. The eye of the storm moved north, then lurched toward land. Late on September 21, Hugo became one of the worst hurricanes ever to bear down on South Carolina, packing 135-mph winds. After a night of terror, twenty-six people died in this state alone, and damage was estimated at several billion dollars. With thousands of homes destroyed or severely damaged, some sixty-five thousand residents had to find temporary shelter.

Now, in the immediate aftermath, Caroline and her Virginia teammates were briefed by local emergency-management personnel and told they were needed to search various islands whose residents had been cut off from communication with or transportation to the mainland. No one knew how many might be missing. So the canine unit's members—thirteen handlers with dogs—dumped their gear inside a firehouse, located near a large bingo hall in which they would sleep that night, and set off in two teams.

Taken out on the water in a military tugboat with three other handlers and their dogs, Caroline and Aly jumped onto one island after another. They were doing a "clearing" job, making sure no bodies were there. It was an incredible scene, with drawbridges terribly twisted and entire homes torn from their foundations. Down closer to the water, houses seemed to have been uprooted before they had been carried by wind and waves up the hillsides.

The searchers were told that initially many island residents had gotten into their boats, thinking they could outrun the hurricane, so Caroline and Aly did water searches as well. They came up with nothing.

That night they slept on the floor of the bingo hall, the windows of which had been broken in the hurricane. There was no running water. The fire company had loaned them a generator to provide electricity.

In the morning the handlers heated their coffee on a little cooking stove they had brought. Over at the command post in the warehouse, the Salvation Army was supplying hot food. They stopped in to get some breakfast and their new assignments.

The Charleston organizers divided them into three search units to cover different parts of the outer counties, where the destruction was the greatest. Caroline's team of four handlers and dogs, with Ralph Wilfong acting as overhead, was told that the only vehicle available for them was a blue prison van. They climbed into it and drove off, stopping at each little village along the way. Most of these communities had mobilized to help their residents. The Baptist churches had soup kitchens running for the newly homeless, and their pastors, part of a well-organized effort, were the best sources for finding out if any local people had not been accounted for.

The handlers had been asked by the U.S. Humane Society to report on abandoned domestic animals; they had cases of donated pet food, which they used to feed the stray dogs and cats they found as they moved from place to place. But they found other animals, too. Wherever the dirt roads were blocked by fallen trees, Caroline and her teammates had to leave the van and hike through woods and swamps with their dogs; as they climbed over logs and branches, she recalled that during the briefing they had been told that poisonous snakes, such as water moccasins, had been driven onto land by the hurricane. And after the floodwaters receded, many alligators had been stranded as well. There was good reason to be cautious.

After finishing their third day of searching, the team got back into the stifling-hot prison van for the ride back to Charleston. After a while they stopped near a field, and they all piled out for a break. Aly and the three other dogs were still romping around when a military truck came roaring down the road and screeched to a halt. A man in green-and-brown army camouflage fatigues bounded out, planted his booted feet apart, and pointed his finger at Caroline: "You're the dogs!"

"I beg your pardon?" she said, suppressing a smile.

"Ma'am, are you the search dogs?"

"That's right, we're a search dog *team*," she said, now laughing.

"Well, I need you in McClellanville—now. I've got work for you guys to do."

"Hold on a minute," Caroline said. She gestured to the driver of the prison van. "This guy needs to take his van back to Charleston, so you'll have to supply transportation for us. And we have to radio our command post and okay it with them. Then we'll go to McClellanville."

"Done," the man said. Getting on his own radio, he barked, "This is Midway One," then issued a stream of orders.

He was in his early forties, about five feet eleven inches, and in top physical shape. His brown hair was cut short, military style, and his piercing pale blue eyes had a glint in them. He seemed to Caroline to be a career military officer, and judging by his age, he had probably served in Vietnam.

By the time Ralph Wilfong had clearance by radio from their own command post, a parade of dark green army vehicles had rolled up to transport the handlers and dogs. They jumped in and headed for the fishing village of McClellanville—which, as they got closer, looked like an armed camp being guarded by military checkpoints at each intersection. But when the guards saw Midway One they were waved through.

He brought them into town, where thirty-four of the forty working fishing boats had been destroyed. The village itself was devastated. Although the basic industry was fishing, there were some bed-and-breakfasts that had been torn apart. Midway One said that local officials had asked him to make sure those places were all empty. Any homes left standing were filled with mud and debris.

They started working methodically through the collapsed structures, then searched all around a boatyard—which, Caroline learned too late, was awash with leaking diesel fuel. The dogs had absorbed it through their paws, she was sure, and would have to be decontaminated. Caroline had her teammates walk their dogs through some salt water, but the residue of diesel fuel would later require a good soaping.

As the searching went on, Midway One did everything he could to facilitate their efforts. When an army helicopter approached and hovered directly overhead, he looked at Caroline with concern.

"This chopper gonna bother the dogs?" he said.

"Yes," Caroline said. "It creates impossible air currents. They won't be able to smell anything."

He got on his radio. "This is Midway One! Get that damned chopper out of here! It's bothering my dogs!"

*My dogs?* Caroline thought, holding back a smile. But she was impressed. Midway One had grounded the helicopter in a nearby field so that they could work. The guy was really efficient. He even went to get food and beverages for the handlers.

When Midway One brought them to another building that he wanted the dogs to search, he told them to wait while he went in first to check it out, and he disappeared inside. Suddenly they heard shots being fired. A moment later he emerged with a big smile on his face.

"Got 'em!" he said. "Got four water moccasins. I didn't want you and the dogs getting tangled up in 'em." Midway One seemed to be having the time of his life.

"We appreciate that," Caroline said.

He had even arranged locally for a full fire-and-rescue team to come in and, if needed, break through wreckage with all sorts of high-powered tools. The firefighters, eager for a chance to use them, remained impatiently on standby. So far the dogs had found no evidence of human life or death in the rubble, but the knowledge that areas were clear was important.

It was well after dark when Caroline radioed back to Bill Dotson. "Hey, Dotson! We need to get back to our bingo hall!"

"Don't worry, I'll find transport," Bill assured her.

"I want you back tomorrow," Midway One said.

"Fine. We'll okay it with the command post and we'll be back."

When Bill showed up in McClellanville around ten-thirty that night, he was driving an ambulance. The team climbed into the back, and Caroline told him the dogs had been exposed to diesel fuel. Although the long-term effects of such exposure were unclear, the handlers were extremely alert to any contamination by hazardous materials, or haz-mats, as they were known. The dogs would have to be washed down as soon as possible. Caroline thought the best way to do that would be to use the firehouse back in Charleston.

"No problem," Bill said.

It was past the curfew that had been imposed in the aftermath of the hurricane for all nonemergency personnel, so Bill was doing more than eighty miles an hour down the highway, passing all the state trooper cars. Every light on the ambulance was swirling and blinking, and the siren was *whoop-whooping* full blast.

"I've never driven an ambulance before," Bill said, chuckling and clearly enjoying himself.

*Crazy Virginian*, Caroline thought, smiling—but also a little nervous. "Don't you think you should slow it down a bit?"

"Ah, hell," he said, speeding up, "if they stop us, we've got a medical emergency here! We need to *decon* these dogs!"

At the firehouse they shampooed all the dogs with Caroline's favorite decontamination soap (which happened to be Dawn dishwashing liquid) and used brushes to make sure the dogs' paws were clean. Only then did the handlers head for the showers themselves.


The warehouse command post was a scene of absolute chaos early the next morning. The bureaucrats from FEMA, conspicuous in their ties and jackets, were being extremely slow and officious in dealing with the people who were filling out forms for their disaster-relief claims, and applicants were booing at the amount of paperwork confronting them. The Reverend Jesse Jackson had arrived in a big black limousine; Willard Scott of the *Today* show was on the air with a live weathercast from hurricane territory.

Caroline and the other dog handlers shook their heads in wonder, then reported for duty.

"Good morning," she said to the commander. "Midway One has requested that we go back to McClellanville. And we think we should send the same team, because the dogs are familiar with the areas already covered."

"Nope!" the man in charge said.

She and Bill looked at each other. "Well, sir," Caroline said, "we've been *asked* to go back. Is there some kind of problem?"

"Yep!"

"Maybe you can enlighten us," Caroline said patiently.

Bill snapped his fingers. "Oh, gosh," he said, "now I get it. President Bush is coming in today!"

That much was true. Bush would be arriving in Charleston, and he planned to go to various hurricane disaster sites, including McClellanville. The Secret Service wanted no extra people there other than police or military personnel.

The commander shook his head. "That's not the problem."

"No transport?" Caroline asked.

"Wrong."

"What is it, then?" she demanded.

The commander looked at her. "We had Midway One arrested this morning."

Caroline and Bill spoke at once: "Why?"

"Well, for one thing, he wouldn't let the state troopers into McClellanville. He had the place barricaded by the army. Second, the guy is an escaped mental patient! And third, we found a whole *arsenal* in the back of his military vehicle!"

Caroline's mouth hung open. Midway One was an imposter, an escaped mental patient, a weapons fanatic? Caroline was astonished. He had been a brilliant emergency manager. The day before, he had directed a full search-and-rescue operation with complete control. He'd been more efficient than a lot of other logistics officers she had known. The dog team's work, under his guidance, had been absolutely thorough. Whatever his story happened to be, and however he'd been able to take over an entire U.S. Army unit, Midway One had singlehandedly cut through all the bureaucratic red tape so Caroline and her team could get the job done. He would have made a good soldier, she thought, and his managerial skills were perfect for disaster work.

The teams ended up searching other areas, eventually declaring them free of any victims—alive or dead—who might have been trapped during the hurricane. Now other kinds of volunteers were pouring in, from as far away as New York and Florida, to help in the long-term process of clearing debris, providing shelter, generating power, restoring water systems, and rebuilding homes. The dogs had been used in the earliest stage of a much larger postdisaster effort that would have to continue for months or years.

They returned on a C-130 to Dulles, but then the dog handlers were on their own. When Caroline tried to hop on a flight directly to Newark, the airline refused to let Aly in the cabin. Bill Dotson and the others had gone home to Virginia, so now she was stranded. She thought ironically that she could have used Midway One at that moment.

"Call up the State Department," she insisted. Finally the airline personnel did, and were told to accommodate her. Relieved that her authorization from the federal government had finally come through and eager to get on with the trip, Caroline asked, "Okay, when is the next plane?"

"Well, at this point you have to go to National Airport and take a Continental flight out."

Caroline could remember few occasions when she had actually broken into tears, but anger and fatigue and frustration were about to make this one of them. She took Aly on a bus over to National and walked with him up to the Continental counter.

"I've just come back from the Hurricane Hugo relief effort," she said, "and another airline at Dulles wouldn't take my dog, but I've flown with you before, and—"

She was losing it. She took a deep breath and tried to stay calm.

"In fact, I've got a card here from one of your supervisors up in Boston, so please call him and verify who I am. I'm really tired and I just want to get home."

Emotionally drained, she waited while the airline people went to speak to the captain. If the answer was no, she thought, she might just lie down right there, using Aly as a pillow, and sleep in front of the ticket counter.

Then the captain came out and saw the pained expression on Caroline's face. He looked at Aly, recognizing the orange rescue vest.

"Put them on board," he said. "Now."

Fourteen months after the Armenia tragedy, Caroline and eight other U.S. citizens received the Soviet Union's prestigious Order for Personal Courage. The honor was conferred by the Supreme Soviet, the Soviet Union's legislature, and authorized by President Gorbachev; the medals were presented to them by Soviet ambassador Anatoly Dobrynin at his country's embassy in Washington, D.C. It was the first time in history that Americans had been so honored.

"You have our deep gratitude," Dobrynin told them. "We are aware that here in the United States, no one stayed indifferent to human suffering."

"This is real proof of friendship," a Soviet Embassy official said. "We have more in common than what divides us."

Caroline remembered her graduation ceremony nearly three decades earlier, when President Kennedy had sounded the same theme: "Let us not be blind to our differences, but let us also direct our attention to our common interests."

"This is a sign of appreciation for those who contributed to the relief effort," the Soviet official added, "and who put their lives at risk for us."

Among the other recipients of the award were Julia Taft, who had since stepped down as director of the Office of Foreign Disaster Assistance; Bill Dotson, coleader with Caroline of the U.S. Disaster Team Canine Unit; and Fred Krimgold, the structural engineering expert. The *Washington Post* reported the next day that "Caroline Hebard was escorted by Aly, the canine hero of last night's reception." If only the paper's reporter had known what it had taken to get Aly there.

The invitation from the Soviets had come by mail in early 1990. Caroline responded with a proper diplomatic-style note, accepting for herself and Art, but then she got on the phone to the Soviet Embassy and asked for Ambassador Dobrynin's office. Her father had taught her, a long time ago, to go right to the top. She could still hear him saying it: "Don't start at the lower levels. Go straight to the chief executive, who can get it done."

An assistant to the ambassador came on the line.

"We have received your acceptance," he said. "We look forward to seeing you and your husband."

"I'm calling," she said, "because I would not feel right about receiving the award unless my partner can accompany me."

There was a brief silence. "Your partner?"

"Yes," she said. "Aly, my dog. Because without him, I could not have worked in Armenia."

Another silence. "Well," the man said at last, "this is unusual, but we will consider your request."

She received a call from the U.S. State Department later that day: "We hear you called the Soviet Embassy about bringing your dog." The voice was stiff and reproachful. The official might as well have said, *How dare you?*

Caroline enjoyed the thought of the mini-crisis she must have caused in the protocol office.

"Look," she pointed out, "*they're* the ones who are hosting it. Isn't it up to them?"

The Soviet Embassy called back a few hours afterward.

"Yes, Mrs. Hebard," the ambassador's assistant said, "it will be fine for you to bring Aly to the reception. We have never had a *dog* in our embassy before, but Ambassador Dobrynin concurs that it would be appropriate."

Caroline smiled to herself when she heard that. Her father's advice still worked.

The night of the reception, Caroline, Art, and Aly arrived at the Soviet Embassy in her well-worn rescue truck. At the unlikely sight of a German shepherd rescue dog, the press and the other guests surged forward. Cameras whirred and flashbulbs popped in Aly's face as the mob of formally dressed men and women crowded around him. Aly took everything in stride and even, Caroline thought, basked in the glow of all the flattery and attention.

A television crew was broadcasting the event live via satellite to the Soviet Union. Aly sat patiently alone on the podium with spotlights in his face while they filmed him. Then Caroline was asked to join him.

"This is Aly, my working partner. He was just one of many search dogs in Armenia," she added. As always, Caroline used the media attention to stress how many volunteers were involved, and how many different nations had cooperated in the rescue efforts.

Ambassador Dobrynin gave out the medals. Then came a reception, with such an enormous crowd that Caroline and Art took Aly just outside the main banquet room, where the Soviet military attaché made sure they received some food. She tried to feed Aly some of the caviar, but after tasting it he looked up at her with an expression of complete dismay, as if pleading, *Can I spit it out?* He swallowed the stuff, however, and Caroline assured him that he would not have to eat any more.

Art returned from the men's room. "It's bugged," he whispered. "They don't even bother disguising it."

Mrs. Dobrynin came over to see Aly. "Oh, I love dogs," she said, "but we are not allowed to have any here at the embassy because we have to travel so much. How is it, Mrs. Hebard, that you managed to bring Aly inside?"

"I insisted," she said, "over the objections of my own government."

When an American official came over to greet them, Caroline recognized his voice: He was the man who had called from the State Department to reprimand her. Now he was all smiles. Bringing her canine partner, he said, had added "another dimension" to the event.

"Could you please fly over the search area?" Caroline was saying. "I'd like to check it out."

Aboard a military Blackhawk helicopter, she was heading over the Panamanian rain forest toward a remote U.S. Army command post.

This time, in early June 1990, the Pentagon had called.

The Department of Defense, through the Office of Foreign Disaster Assistance, had requested help in finding an American G.I. who had become lost while on maneuvers. Surprisingly, the military had no dogs specifically trained in search and rescue. Caroline, responding to OFDA, had put together a team that included three other handlers and dogs, with Bill Dotson serving as coordinator. President Bush's staff at the White House had called Eastern Airlines to pave the way for the dogs to fly in the cabin from Miami direct to Panama, where they had been loaded into the Blackhawk.

Now she went to the open door of the helicopter and stared down at the thick vegetation, thinking to herself, *This is just like Venezuela.*

The mountains were beautiful from above, but Caroline knew that the jungle could be treacherous on the ground, and the conditions in some places would be absolutely horrible. It was the rainy season, and mud would be everywhere down there.

They landed in a field and took their dogs over to the makeshift command post, where members of the 1st Airborne Battalion of the 508th Infantry, also known as the Red Devil Battalion, had congregated with maps and supplies.


A platoon of Red Devil soldiers had gone out on jungle maneuvers, each with heavy survival gear. One of the young men succumbed to heat prostration and needed to be carried back out to the base hospital. Since each man was already struggling under a full load in the blistering heat and deep mud, it was physically impossible for them to carry the stricken soldier's backpack and weapon at the same time. So they left it behind, at a particular spot, and later sent another young man back out again—alone, contrary to military regulations, and without a radio—to retrieve the gear.

The lone G.I. on this mission was fully trained in jungle warfare and survival techniques, so his superiors apparently felt he could take care of himself. But when he failed to return after several hours, a search team was dispatched. They turned up no trace of him. And by the time Caroline and her teammates arrived, the Red Devil soldier had been missing for three days.

The young man had taken a full ration of water, but it wouldn't have lasted long in this incredible heat. He would have become dehydrated by now. Because he'd received survival training, Caroline thought, he probably had headed uphill. He would have sought the highest possible vantage point from which to look around and try to get himself oriented. If he was able to see the ocean, he could determine the direction of the Panama Canal and also that of his military base. That was the theory, anyway.

But climbing through such rugged terrain could be disorienting. In this thick rain forest, even if he had made his way upward and reached a high point, he would not have been able to see very far. Also, the noise from birds, monkeys, and other creatures was often deafening. At times you could stand just twenty yards from someone else and yell, but the chances were that you wouldn't be heard.

The handlers studied the topographical maps to get a feel for where the missing G.I. might have wandered. At the search team's request, some of the soldiers were taken by helicopter to the top of one of the mountains. Those men could start downward while the handlers and dogs began below and worked their way up the gullies.

It was afternoon, and the sun was slowly going down. The ridges and upper air would cool first. The cooler air would start to descend the slopes—and with any luck it would carry the soldier's scent to the dogs as they climbed toward it.

They trudged into the forest, spread out, and began hiking upward as the dogs worked their noses madly. With every two steps forward through the deep mud, however, they slid back a step. With them were young soldiers who, Caroline thought, were "cute kids" like Andrew, now nineteen. "You guys remind me of my son," she said with a smile, aware that they were somewhat bemused by the sight of a suburban housewife and her German shepherd tromping through the undergrowth.

After just one hour, punctuated by brief stops so they and the dogs could drink water and rest, the searchers were nearly overwhelmed by heat and exhaustion. But there was no thought of quitting. And as they continued, Caroline felt she had been transported back to her childhood. At one point she saw a tree that was just like one she remembered from her own garden in Venezuela.

"Keep your dogs away from those soldier ants," she told her colleagues, remembering how she had seen ants that traveled like armies in long columns, capable of overrunning and devouring animals that could not flee their path.

But she was not familiar with, and had not been warned about, the so-called black palms. These plants had sharp, poisonous spikes. As she was sliding backward, Caroline threw out her arm to grab a branch or anything else, winding up with a handful of black palm spikes that hurt like hell. As she walked along trying to pull them out of her skin, determined not to show any pain, she caught up with a young military medic to ask his advice.

The American soldiers, he said, were accustomed to "just letting them fester until they drop out." Then he added, "Are you allergic to bee stings?"

"Why?"

"Well, three of our base dogs just died—from an attack by killer bees!"

"Killer bees?"

"Yeah, just the other day."

"Thanks for the warning," Caroline said, now alarmed that Aly and the other dogs, not to mention the handlers, were unprotected.

Another soldier came over to Caroline holding something in his hand and grinning. "Look at this!" he said, shoving a hairy brown tarantula—its body nearly three inches long, its legs extending several more inches—right into her face. In a flash Caroline remembered the big black spiders that had dropped on her bed in the old house in Caracas. She had been paranoid about spiders ever since.

*Well,* she thought, *I'm not going to give this kid his jollies for the day.*

Caroline did not move. Instead she looked the soldier straight in the eyes. "Aw, gee, son," she said calmly, "that's a *small* one. I used to see much *bigger* ones in Venezuela!"

The young man was speechless.

They had been searching for only five hours, but because of the heat and mud, it seemed more like five days. They kept moving up through the gullies, however, and Aly and the other dogs stayed in front of them, sniffing the air. At one point it was clear that the dogs had picked up a scent cone. The team members continued to work their way upward, following the dogs. Suddenly there was a commotion not far above them. Aly raced ahead to where the others had come upon the missing soldier.

While the dogs were being rewarded with praise and affection and play, medics tended to the soldier. He had gone uphill, exactly as the dog handlers had predicted. He was, of course, dehydrated, and was also suffering from multiple mosquito bites all over his body. He was conscious, although without water it was not likely that he could have lasted much longer.

Despite his own disorientation, he had kept the other soldier's heavy backpack and weapon with him. He had done his job by retrieving them; as a good soldier, he had refused to relinquish them until he completed the job. Then he had simply collapsed.

After being treated in the field, the soldier was evacuated to the base hospital by helicopter. With the mission over, Caroline and the others prepared to leave. But at the last moment the military veterinarian at the jungle base discovered that Aly was the only dog with a health certificate. In order to re-enter the U.S., the three others had to receive full rounds of inoculations all over again.

The dog team boarded a commercial plane back to Florida, and this time the red carpet was out: An Eastern Airlines representative was on hand in Miami to greet them and hustle them through the gate for international arrivals. But then one of the U.S. Customs officials started to protest.

"You can't let these people through!" he said. "I've got to check everything. Where are these dogs from? What is going on here, anyway? This is absolutely out of order!"

The man from Eastern Airlines leaned toward him and glared into his face. "These people and these dogs," he said through clenched teeth, "are *federal property*. You mess with them and you mess with the President!"

They walked on through.


Caroline had been home just a few weeks when she received a Certificate of Achievement from B. R. Fitzgerald, lieutenant colonel of the 1st Airborne Battalion of the 508th Infantry in Panama. At its center was an eagle clutching branches of peace in one set of claws, arrows of war in the other. Above were the words *Fury from the Sky*.

CERTIFICATE OF ACHIEVEMENT
FOR OUTSTANDING SUPPORT
TO THE RED DEVIL BATTALION
Is Awarded to
CAROLINE G. HEBARD

FOR OUTSTANDING CANINE SEARCH AND RESCUE
SUPPORT ON 5 JUNE 1990. DURING THIS PERIOD YOU
DISTINGUISHED YOURSELF BY TIRELESSLY SEARCHING
FOR A MISSING RED DEVIL SOLDIER. ENDURING
EXTREME HEAT AND PUTTING ASIDE YOUR OWN
FATIGUE, YOU CONTINUOUSLY DROVE ON WITH THE
MISSION. YOUR PROFESSIONALISM AND UNTIRING
DEDICATION TO DUTY INSPIRED ALL WHO SAW
YOU TO WORK EVEN HARDER. YOUR SELFLESS
PERFORMANCE IS IN KEEPING WITH THE FINEST
MILITARY TRADITIONS AND REFLECTS GREAT CREDIT
UPON YOU AND THE UNITED STATES ARMY.

It went in a box in the den with the rest of Caroline's growing collection of awards. Maybe someday she would hang them up somewhere, she thought. But the tribute that meant the most to her was the Mother's Day poem she had received a month earlier from fourteen-year-old Alastair:

> *The dogs bark, the trainers yell*
> *The earthquakes rumble, yet the people are humble*
> *The things you see look as if from hell*
> *The danger feels like a life threatening to crumble.*
>
> *The beeper goes off without any clue*
> *The car is packed, my mom is ready*
> *Aly is warned and knows what to do*
> *The team is off, sure and steady.*
>
> *Her love and confidence guides us all.*
> *In her profession there are few,*

*But as a mother, she stands above all.*
*She amazes us how she juggles the two.*

*The family and Aly are showered with love*
*For she holds us in a golden glove.*
*I would like to be a dog trainer too*
*Mom, I love you.*
*Happy Mother's Day!*

*Chapter 20*

# Pascha: Heir Apparent

A SUCCESSOR TO ALY HAD TO BE FOUND.

Caroline had known after Armenia that the Old Man, as she called Aly, had gone on more missions than most search dogs did in a lifetime. But the missions had gone on, through Hurricane Hugo and Panama and dozens of local searches. It was the 1990 earthquake in the Philippines that became a turning point: on the way back Aly nearly died.

They had responded to a call from the Office of Foreign Disaster Assistance, through the National Association for Search and Rescue, with three other handlers and dogs. The rescue component had included the firefighters from Florida and Virginia, the medical team from Pittsburgh, and structural experts, including Fred Krimgold.

Nearly a thousand people had been killed in the central Luzon region. The dog teams and rescuers helped to save several victims who had been trapped in hotels in Baguio, a mountain resort. When Caroline wanted to search through some of the small Filipino villages down in the valley, however, she was told by U.S. military officers that it was "too dangerous, because those people don't like Americans." She went anyway.

It was important, Caroline felt, for the U.S. team to go beyond the wealthy tourist spots and assist the local population. Making his appearance in those poverty-stricken villages, Aly was welcomed like a hero. In places shattered by the earthquake, his work allowed Caroline to reassure villagers that no victims had been overlooked. Once again Aly became a kind of goodwill ambassador.

Before leaving the Philippines, they were taken to an officer's club at Clark Air Force Base. The four handlers were forced to put their dogs in a kennel while they used the club facilities to shower, gulp down a meal, and briefly rest. Then, after retrieving their canine partners, Caroline and the others were confronted by the load master: "These are military dogs, so they have to be crated while in flight."

"No, no," Caroline said. "We don't stick these dogs in any crates. They are *civilian* dogs, used for search and rescue!"

The more they tried to argue, the more intransigent the load master became. Her manifest said military dogs, and that was that. Finally the NASAR representative gave up. Caroline's heart sank as the dog crates were brought from a warehouse. And she was furious when the handlers were forced to guide their dogs into them. These highly trained animals had given their all. They trusted their human partners to protect and love them. But, abruptly, they were being treated like any other cargo for the long flight back to the States. *It's not fair,* Caroline thought as she hugged Aly and told him not to worry. It was almost too painful for her to look at his face as she closed the door.

When they landed at Guam, she took him out for some relief and water. He moved very slowly, as if extremely tired. It could have been a normal response to the mission, perhaps, but a sixth sense told Caroline that he was ill. Then they stopped in Hawaii, at night, but this time the dogs were not allowed out, so Caroline went down to the runway and climbed into the cargo section of the plane. Opening the crate, she immediately knew that something was definitely wrong. She could read it in those sad eyes gazing back at her. She stayed with him until it was time to return to the cabin for takeoff.

They flew to California, then across the country to Andrews Air Force Base. Caroline and Aly checked into a Maryland hotel that night. As he lay down in the room, breathing heavily, she noticed a huge sore on his right rear leg. It was oozing a thick yellowish liquid. In the center of the sore were two puncture wounds that looked like fang marks.

She called her veterinarian in New Jersey. "I'm flying up to Newark first thing in the morning. I'll need to see you right away."

"What's the trouble?"

"Aly's getting sicker and sicker. It looks like he has some sort of snake bite on his back leg."

Aly looked up at her in pain.


"It was a spider," the vet told her. As it turned out, the vet's husband had been in Vietnam, and it was he who recognized the venomous bite.

"All I know is that he didn't have that sore until *after* he had gotten into that military crate. So the spider must have been inside it!"

"That spider is extremely dangerous. It could have killed him."

The vet began calling university labs around the country to find the correct antidote. Caroline waited, terrified that she would lose Aly. Even when the medicine was finally obtained—from the Chicago zoo—it took a month for him to recover.

He was nearly eight years old, but he seemed to have aged considerably beyond that. Even after the crisis was over, he was not at all himself. He was still lethargic; and he was drinking lots more water than usual. The horrible sore on his leg hardened into a thick lump.

Nevertheless, at the slightest hint that another mission might begin, Aly would start pacing and barking, eager to get back to work. His endurance was remarkable—and so was his big heart. But Caroline knew that from now on, she would have to guard against pushing him too hard. The Old Man's heyday as a search dog was over.


Caroline knew she wanted another German shepherd, but even the most spectacular lineage and the best training could not guarantee that she would have with another dog the same kind of bond that she had with Aly. She had been spoiled by his faithfulness and loyalty, by his methodical working habits, by the partnership they had forged. Of course, she told herself, each of her dogs would always be different, as each of her children was, so it was useless to decide in advance exactly what her new canine partner should be like. She had to rely on her instinct; she would know the right dog when she saw it.

To be sure, there were more factors involved than sheer chemistry. Caroline wanted, again, a male shepherd. She also hoped to find one with high drive (or motivation) and enthusiasm, as well as adaptability. Age was a factor, too. Ideally the dog would be about eighteen months old, as Aly had been. On the one hand, she would not have to wait for him to grow out of his puppy stage; on the other, she could do the training and bonding with him during those formative six months before he reached age two.

She had been incredibly lucky with Aly, meeting him for the first time upon his arrival in the United States, but this time she would pick out the dog herself.

And so in April 1991 Caroline flew to Germany.


She stayed in Munich with a friend, Dr. Isabella Kuhn, a veterinarian with the German search-and-rescue team. Isabella and she had planned to devote a week to the search. Every night they went to a different canine club or Schutzhund group so Caroline could meet with breeders, vets, trainers, and other handlers. Word continued to spread that she was on a quest for her new working dog. Isabella had set up a series of lectures for Caroline to give, so club members could hear about the kinds of missions her dogs had gone on. She delivered the lectures in German, accompanied by slides of Aly in Mexico, El Salvador, Armenia, Panama, and the Philippines, as well as on searches in the wilderness. It was necessary, she felt, to earn their respect.

Every day she visited clubs and kennels at which people showed her various German shepherds along with papers documenting their heredity. The few dogs she might have wanted to buy were not for sale—trainers with good working dogs were not about to relinquish them—or were too costly. Caroline was no wealthy dog fancier who could afford to match the premium prices that were being paid for German imports.

As for the others, Caroline shook her head. She didn't like the way a dog looked or moved. Or he was too young, still a puppy. Or he was too old, over age two. Or, simply, nothing clicked. To her, finding the right dog was like falling in love; it happened either right away or not at all.

The week went by quickly. Caroline had looked at more than forty dogs without success, and she was ready to give up. She had brought a crate with her—even if it had been permitted, she did not want to fly with a new, inexperienced shepherd in the passenger cabin—and, back in Isabella's apartment, she pointed to it and said, "Well, it looks like I'm going back with an empty crate."

Then the phone rang. One of Isabella's friends was on the line. "You know, somebody told me that there's this farmer who lives about two hours north of Munich. He has one dog that's a bit older than what Caroline is looking for—two years old—and he also has an eight-month-old puppy. Anyway, the farmer is getting on in age, and his wife doesn't like him handling more than one dog at a time. So he might be willing to sell the older dog. This one has received all the training you could put him through. He's got every degree you could want."

Caroline and Isabella called up the farmer, whose name was Stefan Specht. In a thick Bavarian accent, Specht told them he was very busy. He also had a funeral to go to, he said. But if they could drive up to a certain training field, the location of which he described, he would try to meet them there at six o'clock that evening.

They waited at the training field until dusk fell.

"Well, Isabella, he's not coming," Caroline said.

There was a loud noise. They turned and saw a car roaring toward them on the dirt road. A cage carrier, hitched to its rear bumper, bounced and clattered as the car screeched to a halt in front of them.

The farmer stepped out. Walking with a limp, he went around to the carrier in back. As he opened the cage it seemed to explode. Bursting out was a magnificent German shepherd, now racing around with incredible energy. The effect upon Caroline was electric, and she watched in awe. This dog was strong, lean, muscular—and a whirlwind. The two-year-old shepherd was already on the training field, eagerly pacing in anticipation and barking in short, sharp bursts.

"My God," she whispered to Isabella. "Every nerve in that dog is just ready to work!"

Specht called out, "Pascha!"

The farmer and his dog went through the basic Schutzhund routine. Caroline watched as Pascha systematically searched the blinds, zigzagging back and forth. After that he went to work attacking and tugging the burlap sleeve on Specht's arm, then sitting and barking—a flawless performance. Pascha was clearly enjoying himself, loving every moment and wanting to please his owner.

"Look," Caroline said. "He's *still* going. He's ready for more work. Just look at the *drive* in this dog!"

She loved his black and tan coloring. She loved the way he moved. She loved his spirit. And she listened as Specht, declaring that Pascha had come from a long line of working dogs, listed his impeccable credentials. His name with titles went this way: *Pascha SchHIII, FH, AD, KKI, A, V.*

The final *V* stood for *Vorzüglich*—"excellent." Schutzhund III was the highest level. It meant that Pascha could search eight blinds in a large field. He could bark and hold. He had passed a courage test, proving he did not flinch around sudden loud noises. Most important to Caroline, he had demonstrated the willingness and ability to be controlled by his handler. This meant she could channel his powerful drive and energy into a career as an air-scenting search-and-rescue dog.

"I'm really interested," she told Specht, trying to control her excitement.

He shook his head. "I still have to go home and think about it, and talk to my wife. I need a day. She wants me to get rid of the dog, but I don't want to. So don't count on it."

Caroline waited all the following day on tenterhooks. She wanted that dog, no other. Specht called that evening, but his tone of voice was not happy. "Well," he said, "I asked around about you. I found out what you do with your dogs. And," he added with reluctance, "yes, it will be all right. Come see me tomorrow morning. You can have Pascha."

.  .  .

It was a lovely old farmhouse. Caroline and Isabella were in the immaculate kitchen with Specht and his wife, listening as the farmer told them that since puppyhood Pascha had known only two environments other than the kennel where he had been born: the vast yard out back, where he lived in a dog house, and the training grounds. That was it. He had never been allowed inside the main residence because Mrs. Specht did not believe in having dogs in her clean, orderly home.

"Besides," she said, "Pascha is too wild."

*Now they tell me*, Caroline thought.

Specht brought out photo albums of all the dogs—about thirty—that he had trained. As they sipped coffee he said to Caroline, "You must understand that Pascha is an unusually tough dog. His name is Turkish for 'king'—and he acts like one. To get him to understand, you must pinch and twist his ear!"

*Oh, my God*, Caroline thought. *What am I in for?*

When they got around to discussing price, Caroline tried to act cool. But Specht said the money was not a factor in his decision to let her have Pascha. It was based on her reputation and her previous missions with Aly. He was also impressed by her contacts in Germany. And he liked the fact that she communicated fluently in German with her dogs. Beyond that, she had taken the trouble to come here personally, at her own expense. So he would not accept more than $2,000 from her, Specht said. Caroline let out her breath, relieved.

They all went out to the backyard, where both Pascha and the eight-month-old puppy greeted Specht with eager barking and pacing. The dogs had no toys and had not been taught to play, he said, but they loved to leap up and have a tug-of-war with the burlap sleeve.

The farmer was being overcome by emotion. "I want to have one last tug with him," Specht said, his voice cracking. "That will be my way of saying goodbye."

As Caroline watched, she saw that Pascha was being extremely tolerant toward the puppy. The smaller dog was also jumping up to grab the sleeve, but Pascha didn't seem to mind. Most dogs would not have allowed such interference; they would have whipped around and corrected the puppy. Kindness seemed to be part of Pascha's nature.

Another good point was his size. Aly had been about eighty-five pounds when she got him, but this shepherd was not quite so large. Specht had given his weight in kilos, and Caroline knew that equaled about seventy-eight pounds. As a volunteer firefighter, she had passed tests requiring her to lift two-hundred-pound people and carry them down flights of stairs. She had carried Aly, too, putting her arms around his legs and lifting him up into the truck. One of the OFDA tests she had taken had included carrying him a distance of fifty yards. But Aly was now 96 pounds, close to her 105, and her back wasn't what it used to be. She simply needed a lighter dog.

What really impressed Caroline about Pascha's physical makeup was that his bone structure had been deemed exceptional. Only once in a lifetime did a handler find a German shepherd blessed with perfect hips. And Pascha was poetry in motion.

But when it came time to go and she watched the farmer load Pascha into the crate in the car, Caroline felt guilty over taking his beloved dog. And she felt even worse when Stefan Specht and his wife both began to cry. As Isabella drove away from the farmhouse, Caroline glanced in the side mirror. The couple was standing there, still weeping.

Pascha had never seen a town with cars and crowds, much less a city like Munich. They arrived at Isabella's building, and Caroline got him out of the crate. She held his leash tightly as he tried to race off, pulling her halfway down the sidewalk. *What a lot of dog*, she thought. To get him to pay attention, she used a pronged pinch collar, enabling her to correct him without closing off his windpipe the way a standard choke collar would do.

Caroline had brought some of the farmer's dog food, and she fed him that, not wanting to change his diet right away. He was shedding, so she stayed outside to brush him. She stroked him gently as she brushed, talking to him in German and using a soothing tone of voice. He was still fairly tense, but everything was fine until she moved the brush down his front legs. She heard him make a rumbling noise, a soft warning growl. And then, out of nowhere—*wham!*—he snapped and grabbed at her jacket sleeve.

He did not break the skin, but Caroline was shaking.

*"Nein! Pfui! Platz!"*

Having put him on a down-stay, she walked a few feet away and stood with one foot on his leash, giving herself time to calm down. Pascha had been just warning her, she realized, but he had set up a challenge. She needed to gain his trust. She also needed to assert her dominance. Aly had bonded with her instantly, but this dog was six months older and fiercely independent.

Caroline knew that all dogs needed some time to adjust to a new owner, some more than others. For Pascha there were several other factors involved as well. He had gone from the country to the city, experiencing a jarring change of environment. He had gone from a tough male handler to a female handler whose approach and methods were softer. And that night he'd be sleeping not in a kennel but in an apartment with human beings as well as Isabella's own German shepherd.

It was difficult to judge how disoriented Pascha might be or for how long. Did he miss the kennel and the fields behind Specht's farmhouse? Was he in mourning over having been taken from his owner?

There was something else, too. He had been warning her, but what about? What was it about brushing his front legs that had set him off?

She thought about the German Schutzhund methods, and suddenly she realized what had happened. When a dog bit into the burlap sleeve, he was supposed to release on command; if he failed to let go right away, the trainer would hit him with a stick across his front legs. *No wonder Pascha reacted*, Caroline thought. Any touching on his front legs would be associated with pain and punishment. Even her gentle brushing would have triggered his instinct to protect himself.

Caroline reached in her pocket for some German sausage that she had chopped up. Sitting next to him, she petted Pascha gently and fed him the pieces of sausage. His paws and body muscles—but not his ears—gradually began to relax. She proceeded to brush his front legs again, talking calmly and feeding him sausages the whole time. But he did not relax completely.

*What a challenge*, she thought.

. . .

In Isabella's apartment, she put Pascha's blanket inside the crate and told him to enter. He did so without hesitation, and she shut him in. It was best to keep him crated for the first night, not only because he was a kennel dog but also to give him a sense of having his own domain until they got to know each other. She would never rush a dog.

And he would have to win *her* trust, as well.

Caroline did not want to fly home with him right away. She took him for long walks, just the two of them. She could make him her dog, but only if she took things slowly. Whereas Aly had attached himself to her from the first moment, Pascha clearly needed to bond gradually. He needed space; she could not crowd him. He was thoroughly independent, and that was that.

The second night Caroline put him in the crate again, but she left the door open. He slept there without coming out.

They joined Isabella and the German canine team the next day so that Pascha could learn to be around other working dogs. With proper training, his independent spirit could be channeled into the tasks that Caroline's missions required.

The third night, he slept on her bed.


So Pascha joined Aly—along with the aging Mad Max and the retired Sasquatch—in the Hebard household. Pascha seemed to understand from the start that Aly was the dominant dog and that it wouldn't be wise to challenge him. He came into the kitchen and sniffed the other dogs, including Aly, and they sniffed him, but it was Aly who set the rules—silently communicating, through his regal and aloof manner, that the hierarchy of his kingdom must prevail.

At one point Pascha barked at Aly, who barked back at him. Pascha fell silent. He barked again, not so loudly, and Aly barked back only briefly. Pascha, the potential challenger, was silent. Then, as if the issue had been settled, he walked away. At that moment Caroline knew it was going to work out all right.

"If someone could totally understand how these animals communicate," Caroline told Art, smiling as they watched, "maybe we'd find a way to achieve world peace!"

As she had done when Aly arrived, Caroline made sure to get up early and be the first person to greet Pascha in the morning and handle him—give him food and water, interact with him, and take him for walks—before the rest of the family was up. It was an essential part of the bonding process.

It had not taken long for her to realize that while Aly was a one-person dog (that person being Caroline), Pascha was not that way at all. He went right up to everybody—all the members of the family, even strangers—and bumped his head against them with affection. Aly would stick with Caroline wherever she went, but Pascha raced around to get love and attention from everyone else as well.

When Caroline drove away from the house, Aly would scarcely eat until she returned; Pascha never felt abandoned or lonely when she was gone. If she was with Aly in the backyard and stepped into the kitchen, Aly would not move from the back door; Pascha felt no such tie to her, even when she was home. With or without Caroline around, he ate heartily and ran all over the yard, enjoying his freedom.

It was Alastair, now fifteen, who taught Pascha how to have fun. The two of them quickly became attached, possibly because their personalities were so alike. Alastair had been full of energy from day one, never sitting still, getting into everything, and that was exactly the way Pascha was. At the edge of the swimming pool they would play tug-of-war with one of Alastair's shoes until one or the other finally won the game and fell into the water.

No one knew why Pascha loved shoes, but he did. What turned him on especially was the sight of old sneakers. Caroline and Alastair went to flea markets and bought whole boxes of them so that they could teach Pascha to play. Aly had known from the beginning how to have fun with balls or sticks, because he had been played with as a puppy, but Pascha had known only his training with Specht. An essential part of his personality had been left undeveloped.

Pascha's training had begun—and to Caroline, the ability of a dog to have fun was an essential aspect of it. Any good search dog needed a high play drive in order to win the "game" of find-the-victim. And it was necessary for him to have the desire to please his handler. When she threw a ball or Frisbee and Pascha fetched it, she praised him and then rewarded him not with a treat but by throwing it again, until he got the message that such interaction with her resulted in benefits beyond the limited scope of food.

Pascha needed time. Caroline would not put him through any search-and-rescue tests until she had a gut feeling that the dog was motivated to be with her, to please her, to listen and respond and never quit on her.

When he went for a gopher hole in the woods behind the house, there was nothing she could do to get him back. It was necessary to set him straight: "Hey, *I'm* supposed to be more important to you than a *gopher!*" The only way to win this battle was to work at it with him over time: doing consistent obedience work, spending quality time together, over and over. Only then would she know for sure that Pascha's impulsiveness was not, as Sasquatch's had been, incurable.

"*Nein,*" she called sharply when he raced off to chase a deer, which was all too often. "*Hier!*" When he came back, which was all too seldom, she told him he was a good dog: "*Feiner Hund!*"

If he bolted off to inspect some animal in a tree, she called out, "*Pfui!* No, leave it!" He might even turn and come toward her, but often temptation would overcome him again and he would race back to the tree.

When she let him out to play in the unfenced backyard, he might spot a deer—or even smell one—in the surrounding woods and take off. Sometimes he was gone for hours, and Caroline would drive off in the Suburban, searching for him, in tears. Most of the time these escapades ended with a call from some other family miles away, saying, "Your dog is in our swimming pool!"

Or he would come back with his tongue hanging out from running so fast and far. Caroline never punished him upon his return. If he ran away and came back on his own, she would simply put him into his outdoor pen and leave him there, ignoring him.

If, however, he started to chase a deer but came right back when she called him, Caroline would become effusive with her praise. She might also give him a treat and then play with him. He would learn, over time, that it was much more fun to come back when she told him to.

Pascha was stubborn. As a Schutzhund dog, he was a lot more obedient than ordinary dogs, but he was accustomed to Specht's handling and needed to adjust to Caroline's less forceful training methods. Also he was a fully mature dog, so it was more difficult to mold his behavior than it had been with Aly. Caroline was thankful that she herself was not a novice trainer; Pascha was certainly not a dog for any beginner to take on and try to tame.

He was so stubborn that even when she gave him a *platz* (down) command, he would protest with a rumbling sound. The down position forced him to assume a submissive attitude, and he didn't like it.

Sometimes she loaded him into the Suburban and they went to wilderness sites, where she felt compelled to reinforce her verbal commands with a whistle—something she had never needed to do with Aly. The piercing sound made Pascha's sensitive ears shoot up, and he could neither ignore it nor block it out. One blast meant, "Look at me! I might want to direct you." Two blasts meant, "Get your nose and tail over to me! Now!"

In time, she would simply reach for the whistle and he would become fully alert to her. If he couldn't see Caroline but heard two blasts of the whistle, he knew that Caroline meant business, and he responded. When he was bounding over a distant hill, moving incredibly fast and disappearing from view, it was impossible to yell against the wind and expect him to hear her voice. But he heard that whistle.

As Caroline continued her training with Pascha, she began to see how his remarkable independence would also make him a remarkable work dog. He already knew, from Schutzhund, how to range and work on his own to find the person who was hiding. But he insisted upon creating his own zigzag pattern, which ranged much wider and farther than that of any other dog she had known. Caroline had seen dogs that would not range even four feet ahead of their handlers, but Pascha would take off and cover a full acre while she herself walked in a straight line.

She gave him his freedom, and, in turn, Pascha proved he would work for her until he dropped. Nothing could stop him when he was moving toward his goal. Aly, always more sensitive, would look at her and try to communicate what he was doing, but Pascha never looked back. He just took off, as if to say, *I've got it, I know where to go, and I'm on my way—so you'd better follow me!*

It was a totally different attitude.

Yet she and Pascha were growing so close—and she was establishing her dominance so thoroughly—that by this time she could lean toward his face and tell him directly what she wanted. If it was necessary to gain the upper hand, she just kept staring him down until, finally submitting, he averted his eyes.

A woman and her dog, both proud and stubborn as hell, were finally coming to terms.

In the first weeks Caroline had trained with Pascha alone, but by June she was bringing Aly with them. The older dog, working with his usual precision, became Pascha's teacher and role model. With a "victim" hidden far away in the woods, Pascha would watch Aly for a short while to see what he was doing. Then the younger dog returned to his own style, heading off by himself to cover a much wider area, while also racing to get there ahead of his mentor. And he usually did.

Pascha completed all phases of his wilderness training by July 1991, three months after leaving Germany, proving he was a natural at searching. During the rest of that summer Caroline worked with him nearly every day, if only for half an hour. That fall the Federal Emergency Management Agency sponsored a five-day training session in Montana, and Caroline took only Pascha with her because the airline would not take two dogs; but a few weeks later, when she drove to Maine to teach at a school for police dogs, she was able to bring both of her working shepherds.

In November she brought Pascha by himself to the fourth International Disaster Dog Symposium, held in Berlin, where she had been asked to give lectures on water-search techniques. They also trained on the site of the Berlin Wall, large chunks of which still lay where they had been bulldozed two years earlier. Pascha went through the disaster dog test on a specially constructed site using remnants of the infamous wall, as well as other debris. The tests gave him his first chance to practice agility and do air-scenting work on dangerous surfaces.

Of course, Caroline knew that *her* training was ongoing as well. And there on the Berlin Wall she had a chance to appreciate that fact more than ever.

One lesson she learned began with her observation that with live "victims" hiding under the debris, Pascha moved unusually fast from the outset. At first, not realizing he could cover rubble accurately at such a pace, Caroline kept calling him back to search for the human scent again. She wanted him to work more methodically—the way Aly did—to make sure he didn't miss anything. Then a Berlin police officer and dog trainer who had been watching came over to her.

"You're going kill the drive in that dog," he said. "Just let him alone. He's already checked the area in his own way."

"How can you tell?" she asked.

"I was watching that dog's head move," he said, indicating that Pascha had worked his nose in all directions. "If anything had been in there, he would have zeroed in on it."

"You can read my dog?"

"He's a wonderful animal. Just let him work the way he wants to. If there's a scent down there, he'll find it, no matter how fast he's going."

Although she considered herself a highly trained professional, Caroline was more than willing to listen and take correction from someone else—if the advice made sense. In this case, she followed the officer's suggestion and gave Pascha all the room he wanted. And it worked.

Back home, Caroline began teaching Pascha to discriminate between different human scents. Devising a game with the old shoes from flea markets, she took one of her own sneakers and hid it deep in the pile. Then she gave Pascha a brief whiff of the matching sneaker. Next she pointed to the box and said one word: "*Such,*" which meant "go find." Suddenly Pascha was at the box and all the shoes were flying up in the air—sneakers, men's shoes, high heels, sandals, slippers—until he had flung them all away except for the matching sneaker, which he brought back in his mouth to Caroline with immense joy and pride.

Next Caroline pulled from the box a pair of shoes that were not her own. She buried one shoe in the box and scented him on the other. This time Pascha was searching for the smell of someone he had never met. "Go find," she said, and again everything flew up in the air and he came back with the matching shoe.

She also used a pair of hard red rubber balls to increase his scent discrimination. First she dropped them in boiling water long enough to sterilize them. This would destroy any human scent clinging to either ball. She picked one up with sterilized tongs and, while Pascha was still outside, hid it somewhere in the house. Next she took the other sterilized ball and rubbed her own scent all over it. She hid that ball in the house, too. Then she let Pascha in and gave him the command to "go find." Invariably he found the ball that had her scent on it, while the other remained hidden. This test satisfied Caroline that rather than trying to find a ball per se, the dog was strictly going after the human scent.

Aly and Pascha became buddies. In the kitchen together, *both* dogs began to pace when they heard Caroline upstairs at her search-and-rescue closet. Pascha would actually go up the back stairs, knowing this was not allowed, to try to catch a glimpse of her. Aly, not to be outdone, would go along with him. Caroline would look down the hall and see their two heads peering around the corner—ears forward, eyes wide, guilty looks on their faces—as they both panted and let out little whines of excitement. If it happened to be a false alarm, with no actual training session or mission to go out on, the Old Man and his successor would retreat down to the kitchen in disappointment and silence.

# Chapter 21

# Close to Home

ONE SUNDAY MORNING CAROLINE HAD JUST AR-
rived back home with Aly and Pascha from another search, one of those all-nighters. Art was
standing at the door with a strange expression on his
face. Caroline, suddenly afraid that something had
happened to one of the children, waited as he walked toward her.

"Max is dead," he said.

Her relief over the children was quickly replaced by shock and
disbelief. She had seen Mad Max only the day before. He had shown
no signs of illness. In fact, he had been full of energy, in top form. Was
this some kind of sick joke?

"Aw, come on, Art. I'm too tired for that."

"I'm serious," he said as tears started from his eyes.

She had never seen her husband cry over the death of a dog.
Sasquatch had been put down in the vet's office only three months
before, at age thirteen; but he had grown old and senile, so his death
had been accepted. Losing Max was different. On top of that, Art had
become especially close to Max. He was accustomed to their walks
together, and to Max's greeting when he went outside in the morning
or came home at night. The two had become buddies, keeping each
other company, especially during the periods when Caroline had been
away with the other dogs.

"He's still in his pen," said Art, who was so devastated that he had not known what to do except to wait for Caroline to come home.

She took Aly and Pascha around to the back of the house and returned them to their pens, where they began to pace restlessly and whine and whimper, while keeping their distance from Max's pen. As Caroline got closer, she saw that he was just lying on his side as if he were sleeping. Max must have succumbed to cardiac arrest or, perhaps, a massive aneurysm, she thought.

Going back into the house, she realized it was Sunday and that the vet was closed. They needed to bury Max right away, and they would have to do it themselves.

This was the first time any of the dogs had died at home, with Art and the children around. She had always shielded them from the grief of having to deal with the loss of a dog, but that was impossible right now. Max had died too suddenly, right there in his pen, and the emotional impact on everybody was intense. What they needed, she felt, was some kind of ritual that would offer them a way to release their feelings. This was a family affair, an event to be shared.

She called a friend, a dog lover who owned a farm about an hour away: "I've got a real problem. Max is dead. I can't leave him here, because the other dogs are getting upset, and Art and the kids are upset, too. Do you have a spot where we can bury him?"

It was a group effort to put Mad Max in a plastic bag, then carry him around to the front of the house and lift him up into the Suburban. Caroline and Art, with the four children, drove out to the farm. While Aly had always been Caroline's dog, Max had belonged to all of them. The kids had loved him, and she felt it was necessary for them to say goodbye to him.

Art and the friend went into a field and dug a hole in the ground. They lowered Max into it, and each of the kids made a little speech.

"Max was part of our family," Joanne said. "Mom always taught us to respect our dogs. We respected Max, and we gained his trust and respect in return. We loved him and he loved us."

Andrew recalled how Mad Max had run after a terrified jogger. "All the dog wanted to do was say hello. The guy was afraid of him, though, and tried to run faster, but he tripped and fell. Big old Max felt real bad about that, so he went over to the jogger and started licking his face!"

The others laughed through their tears.

Finally, after Alastair and Heather had said a few words, too, they all threw flowers from the garden into Max's grave. When the hole had been filled in, they placed a little cross on top with some more flowers encircling it.

Art could barely speak. "You get very, uh, attached to these animals," he said, wiping his eyes.

"Come on, Art," Caroline said. "Let's get you home."


Aly and Pascha would not go near Mad Max's pen for days afterward. They too seemed to be in mourning. Dogs are social animals by nature, Caroline knew, and Aly and Pascha had enjoyed Max's company. At least they still had each other.

The two dogs occasionally went on searches together. When they did, Aly and Pascha automatically divided up the territory between them. Caroline felt that they did so out of a pack instinct that went back to their distant roots in the wild. The wolf strain was still in them. Their behavior was inborn, inherited from ancestors that had used similar tactics for hunting. Aly and Pascha zigzagged over their separate areas, working the way wolves did, usually without any direction from her. When she needed to assert her authority, the dogs obeyed, treating Caroline as the pack leader.

Each dog, she believed, understood the other by watching the other's behavior. For example, if Aly's nose went up and he suddenly moved out, Pascha, watching the Old Man, picked up the same air scent and headed in his direction. They were totally attuned to each other, with Aly somehow knowing that Pascha was following.

But their responses, like their personalities, were different. If they made a live find in the woods, it was Pascha that *immediately* needed his stick reward, while Aly was usually not in such a hurry. Only Zibo had been more impatient than Pascha, to the point where he had rewarded himself by finding his own stick.

Neither Aly nor Pascha was jealous of the other. Both were dominant males, but Aly, the elder statesman, maintained certain prerogatives. If, say, he felt the need for an extra pat on the head from Caroline, he shouldered his way up to her and pushed his nose right under her hand. Pascha, the independent spirit, would not mind. He knew that within the pack he was below Aly in the hierarchy, and he reacted with the appropriate respect.

Although Aly had a proprietary feeling about Caroline, and Pascha acknowledged that, Pascha still made sure he was included. When a magazine photographer came to the house and Caroline posed between the two dogs, Aly put his paw on her—and then so did Pascha.

"They are both absolute hams," she joked.

And both were absolutely protective of Caroline and any territory they saw as theirs. One time, when Caroline had finished a search in Pennsylvania late at night and was on her way home, she decided to stop at a rest area on the turnpike around two o'clock in the morning. She was driving a rental car, since her Suburban had broken down. Leaving Pascha half asleep in the back, she went inside to use the bathroom. On her way out, she heard frantic barking. Approaching in the darkness, she saw two men walking around the car. They were looking inside, as if wondering what they could steal, while Pascha was going crazy, barking furiously and baring his teeth at them.

She sneaked up behind the car, remembering that she had left one of the rear doors unlocked. She quickly opened it, releasing Pascha, who burst out, raced around the car, and leaped at the two men. They ran toward the trucks parked in another part of the rest area, but Pascha grabbed one of them by the pants.

"Pull him off!" the trucker yelled. "Pull him off!"

Caroline blew her whistle. Pascha let go of the man and came back to her. She put him on a down-stay.

"You'd better get in your truck *real* fast," she told the men, who raced off.

When she got back to the rental car, she surveyed the damage: Pascha had chewed off the vinyl covering of the steering wheel, torn up the seats, and brought down half the fabric that lined the roof. When Caroline returned the battered wreck of a vehicle, she walked up to the rental counter and said, "I'm sorry, but my dog ate your car."

As if coming full circle back to her early days with Jaeger and Zibo, Caroline began to work more with police officers. The difference, nearly a quarter-century later, was that now she arrived as an expert to share her knowledge and experience while learning from them as well. She worked with FBI agents; with state troopers from New Jersey, Connecticut, New York, Pennsylvania, Virginia, and South Carolina; and with sheriff's departments and local police groups. She helped train dogs and handlers from the New York City Police Department and, working with railroad officials, became a resource for Amtrak's disaster-response team.

As law enforcement agencies had come to rely on air-scenting dogs to help find missing persons, they also began to seek more assistance in kidnapping or homicide searches. In the event of a suspected murder, the dogs could help find the victim. Here was a new and developing aspect of her field, so Caroline plunged into a fresh round of seminars, workshops, and courses to trade information and pick up the special education she needed.

She took Pascha through a cadaver training course sponsored by the Federal Emergency Management Agency. Later she brought him to an FBI workshop on the detection of human remains. Caroline also took Pascha through a two-week cadaver course run by the recently retired commander of the Connecticut State Police K-9 unit, Andy Rebmann, the same man who had almost prevented the volunteer dog handlers from working during the L'Ambiance Plaza collapse in Bridgeport. As police understanding of trained disaster dogs had grown, she and the former K-9 chief had become friends and colleagues based on mutual respect.

Cadaver work involved training dogs with scent articles from human victims—hair, teeth, dried blood—or with soil retrieved from beneath bodies. Caroline obtained her own stash from various police sources. She kept these items in a small metal ammunition box, which could be sealed airtight. During training, the scent article was placed in a different container and concealed somewhere—hung from a tree or stuck inside a hollow concrete block or buried in the ground to a depth of a foot or more.

Training centered around having the handlers read the body language of their dogs, each of which reacted individually to the scent of human death. All search dogs showed a preference for finding live victims, so beginners had to be "introduced" to cadaver scent and made to feel (through praise and rewards) that it was desirable for them to find it. A few dogs displayed no aversion, but most (about eighty percent) became visibly upset. Caroline recalled how the fur on Zibo's back had risen as he approached a site where someone had died. She was very familiar with Aly's total aversion—ears down, tail tucked, a hangdog look—which made it easy to read him.

Pascha's aversion to cadavers was far less intense than Aly's. He didn't back away, but stayed right there, barking at the scent and even digging for it. Caroline did not try to change that instinctive reaction, but she needed to prevent him from destroying evidence at a crime scene. So she taught him to return, bark at *her*, and then lead her back to the location. To ingrain that habit in him, she carried his burlap tug toy; as soon as he nosed or scratched at the scent source, she produced the toy and held it up as his reward. Seeing it, he'd bark at her until she gave it to him.

Going through this routine consistently, Caroline taught Pascha to realize, *When I find a cadaver, I bark at my partner!* He needed instant gratification, so she made sure to have the toy ready before he ripped it from her pocket or rewarded himself by grabbing someone's shoe.

Caroline also began working with scientists who were developing chemicals to simulate the scent of dead bodies. Aly and Pascha were among the first field testers of synthetic products made by the Sigma Chemical Company of St. Louis, Missouri. The initial batch was not very effective, so Caroline helped the company refine it into a workable training aid. The result was Sigma Pseudo Corpse Scent, Formulations I and II, representing human bodies in different stages of decomposition. But Caroline pressed for more varieties.

"If you ride ambulances, as I do," she told the chemists, "you know that people coming out of a bad accident have a certain odor about them. It's the scent of someone who's not dead but is seriously injured and may be in shock. Could you bottle that?"

So they created a product called Distressed Body Scent.

There was also a Drowned Victim Scent for water-search training, in the form of effervescent tablets that could be dropped into the water, and Pseudo Burned Victim Scent, so handlers could be taught to read the reactions of their dogs to bodies at fire or explosion scenes.

Caroline took both Aly and Pascha on several police-related missions in 1992, each of which demonstrated once again that search-and-rescue work was rarely glamorous and often frustrating or agonizing or both. In April of that year, they helped the FBI and other agencies in their intensive search for Sidney J. Reso, president of Exxon International, who had been kidnapped from the driveway of his home in New Jersey. With other K-9 teams, Caroline and her dogs searched through acres of parking lots at Newark Airport—from before midnight to dawn, to avoid attracting attention—after an anonymous tip was received that Reso's body might be in the trunk of a car there. On subsequent days she took both dogs through several wooded areas, again coming up with no clues. It was only after one of the kidnappers confessed that the Exxon executive's body was found.

The unresolved searches were especially taxing. Two that summer were for missing boys in New Jersey. In one case, the child was never found. In the other, police suspected that the boy had been killed by his mother, but his body was recovered months later, far from the designated search area, and the police did not have enough evidence to charge her. In September, Caroline and Pascha were called to a search in the wilderness of Ontario, where a young Minnesota man on an end-of-summer fishing expedition had taken out a boat alone and apparently fallen overboard and drowned. Joining another handler and her dog, as well as Canadian police divers, they searched a vast, deep lake by boat and from shore, sometimes working all night when heavy rain and wind kept them off the water during the day. The young man's father-in-law tried to help, going over the details of the tragedy, pointing out where the empty boat, its motor still running, had come aground. "It's my fault," he kept saying, even though he had done nothing more than invite his new son-in-law to come along with his fishing buddies. But after a week of frustration, they left without recovering the body, and the older man had to go home to confront the young man's family and his own widowed daughter.

The final search of the year, beginning in December and continuing into January 1993, involved a young woman reported missing in Trenton. Caroline brought both dogs, using Aly for extra protection. After being given the woman's clothing as scent articles, he and Pascha searched day after day for two weeks through rubble-filled lots, abandoned factories, and crumbling row houses. Then, for another grueling and fruitless week, Caroline brought Pascha out on the windswept Raritan Canal aboard an inflatable rubber boat. The victim's body was found later in a vacant lot near the canal, because of a tip given to the police.

Caroline knew she was exhausted. In the past at these times, she had relied on her ability to go into what she called her "robot mode" to block out the fear, uncertainty, and sadness of her work. It enabled her to keep going, but it also contributed to the illusion that she was both indispensable and indestructible. This was a potentially dangerous road that could lead to an emotional breakdown.

Now she was having flashbacks. Over and over, she would see Pascha alerting on the scent of a man's body nearly two hundred feet under the water, at the bottom of a quarry. And even while that experience replayed in her mind, another image would intrude. They had been helping police search through the wreckage of a burned building in Irvington, New Jersey, when Pascha had pawed the charred rubble and made a face as if he were in mourning. Then Caroline had felt something strange under her foot; looking down, she'd discovered that she had kicked open a small burned skull.

The scene kept replaying before her eyes, like a series of colored slides. *It was an accident*, Caroline thought, but the mental image would not go away. It started to appear in nightmares. *I accidentally kicked the skull and it broke apart. It was a child's*, her own voice was saying—then she would wake and sit up in bed, sweating and shaking.

Caroline had taken Jeff Mitchell's course in Critical Incident Stress Debriefing, and she was aware that rescuers often needed to recover from their own trauma. Having seen so much suffering and death, their psychological world could collapse. The concept of post-traumatic stress disorder, or PTSD, had become recognized and accepted only in the years after the Vietnam war. Most people already knew about the devastating effects of trauma experienced in early childhood, but the experiences of Vietnam veterans led to studies of those who had suffered unusual shock or stress in adulthood.

In the emotional aftershock, survivors and rescuers alike experienced symptoms that could include fear, sadness, grief, anxiety, insomnia, anger, rage, denial, depression, and even suicidal tendencies. Some experienced disorientation, memory loss, flashbacks, disturbing dreams, and cold sweats. There could be abrupt changes in behavior patterns or lifestyles, too, most involving relationships or careers. Caroline had seen this at first hand. Some dog handlers she knew had left their marriages or jobs, unable to cope with the demands of ordinary life.

At last Caroline acknowledged to herself that she needed to find a sense of personal peace and tranquility. Paradoxically, this inner journey had to do with reaching out—with becoming more involved with the survivors of the tragedies she witnessed. In the past she had almost always just done the job and then left, trying to protect herself from feeling too much. She had been an absolute artist at pushing down her own emotions, she admitted, as if she could merely open a book, turn to the page that contained the instructions she needed in order to function, read and follow those directions—and be done with it. That was how she had gotten through so much without falling apart. But now the only way out was to open up to those emotions and let herself be touched.

What she needed, Caroline believed, was to have the courage to drop her protective guard. She had always extended herself, with complete empathy, to her own family and to the dogs—but getting close to survivors had been too much. She had needed to escape, to go home, to remain strong enough for the next tragedy. Now she needed to become part of the lives of those affected, as well. In doing so, she hoped, she would come back to herself.

As the number of volunteer dog handlers in the United States had grown to more than five hundred, in more than a hundred search groups nationwide, the Federal Emergency Management Agency had stepped in to organize them as a resource. FEMA provided funds for regional task forces—each with canine, rescue, and medical components—that could respond quickly and efficiently to domestic catastrophes. Caroline helped FEMA put together guidelines for both handlers and dogs, and she participated in a series of pilot programs around the country, consisting of five-day courses designed to "train the trainers" of federally sponsored volunteer canine units.

Closer to home, she had begun putting together her own small team of dog handlers, some of whom were park rangers in Somerset County, New Jersey. She would teach them what she knew. She would encourage them to be open-minded, to keep learning and growing. They would work together as an independent unit, going on searches when called and helping in whatever ways they could.

In the early morning hours of March 23, 1994, an explosion in a natural-gas pipeline leveled eight nearby apartment buildings in Edison, New Jersey. First there had been a deafening roar, then the red-orange glow of a vast firestorm, with flames leaping hundreds of feet as more than a thousand residents fled for their lives. Reaching the scene only hours after the blast with two of the park rangers on her team, Caroline saw that the explosion had carved a crater fifty feet deep, filled with smoldering concrete, crumpled appliances, and raw sewage. In some places it was still too hot to search for signs of possible victims, but after two days the dogs confirmed that, miraculously, all residents had gotten out alive.

The explosion drew national news coverage, with Caroline and Pascha on front pages across the country, and she returned home to find that she had been named the ABC News Person of the Week for her efforts in Edison. But even while she was answering questions about search dogs, her mind was with the survivors, especially the children. They and their parents were still alive, but their entire familiar world had been obliterated in a single terrifying moment. Now their parents would be preoccupied with getting their lives back in order. How would the children cope with the trauma?

Caroline recalled how children who had survived the Armenian earthquake had been encouraged to express their feelings through artwork; she had gone to Washington, D.C., for an exhibit that had haunted her for days. One painting in particular had made such an impression on her that she had bought it and taken it home. Now she took it from a shelf and examined it once again.

On the front were the words "Portrait of Ani: A Four-Year-Old Earthquake Survivor's Remembrance of His Perished Friend." The painting, filled with bright reds and yellows and blues, reminded her of Picasso's work. The girl in the portrait, Ani, was depicted wearing a traditional Armenian dress with lace along the bottom, and black boots. On the reverse was an inscription:

When four-year-old Hovhannes Manoukian returned to Leninakan, Armenia, after visiting his grandmother in Yerevan, he found the world as he knew it had been shattered by the earthquake that struck northern Armenia in December of 1988. He could not find the little girl next door, named Ani, who was his friend. Ani had perished in the rubble along with the many thousands of victims of that unspeakable tragedy. Weeks later, Hovhannes painted her portrait to help him remember.

Caroline turned the painting over again, staring at the portrait of Ani. The girl's complexion was not the warm olive shade usual for Armenians but, instead, was white and gray—the colors of death. In the boy's painting she had big black eyes, with black eyelashes, and a smile that was larger than life. Hovhannes Manoukian, age four, had painted his little friend as dead and gone, yet, simultaneously, as still alive and joyous. The portrait was his remembrance of Ani, and it was also his goodbye to her. He had released some of the turmoil inside himself—and, Caroline thought, the children who had survived the recent gas explosion needed to do the same.

So she and two of the Somerset County park rangers returned to Edison that weekend, bringing shopping bags full of art supplies. They spent the day with about two dozen young children at a temporary Red Cross center in a hotel conference room, helping them vent their fears and anxieties through games, drawings, and paintings. Many of the children drew their versions of the giant flames. Others drew pictures of their favorite teddy bears or stuffed animals, which had been lost in the explosion. And as she played and talked with the children, helping them to release their emotions, Caroline quietly released some of her own.

.  .  .

Several months later, Caroline and Pascha responded to a call from Bridgewater, New Jersey, where a recent immigrant from Brazil had drowned in a reservoir. The young man's family members spoke only Portuguese, so Caroline became their communication link to the other rescuers. Pascha had made many alerts in one spot, and now there was only the ordeal of waiting for divers to recover the body. Caroline began returning each day to spend time with the family by herself, without her dog. Along with three of the park rangers, she sat with the relatives—six or seven at any given time—on the dam overlooking the reservoir. She listened to them speak about the man they had lost, about how his dream had been to bring his eight-year-old son to America for an education. The man's sister, weeping, vowed to do everything she could to achieve that goal for her dead brother and for the boy in Brazil, and Caroline felt the young woman's emotions as if they were her own.

The vigil lasted a full week, and Caroline virtually became part of the family. When the body was finally recovered, a priest came to conduct a short service at the reservoir. Caroline then accompanied the relatives to the morgue, staying with them in the small waiting room for nearly two hours, until it was time to go in and identify the body, which would be flown to Brazil for burial. At the sight of it, their grief swelled over, and Caroline wept, too, as she supported the wailing sister.

Outside in the parking lot, she hugged each of them again, as they thanked her over and over. This time Caroline had reached out all the way. On the surface it had been just another mission, and she could have held back, as she had done so often in the past. Instead, she allowed herself to share the intimate, chaotic emotions of people who, not long before, had been complete strangers.

As she drove slowly away, the pain of that family's loss burned in her stomach. It was harder this way, but it brought her closer to herself, as well. She took deep breaths in silence and gripped the wheel, blinking to clear her eyes. Then she sped up and headed home.

The Hebard household was quiet in the fall of 1994. Joanne, the oldest, was living and working in Florida. Andrew was in graduate school. Alastair had just gone off to college. Heather was in high school. Art Hebard still worked long hours at Bell Labs, by now one of the prominent figures in his field.

Caroline had celebrated her fiftieth birthday. She had spent nearly half her life in search and rescue. Because of her, in many ways, the entire field had come of age. Now, working with a small network of handlers and rescue workers in the United States and around the world, she was striving to maintain the highest standards. She was also expanding her teaching role, with the aim of training a new generation of caring, competent, and highly qualified dog handlers. If her basic values could be transmitted to them—as, indeed, many of those same values had become part of her own children's lives—she would feel fulfilled. And she would continue to serve in the American tradition of volunteering, of reaching out as an individual, believing that one person can make a difference.

Aly was quiet, too. His muzzle was almost white, and his bark seemed to come from deep inside him. There was a film over his eyes, and Caroline could tell that he was going blind. Now she often had to call him four or five times before he responded. The Old Man spent a lot of time sleeping, these days, or else he lay in the yard panting, and he no longer barked insistently to go on missions.

Yet even without his old energy and mobility, Aly maintained his royal presence and bearing. When he gazed in her direction, Caroline felt his dignity shine through as it always had. He was more than halfway through his twelfth year, but what he had given of himself could not be measured in years. One night, after stroking his head, Caroline found herself in the den, rummaging through the boxes where she stored the tributes to him from around the globe. There were plates, plaques, mugs, medals, and certificates from grateful governments, companies, and communities. There were letters from heads of state, from families and individuals, all thanking Aly for his help.

Aly would always have a special place in her heart, but Caroline came sadly to terms with the fact that soon it would be Pascha alone receiving the tributes. Although initially he had challenged her authority by displaying his fierce independence, he had become one of the strongest and most reliable air-scent search dogs in the world.

When a powerful earthquake struck Kobe, Japan, in January 1995, Caroline guessed correctly that the United States would not send dogs. After the 1990 earthquake in the Philippines, the State Department had stopped sending the U.S. Disaster Team Canine Unit to foreign countries.

The responses in the 1980s, to Latin America and Armenia, had occurred during Ronald Reagan's second term, when Julia Taft had led the Office of Foreign Disaster Assistance, displaying personal commitment and dynamic leadership. The mission to the Philippines had taken place when George Bush was in the White House, but there had been no others during his term and none in Bill Clinton's—not even when, in 1993, India had been hit by its most devastating earthquake in half a century.

Maybe, Caroline thought, the U.S. government had felt no diplomatic urgency. There was nothing to gain, politically, from India. Much more had been at stake in relations with Mexico, El Salvador, the Soviet Union, and the Philippines. Maybe helping just for the sake of helping, for humanitarian reasons, was not a priority. And maybe the United States, embroiled in its own domestic problems, was moving away from a global vision of its role.

After the Kobe quake, the Japanese government at first refused foreign assistance. But then Caroline received a call from Paris, inviting her to join the French canine team at the disaster. She left for the airport before five the next morning, paying her own way. Caroline and Pascha became the only U.S. handler-dog team in Kobe. And when the French unit that had called her failed to appear, Caroline found herself working as a "nongovernment operation"—the equivalent of a female Lone Ranger with her German shepherd.

Joining forces with the British rescue team, which had no search dogs, Caroline spent a week sleeping on floors and hitchhiking, sometimes at night, to scenes of wreckage where victims might be found.

Pascha worked entirely off-leash, making his way over sharp glass and nails without the slightest injury, and he identified at least nineteen bodies in the rubble.

In the tragic aftermath of the bombing of the Alfred P. Murrah Federal Building in Oklahoma City on the morning of April 19, 1995, an anxious nation was introduced to the phenomenon of search dogs that could guide rescuers to the living and help them locate the dead. Dozens of handlers, many working with FEMA task forces, rushed with canine partners of every description to aid in the desperate search for survivors. Among them, working as an independent team, were Caroline and Pascha.

Again she had financed her own trip.

The dogs were credited with leading emergency crews to the bodies of at least fifty victims of the bomb—and, too, with lifting the spirits of rescue workers who had been numbed by the devastation. Caroline was deeply impressed by the outpouring of volunteer support at the scene by the people of Oklahoma, and she felt that local law enforcement officers and their K-9 units were special heroes who never gave up. These officers and their dogs continued to search after the other canine teams had left, working on the rubble until the last three bodies were finally found, bringing the total number of those who had been murdered to 167 men, women, and children.

Caroline spent much of her time debriefing rescuers who had become emotionally overwhelmed. Near the end of the fourth day she noticed a tall, rugged officer from the sheriff's department who kept staring off with a pained look in his eyes. When he came over and patted Pascha, she decided that he probably needed to talk.

"Hey," she said, "I've been on my feet all day. What do you say we go over there and sit down?"

Caroline led the way to a grassy area, where Pascha joined some of the other dogs that were playing or resting. They sat down on the steps in front of a red brick building and the sheriff's deputy started, slowly at first, to tell her what he had seen. He had been one of the first people to try to get into what had been the Federal Building's day-care center after the building had been blown apart. He recalled coming upon a boy whose horribly torn body was still beside the tricycle he had been riding.

"I brought him out," the deputy said, "but he was dead and I, uh, I . . ." Unable to go on, he reached into a pocket and pulled out a light blue baseball cap. After staring at it awhile, he continued. "This is his hat," he said with intensity. "Look, there's no blood on it, none. I've been carrying it around, and, do you see, no blood . . ."

Caroline was beginning to realize fully how much emotional turmoil was inside this physically strong man, who had felt so utterly helpless. "Nobody could have done any more than you did," she said.

"I couldn't save him. I couldn't, I . . ."

"No. But at least you helped that family to bury their child. That was so very important to them."

"I can't give this hat back. I want to, but I can't."

"You'll do it," she told him. "You'll know when it's time."

"I'll take it home first," the deputy said.

"You have kids of your own?"

The man gazed intently at the small blue cap clutched in his large hands. He nodded. "Yes," he said.

"I bet you look at those kids now and just want to hug them all the time."

The deputy looked away. "Yes," he whispered, and at last he broke down and wept. As the officer's body shook with grief, she stared at the blue cap that represented one specific child, one individual boy whose life had been precious beyond words. The boy had a name and a history and—until it had been taken from him—a future. The officer who had tried to save him, even as he was trying to let go of his grief and pain, could not let go of the baseball cap.

*No, you could not save every one*, Caroline thought, and for a moment the terrible precariousness of life overwhelmed her. *You could not save every one—but you could come, and you could do your best to help.*

Somewhere, right at that moment, there was another child, with a name and a history and a future, whose life might someday depend upon her skill, dedication, and teamwork with her dogs. And when the pager summoned her again—and yet again, for as long as she was able to carry on—Caroline Hebard and her partner would be on their way.

# *Afterword*

# So That Others May Live

## HOW TO FIND OUT ABOUT CANINE SEARCH AND RESCUE

Across the United States and around the world, there are groups of dedicated men and women devoted to all aspects of search and rescue. These volunteers take the traditional SAR pledge to be "always ready, so that others may live."

The clearinghouse in the United States for new developments in the field is the National Association for Search and Rescue (NASAR), which also acts as a referral base for anyone interested in joining a response group, including canine search-and-rescue units. For membership information and to find out about groups in your area, write or call:

NASAR
4500 Southgate Place, Suite 100
Chantilly, VA 22021
703-222-6277

Another organization offering training and information about local units is:

American Rescue Team
P.O. Box 489
Alameda, CA 94501
510-523-5493
**E-mail**    AmerRescue@AOL.com
**Internet address**    http://www.acosta.com/
AmerRescue.HTML